The FRATERNITY of the BUILDERS

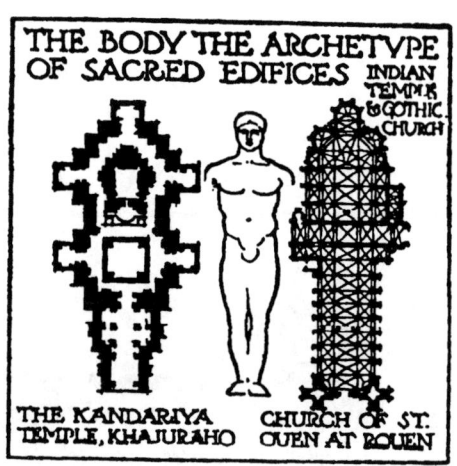

Discover in this rare and scarce book on Freemasonry the secrets of: Atlantis; Egypt; the Druids; The Mother; Vishnu; the Zodiac; the Cherubim; The Mysteries; Masonic, Rosicrucian and Kabbalistic Orders, Including the Tarot; The Tabernacle, Solomon's Temple, the Tower of Babel; Builders of the Middle Ages; Architecture; Medieval Masons; Early Masonic Regulations; Symbols; The Faculty of the Abrac; Masonry; Legendary History of Masonry; A Phoenician Tradition of Sanchoniathon; Fragments Suggesting the Atlantean and Biblical Connection. Written by the author of THE CELESTIAL SHIP OF THE NORTH.

E. Valentia Straiton

ISBN 1-56459-501-3

Request our FREE CATALOG of over 1,000
Rare Esoteric Books
Unavailable Elsewhere

Alchemy, Ancient Wisdom, Astronomy, Baconian, Eastern-Thought, Egyptology, Esoteric, Freemasonry, Gnosticism, Hermetic, Magic, Metaphysics, Mysticism, Mystery Schools, Mythology, Occult, Philosophy, Psychology, Pyramids, Qabalah, Religions, Rosicrucian, Science, Spiritual, Symbolism, Tarot, Theosophy, *and many more!*

Kessinger Publishing Company
Montana, U.S.A.

TABLE OF CONTENTS

Chapter	Page
I - ATLANTIS	1
II - EGYPT	13
III - DRUIDS	23
IV - THE MOTHER	37
V - VISHNU, THE ZODIAC, THE CHERUBIM	50
VI - THE MYSTERIES	59
VII - MASONIC, ROSICRUCIAN AND KABALISTIC ORDERS, INCLUDING THE TAROT	72
VIII - THE TABERNACLE, SOLOMON'S TEMPLE, THE TOWER OF BABEL	89
IX - BUILDERS OF THE MIDDLE AGES	100
X - ARCHITECTURE	113
XI - MEDIEVAL MASONS	133
XII - EARLY MASONIC REGULATIONS -- SYMBOLS	145
XIII - SYMBOLS	159
XIV - THE FACULTY OF ABRAC - SYMBOLS	173
XV - MASONRY	186

APPENDIX

A - LEGENDARY HISTORY OF MASONRY	i
B - A PHOENICIAN TRADITION OF SANCHONIATHON	v
C - INTERESTING FRAGMENTS SUGGESTING THE ATLANTEAN AND BIBLICAL CONNECTION	vi

ERRATA

Page	Paragraph	Line	
4	2nd	9	Change iniators to initiators.
8	1st	last	Change invest to invent.
16	2nd	6	Change Hedes to Hades.
18	3rd	7	Change robes to ropes.
19	1st	2	Change IAO to IAO (I A O).
33	1st	5	Change Asic to Asia.
46	6th	2	Enclose the following in quotation marks: "She is the Mystic Rose of many petals; all living things that tend to God are gathered in her heart.... Within that Mystic Rose, Dante saw Eve sitting at the feet of Mary; healed and made radiant by the reflection of her transfigured countenance." This is a quotation from "The Spiral Way," by John Cordelier, Pages 173-4.
64	2nd	1	The word should be Zoroastrian.
73	2nd	4	Change Kaph-Resh-Kash to Kaph-Resh-Kaph.
81	3rd	6	Change initetes to initiates.
84	1st	2	Change treasurer to treasures.
88	1st	1	Change twentiety to twentieth.
102	4th	3	Should read: services, but they continued to be tolerated.
116	5th	10	Change emperor to Emperor.
130	1st	3	Change Henry VI-i to Henry VI-I
133	4th	6	Change Auchinick to Auchinlock.
137	7th		Under "Item" the reference (2) belongs to A tiler and should not follow the word Knave.
139	1st	5	Take out parentheses from (and Free Masons).
140	2nd	5	Change unitiated to uninitiated.
169	2nd	3	Change was to wax. Line 4: Insert the before the word bees.
181	3rd	12	Take out the word the: "the acacia was ... emblematic."

APPENDIX

i	1st	3, 6 & 7:	Change Lemech to Lamech.
i	5th	3	Take out last word - for.

Fraternally and gratefully I dedicate this book to C. E. K., whose profound knowledge of, and faith in The Builders have been my inspiration, leading me into realms of celestial realities and the unfolding of the backward path which I found strewn with leaves of wisdom for the gathering.

FOREWORD

YEARS OF LABOR are needed in <u>living back</u> to unearth Truths of antiquity -- Truths that are apparently <u>the</u> least wanted but greatly needed to lead through earth-shadows to the Realities, -- found in that GREAT BOOK OF GOD, THE HEAVENS. There are seekers of these truths who never rest in their search for that which had perhaps seemed unattainable; but who are always hoping for attainment. Natural origins found in this GREAT BOOK OF GOD in the past are needed to teach a doctrine of development, as nothing short of primal natural sources can elsewhere be found in their true values; and this doctrine is the battlefield for the evolutionist who looks beyond the historical. Many footholds have been lost in the phenomena of Time and Space, where Ancient Wisdom lives eternally.

In the Apochryphal Chapter IV of The Wisdom of Solomon it is asked of Wisdom: "What is she, and how came she up. I will tell you, and will not hide mysteries from you: but will seek her out from the beginning of her nativity, and bring the knowledge of her into light, and will not pass over the truth." Also, "Whoso seeketh her early shall have no great travail: for he shall find her sitting at his doors."

Wisdom was ever the name of the Mother. The GREAT WORLD MOTHER did not arise out of religion; pre-eval matter is never historical; Motherhood was known long before Paternity had been identified. The Seven Sons of God, called Creative Forces or Powers, were the offspring of this GREAT MOTHER; they were her Celestial Messengers, her Sons of Light, known as "THE FRATERNITY OF THE BUILDERS." They are the Seven Officers belonging to all Masonic Lodges today, for, "as above, so below."

I have endeavored to give fundamental facts in tracing the origin of MASONRY to its source -- these facts are verified in the rudiments of beginnings where the genesis of signs, symbols, and the doctrines of The Ancient Wisdom is discovered.

I am deeply indebted to the few Great Souls I have frequently quoted in this book -- souls who have also traveled the backward way into the Primal Avenue of the GREATEST OF ALL BUILDERS.

Many milestones have been indicated for the earnest student of research, that he may seek for himself and further the Truths brought from the Past. These belong to, and should be taught in every Masonic Lodge throughout the world.

Valentia Straiton

"And I said: I will find the Great Temples in space. The Temple of Temples, whose spires gleam silverly on the loftiest mountain.

Thither will I take my way. Thither will I direct my course.

For though the heart faints mightily, the footsteps falter, and from every pore the spirit bleeds,

Yet would I go upon the Road to the Temple --

Yet would I hasten lest the night-shadows close in about me and the earth-course be ended ere yet I have won to the Holy Heights."

-- Mary Siegrist.

ATLANTIS

A BIRTHPLACE in the heaven of Eternity is portrayed in the constellation we know today as the Great Bear situated in the North with its Seven Great Stars, those marvelously recorded Seven Stars of the ANCIENT FRATERNITY. The starting place was always in the North, where the Ancients noted the revolving of these Great Stars around the Pole of heaven. They were one of the first mystical Seven renowned throughout the entire world, and were called Creative Forces or Powers. As Sons of God they were the offsprings of the Great Mother -- Mother of the World. Primitive peoples called the sky the Temple of the Supreme.

These powers and forces were later recognized as gods, and the higher gods of antiquity were always known as the Sons of the Mother. They became the "Bringers Forth" of creations; they were the first creators of form in space; and these Seven Royal Stars in the course of evolution were called spirits, genii, the angels of the Christians; and finally, through Masonic significance, laid down the rules for the planetary world in perfected laws as the Masonic officers use them today. As planets they belong to the entire world. Stars, Spirits and Humanity are indissolubly bound together. The Sanctus Sanctorum was the Ark of those Seven -- the Ark to build the Covenant to keep -- and the Seven Great Stars, offspring of the Mother, were known as THE FRATERNITY OF THE BUILDERS.

Every early religious scripture gives evidence of a time when the gods gave birth to, and instructed mankind in, these beginnings or early periods when the Great Mother was called "The Living Word." Ancient symbols, myths, legends and allegories of the Ancient Wisdom were created by men who dealt with nature and who were profoundly spiritual in thought and aspiration -- men who taught that the "gymnastics of eternity" meant how to suffer and how to die. Nothing short of the knowledge of remotest beginnings can be sufficient for instruction in the origin of all rites and doctrines where man had attained his expressions through external phenomena. Yet we are still in an age of symbolism; everything seen is a symbol; symbolism should dominate the mind of man today.

Every rite, every ceremony, in fact all things ancient had special symbols to support them, though many of their inner meanings have been lost in the night of time. Masonry became co-eval with man, and the Masons today have the same signs and symbols given them by The Great Architect through His Builders.

Masonry with its ritualism began in the dawn of creation, when the spirit of Masonry was with God as Father-Mother, and though the mists of ages may have enshrouded some of man's first knowledge belonging celestially to THE FRATERNITY OF THE BUILDERS, who had worked under the plans of the Master Architect of Heaven, that Ancient Wisdom has persisted through endless periods of time to the present; and though the old imagery is still apparent throughout the world, much remains undiscovered. The human race is today bringing to light many buried secrets and records belonging to those primeval days.

From this celestial origin, as an earliest form of language, came Sound, which was followed by a Gesture, or Sign Language, -- roots of which were planted, grew, and became established in the early Root Races of the mundane world. The first cell representatives of human life could only receive an answer from the Creator. Those of the First Root Race were said to be beings so ethereal in constitution as to be impervious to the elements; neither flood nor fire could destroy them. They were known as the "shadows of the bodies of the sons of the twilight," showing how very mystical they were -- astral beings devoid of mind, intelligence or will -- ethereal images, as it were. Death came only after man had become a physical creature. Those of the First Race and also the Second dissolved and disappeared into their progeny.

The Second Root Race had a sound language, as if composed only of vowels -- a sort of chant-like sound. This race is only alluded to, therefore very little is known of it.

Hyperborean was the name chosen for the second continent which stretched out towards the North Pole, known as the Land of the Gods, and said to be the birthplace of the first Giants and the Pygmies. These Polar lands were pre-Lemurian. The Lemurians were said to gravitate toward their progenitors the Hyperboreans, who were called "the Dwellers beyond the North Wind," or those who lived above the mountains -- mystically meaning the heavens where Paradise was said to be located. It was an Elysium inaccessible by land or sea. (Some of the Australian tribes are said to be descendants of the Hyperborean region.) *1

It is said the Pygmies came from the Dwarfed Races of the Pole. They began millions of years ago to build a sign language which they evolved from articulate sound. The Red Men of the Paleolithic Ages were Pygmies. Remnants of these are found throughout the world. African tribes were the offshoots of the Atlanteans. The earliest Paleolithic men of Europe were of Atlantean stock, while the Aboriginals were an exodus from the earliest Nilotic Negroes. Paleolithic represented the age of unpolished stone; the Neolithic, polished stone.

The Third Root Race improved the sound language which became monosyllabic. Gesture and sign language supplemented sound, an outlet for the image-making faculty. Knowledge of things came through pictures which represented visualized thought, a mental reflection before the use of words. Towards the end of this Third Root Race beings were human in their Divine nature. The Human Race, known as the Lemurian Race of peoples, originated at the end of the Third Race. Sex appeared in the Third Race. It appears in embryo in the third month of its pre-natal existence. When primitive man first began to think, he observed the laws of nature from which came his spiritual ideas, and from the need created by articulate sound he began to represent things by gesture, sign and symbol. His first mode of worship was a propitiary one to the Elements -- Fire, Earth, Air and Water. Awe and wonder created a spiritual instinct, which was greater than a religious one. Time has added to, but taken much from, the simplicity and depth of man's first mystic realizations.

The Lemurians in their Sixth Sub-Race were known to have put up buildings or the first "rock cities" from stone and lava; hence the stone

---

*1 After the Hyperboreans of these early first ages came the primitive Lemurian men. Next came the Atlanteans; then the Aryans.

relics on the Easter Isles. "The oldest remains of Cyclopian buildings were all the handiwork of the Lemurians of the last Sub-race." [1]

Man of the Third Root Race were originally androgynous beings, but slowly developed into separate ones at its close; they were known as the "Golden Colored," and secret knowledge tells us that they built boats and flotillas before the building of houses began. The later Lemurians and their Continent became the center of human development. They preceded and completed the Human Races of the Fourth and Fifth. They had unlimited control over the Elements and lived with ease in Water, Air or Fire; and it has been stated that they understood the most weird secrets of nature. They are said to have imparted the ineffable Lost Word, which lingers as a "far-off dying echo" in the hearts of a privileged few. This sacred Word, which came through the Third Race, has been orally given from one generation to another, and the Disciples or Initiates of the Fourth Race -- the Atlanteans -- gave it to the Fifth; and this Fifth Race, or continent, is America. When America was discovered it was called Atlantis by some of the natives.

A few records, half a dozen columns, and old Cyclopian ruins are all that is left of Lemuria --- now submerged due to earthquakes and subterraneous fires. It is prophesied that Great Britain and Europe will one day meet with the same fate. The beginning of the sinking of Lemuria was near the Arctic Circle (Norway). Scandinavian legends play an important part in the ceremonies of Masonic Lodges today. Lemuria ended its career in Lanka, which became the Lanka of the Atlanteans. The Giants of Genesis are the historical Atlanteans of Lanka, who later became the Greek Titans.

The Book of Genesis should be regarded "with increased veneration, as a relic dating from the most ancient days of man's history on earth; its roots cross the great ocean; every line is valuable; a word, a letter, an accent may throw light upon the gravest problems of the birth of civilization.[2]

There are small groups of islands in the Pacific Ocean where we find the remains of a once great civilization. Enormous roofless temples are still there which had permitted the rays of the sun to fall on heads bowed in supplication and prayer. Great Cyclopian walls and Monoliths still remain -- all that is left of that marvelous age. Today only savages linger among the ruins which are now but footprints on the sands of time. The Easter Isles, though submerged by a volcanic disturbance, have been raised untouched, and upon them are the relics of primeval Giants, eloquent, magnificent memorials, both grand and mysterious -- some carved in red stone, some with crowns upon their heads ten feet in diameter -- the work of the Cyclops, those Giants of of old. The divine perfection of architectural proportions of the Great Pyramid, cromlechs, Druidical circles, dolmans, temples in India, altars, and other enormous works of stone is due to the work of the Cyclops -- gigantic engineers using neither mortar, cement, steel nor iron with which to cut their stones. As engineers with their marvelous works they still remain a mystery, almost unknown today. They were the Initiated Priest-Architects who were justly called "The Builders."

---

[1] - BLAVATSKY, H. P. - THE SECRET DOCTRINE, Vol. II, page 317.
[2] - DONNELLY, Ignatius -- ATLANTIC, THE ANTEDILUVIAN WORLD - page 212

In a small half-ruined town in Central Asia, called Bamian, which lies at the foot of a great mountain, there is a valley hemmed in by colossal rocks, some of which have been carved into caves or grottoes, though others are natural. At the entrance to one of the caves there are five enormous statues which have been claimed to be the work of the Initiates of the Fourth Race who had sought refuge there after the submersion of the continent. These five statues give "an imperishable record of the esoteric teaching about the gradual evolution of the races. The largest is made to represent the First Race of mankind, its ethereal body being commemorated in hard, everlasting stone for the instruction of future generations, as its remembrance would otherwise never have survived the Atlantean Deluge." (This statue cut in rock is 173 feet high.) "The second -- 120 feet high -- represents the sweat-born; and the third -- measuring 60 feet -- immortalizes the race that fell, and thereby inaugurated the first physical race, born of father and mother, the last descendants of which are represented in the Statues found on Easter Isle, but they were only from twenty to twenty-five feet in stature at the epoch when Lemuria was submerged, after it had been nearly destroyed by volcanic fires. The Fourth Race was still smaller, though gigantic in comparison with our present Fifth Race, and the series culminated finally in the latter." 1

Enormous blocks of granite are strewn over Southern Russia and Siberia where there is neither mountain nor rock, showing that these must have been brought from a great distance with gigantic effort. The circular arrangement of the stones would seem to indicate Atlantean or Lemurian origin. Giants they must have been who carved and carried these enormous granite monoliths. Traditions about a race of early Giants in days of old were universal and exist in both oral and written law. The Cyclops were the true Giants who had flourished millions of years before. They were called Builders. Occultism calls them Iniators. They laid many foundation stones of true Masonry. This should be of special interest to Speculative Masonry today.

Allegory tells us that the gradual passage from the Cyclopian civilization, the age of colossal structures in buildings, to the more sensual and physical culture of the Atlanteans caused the last of the Third Race to lose the third eye.

The one-eyed Giants were the last Sub-Race of the Lemurians. One eye was always regarded as the Wisdom Eye, or the All-Seeing Eye. The two front eyes were fully developed as physical organs in the beginning of the Atlantean Fourth Race. Millions of years ago the organ of consciousness known today as the pineal gland gave man knowledge of invisible worlds. It was closed during the Lemurian period, when man became more human, more material; but the student of occultism should know that the third eye is indissolubly connected with Karma -- the tenet being so mysterious that very few seem to know of it.

"The Lemurians gravitated towards the North Pole, or the heavens, to their progenitors -- the Hyperboreans. The Atlanteans gravitated towards the South Pole -- the pit, cosmically and terrestrially." The Lemurians

---

1 - BLAVATSKY, H. P. - "THE SECRET DOCTRINE." - Vol. II, page 340.

were called the Children of Heaven and Earth. The Atlanteans were Giants of physical beauty and strength at the middle of their Fourth Race. Lemuria was destroyed by fire; Atlantis, by water.

The Lemurians merged with the Atlanteans and formed what was known as the Lemuro-Atlantean Race. Ancients knew the Secret Wisdom. The orally-given words of the inhabitants of this Race have been perpetuated through the ages, whispered from mouth to ear, and given orally to those worthy to receive such knowledge. In no other way could the truths of the Ancient Wisdom have been preserved. The Lemuro-Atlanteans were originally known as Divine Kings and Gods; they possessed superhuman powers. So sacred and secret was their knowledge that to divulge it was punishable by death.

The Atlanteans were the first really human and terrestrial race, as those who preceded them were more ethereal and divine than human. These semi-divine beings were only human in appearance, but became physiologically changed and, as the Bible tells us, took unto themselves wives fair to look at but mindless. They fell victims to their animal natures when magic and sorcery became prevalent. Creuzer states, in part: "They <u>commanded the Elements, knew the secrets of heaven and the earth, of the sea and the whole world, and read futurity in the stars</u>. . . . It seems, indeed, as though one has to deal, when reading of them, <u>not with men as we are</u>, but with Spirits of the Elements sprung from the bosom of Nature and having full sway over her. ... All these beings <u>are marked with a character of MAGIC and SORCERY</u>." [1] Time is proving the existence of a true race at that period.

The Fourth Race developed monosyllabic speech; they had unlimited sight and therefore knew all things at once. They were the originators of speech, but the primitive speech of the civilized Atlanteans has almost died out or has decayed. It was in Atlantis that so much arose of purity and power. The true Illuminati were warned of the destruction to come and departed to different parts of the world that they might preserve this truth for future generations. It is said "The light still shines on the true Atlantis." The Golden Age of Saturn was the happy age of Atlantis.

The religion of Atlantis was pure and simple; her people made no sacrifices but worshipped the Sun. It was the common center from which arts and sciences came; and the Atlanteans eclipsed all others in sciences. Nearly all arts essential to civilization which we possess date back to Atlantis. The powerful ancient civilization of Egypt was an outgrowth of Atlantis. As heirlooms we have an advanced knowledge of the zodiac; also, astronomy and symbolism. The entire history of the world is in the zodiac. All antiquity believed that humanity and its races were intimately connected with the planets and the zodiac.

Marvelous temples were erected in Atlantis from which we have our knowledge of the sacred mountain over which the twelve gods ruled. Atlantis is the first historical land in the traditions of the Ancients. The last of Atlantis that went down beyond the Pillars of Hercules is Plato's Island of Atlantis, only a fragment of the great continent, named after its parent. Berosus

---

1 - BLAVATSKY, H. P. - THE SECRET DOCTRINE, Vol. II., Page 285.

tells us that the god who gave warning of the Deluge was Chronus (Saturn). The Pillars of Hercules were called the "Pillars of Chronus." Chronus was an Atlantean god, and the ancient Romans called the Atlantic Ocean "The Chronian Sea."

The Ram with the Golden Fleece was an offspring of Poseidon, who sat as the first King of Atlantis, according to Plato. Trying to separate the great continent of Atlantis from this last little island of Plato's has been both trying and confusing. The old records tell us that when Atlantis was submerged "the ends of the world got loose."

Atlantean civilization reached the highest level. Its fall came through the degenerate descendants of the nation of Plato's Atlantis. The Atlanteans' knowledge led them to build, before the coming of the Flood, subterranean passages and retreats for the preservation of their records, lest the memory of their sacred ceremonies should be lost.

"The Fourth Race had periods of the highest civilization. Greek, Roman, and even Egyptian civilization was nothing compared to the civilization that began with the Third Root Race," it was said, by a Master, after its separation.

There were different colored Atlanteans, among them Giants and Dwarfs. The last of the Giants perished some 850,000 years ago, towards the close of the Miocene Age. The last of the lands of Lemuria perished about 700,000 years before the beginning of the Tertiary period; and the last of Atlantis, Plato's little island, about 11,000 years ago. Orientals never doubted the ages; they recognized the early original races and their cycles. Only the skeptic Westerner still doubts; but the veil is constantly being lifted, for nothing stands still.

All ancient writings are filled with traditions, fables and myths of Lemuria and Atlantis. They were divided into two distinct classes; "Sons of Night" or the dark, and "Sons of the Sun" or light.(1) All allegories are based on the battle between light and darkness under myriad names -- the Sun going down in the West, into the dark, and arising in the East, into the light. We await the time when astronomical significance will release its place in the spiritual and the divine. Ancient deities were of Light and Wisdom, symbolized by the Sun and the Moon, whose influences cyclically change the axis of the earth, -- hence, deluges and cataclysms. Continents perish in turn by Fire and Water -- fundamental Elements. Earthquakes, becoming more and more prevalent, hold their warning in sudden changes in climate or position of continents. Our whole globe is convulsed periodically, transforming the face of the earth. However, very little change has taken place at the Poles, for Polar land breaks off into islands and peninsulas which remain the same.

The power and importance of names having been recognized by the Divine Masters, Atlantis was often mentioned under different names.

---

(1) - Earliest legends of India speak of two dynasties, those of the kings of the "Race of the Sun" and those of the "Race of the Moon." In Egypt the Sun was especially emphasized as Osiris, and Osiris and Horus are never mentioned, unless with the Sun. They were "Sons of the Sun" or Light.

Occult science shows that the founders of the Root Races had been connected with the North Pole. "The Aryan Race was born and developed in the Far North, though after the sinking of Atlantis its tribes emigrated further south into Asia." They trace their descent through the Atlanteans and the more spiritual race of the Lemurians, in whom the "Sons of Wisdom" were supposed to have incarnated; but from the Fourth Race they received their knowledge of the sciences. Before the Veda of the earliest Aryans was written, the Ancient Wisdom of the Lemuro-Atlanteans was sowing the seed of many of the existing religions in every nation. These religions were the offshoots of the Wisdom of the Great Mother -- the never-dying Tree whose leaves have been scattered over the whole world.

There were four distinct Races that preceded the Fifth Race. Nothing regarding this is mystical, except the ethereal bodies of the first Races, those of legendary origin. Legend is universal and belongs to every ancient country. Having become historical, the traditions of Atlantis are still being told and must be accepted. They have come down to us from time immemorial, from the dawn of creation, where the first ritual of Masonry had its birth, and the Great Mother from her throne among the stars gave her messages of Wisdom through her Sons of Light -- THE FRATERNITY OF THE BUILDERS -- to their prototypes below.

The capital of Atlantis was called the City of the Golden Gates, and has been preserved among many religions as the City of God, or the Holy City. This Sacred City has ever been called the archetype of the New Jerusalem with its twelve gates of precious stones and its streets paved with gold.

Monotheism was first preached in Atlantis. Nearly all existing creeds are offshoots or modifications of pure monotheism. In the oldest book of the Egyptians are the proverbs of Ptah-hotep, showing that her ancient colony came from, and received its original pure faith from the Mother Land, Atlantis. This book proclaimed the doctrine of the One God. "And over the heads and over the ruins of Egypt, Chaldea, Phoenicia, Greece, Rome and India, a handful of poor shepherds, ignorant, debased and despised, have carried down to our own times a conception which could only have originated in the highest possible state of human society." Kindred Nomadic tribes are gone, and their land of promise is in the hands of strangers.

The center of worship of the Atlantean Wisdom Religion was in a great pyramidal temple built upon a plateau which arose from the center of their capital city. The construction of all pyramids originated in Atlantis; and this construction is a problem not yet solved. Pyramids, tombs, temples, were all dedicated to the Sun, or Fire Worship, which Masons today look upon as the Fire Principle. Wherever the Atlanteans went they erected pyramids after the pattern of the great sanctuary in their City of the Golden Gates. The pyramids of Egypt, Yucatan, Mexico, Central America, Normandy, Britain, and of our own Indians, originated with the Atlanteans. "Nearly all the great cosmologic mysteries forming the foundations of the various books of the world were based upon the Atlantean Mystery Ritual," derived from THE FRATERNITY OF THE BUILDERS.

Atlantis has left a heritage not alone of science, ethics, philosophy, et cetera, but, owing to her downfall, of hate, war and perversions. When the Initiate Priests realized the steady degradation and doom of their country, when she slowly but surely departed from her Divine path, they withdrew from their homeland, carrying with them to the uttermost parts of the earth the keys of their Ancient Wisdom, their Secret Doctrine, enfolded in the sanctity of their symbols held so sacredly in Masonry. Many traveled into Egypt and established themselves there as Divine Rulers. "Phoenicia, Egypt, Chaldea, India, Greece and Rome passed the torch of Wisdom from one to another, but in all that lapse of time they added nothing to the arts which existed in the earliest period of Egyptian history. Egyptian civilization was an outgrowth of Atlantis, but thousands of years passed when no advance was made from this civilization. In the future it will be said that between the birth of civilization in Atlantis and the new civilization there stretches a period of many thousands of years during which mankind did not invest but simply perpetuated." (1)

Sun Worship (2) was the religion of Atlantis; it was also the primitive religion of the Red Men of America, and remains today, as those who know can testify. From the greatest antiquity red was a sacred color. Gods of the Ancients were painted red; early branches of the Atlantean stock were Red Men. Adam stands for the first, Ad-Ad meaning "the Only One," the virgin earth or primordial matter (which was red) from which we have the name Adam, who was said to be red. The color red denotes life, action, service; and red belongs to Masonry; it is a part of their Fire Principle.

In Atlantis women dominated and set the record of their time. Through many cycles men forgot, but women artists created the wavy designs used/upon their pillars; they designed the flowers interwoven with the mystic design of those distant ages so well preserved in our temple pillars today; and there in Atlantis the Mother was first, the Mother reigned. She was called the Mother of Wisdom; and the Mother was queen, Labor was royal.

It was said, "Thou shalt return, for Atlantis holds thee dear." If her people should return, they would see water, only water, for Atlantis lies asleep on the ocean-bed; but, "Atlantis though dead yet speaketh." Among our American Indians, the Chaldeans, the Mexicans, Central Americans, and from other pre-historic races primitive men remembered the glories of Atlantis, the golden ornaments and their source in the City of the Golden Gates, and many tales and legends are told about the gods who came up out of the sea. Isaiah and Ezekiel frequently refer to the Islands of the Sea. "The Initiate Priests of the sacred Fathers who promised to come back to their missionary settlement never returned." Atlantean tradition states that Atlantis perished in one night through a great cataclysmic condition. Some of the people escaped in boats and were called the "men of the sea." They spread over many parts of the world.

---

(1) - DONNELLY, Ignatius -- ATLANTIS, THE ANTEDILUVIAN WORLD, Pages 130-131
(2) - Atlantean Sun Worship is perpetuated in the Ritual of our Christian Churches. The Atlanteans were the keepers of the most sacred mysteries. As Sun Worshipers they were called those who "Were enamored of the light and beauty of the Sun" who built their temples on the heights; and these temples showed a finished type of sacred art worthy of their sacred Ritual. The people of Atlantis are remembered as belonging to a great civilized race of gigantic stature. They were architects, builders, Masons, who moved enormous stones -- as fragments of their work indicate.

Zodiacal knowledge handed down from time immemorial was perfected in Atlantis. Invention of fire and making of brick were first known there. Alchemy had its birthplace in the Fourth Race; the rite of circumcision had its origin then, and was imposed upon the Egyptians, Ethiopians, Phoenicians, Hebrews, and other ancient races. The mythology of Greece is a history of the kings and queens of Atlantis; Poseidon, god and founder of Atlantis, was also called the founder of Athens. The Eleusinian mysteries were Atlantean. They held an extraordinary influence and represented the Masonic Ritual traced back through Atlantis to its celestial origin.

There existed in the middle of an island located in Atlantis a very sacred and lofty mountain. "This mountain cast a shadow 5,000 stadia in extent. Its summit touched the sphere of ether." On its summit a temple to the gods was built -- from which is traced the origin of the legends of Meru, Olympus, and Asgard, with their twelve gods. In nearly all religions twelve gods, or twelve brothers, belonged to a sacred mountain. Asgard with her twelve gods was watered by four primoval rivers of milk flowing in four directions representing the cardinal points of the world. It was an abode of happiness and peace. Also, there was the enchanted garden of the Chinese with its four rivers radiating from one parent stream. Many legends tell of sacred eminences in the midst of superabundance. Indeed, this tradition of four rivers springing from a central source and forming the cardinal cross is found among the Singalese, the Tibetans, the Buddhists, the Brahmans and the Hebrews.

Atlantis was called the "axle mountain" of the world; among many nations it was symbolic of the human head as it rose out of the four elements that composed the body. It has been called the Garden of Eden; but in the story of creation, "a river went out from Eden (to water the garden) and was parted thence and became four heads." The Ancients regarded the rest of the body as the Garden of Eden; and when it is understood that the head is Eden and the rest of the body the Garden of Eden, and <u>all the Garden of Eden that ever was</u>, its solution may easily be seen and found in the four currents of the body.

"Atlantis had its four rivers and its four kings where the four sacred elements were formed; and there began to manifest man as we know him today. Man has latent within him both male and female; and when these are balanced there will be moments when a merge or union is made, and then flashes of real consciousness will follow, for man carries within him that part of the WORD of which he is an expression, that brings thoughts from the unmanifest into manifestation, and so fulfills his destiny."[1]

The Book of Genesis states clearly that God created man male and female and called <u>their</u> name Adam. The people of <u>Ad</u> were Atlanteans, and these two letters prefixed many other names representing nationalities all over the world; hence it became a common tradition for lands where four rivers are found going in opposite directions, as North, East, South and West, to create the four cardinal points of the world, as well as the cross belonging to all the nations of the world; and the cross that was surrounded by a ring belonged to, and was pre-eminently the symbol of Atlantis. The

---

(1) - WIGGS, George W.

mystical Tau, the Crux Ansata, represented the Hidden Wisdom of many ancient countries, and the cross, we are told, was a remembrance of the celestial Garden of Eden, originally called "The Garden of God and the Beautiful" (the Mother) where the Seven Great Stars encircled the Pole and became especially reminiscent of THE FRATERNITY OF THE BUILDERS. These builders originated the cross of creative power, eternity, and immortality, as an emblematic type of "The Soul of the Universe," the Mother -- the Mother who gives everlasting evidence of Divine Unity.

A phonetic alphabet is a system of signs representing the sounds of human speech. The Second Root Race had the first sound language that we know of, and from it knowledge of our civilization has been made possible. The old and enlightened Chinese never had a phonetic alphabet which might have helped as a guide and shown the greatness of the people who had invented it. Semitic and Phoenician characters were developed through a phonetic alphabet originating from early picture-writing. A phonetic alphabet is found among the Mayas, an ancient people belonging to the Peninsular of Yucatan, "who claim that their civilization came to them across the sea in ships from the East, that is, from the direction of Atlantis." (1)

Lando, the first Bishop of Yucatan, wrote a history of the Mayas which contains an explanation and a description of this phonetic alphabet, as great in its usefulness as the finding of the Rosetta Stone.

Phoenicians and Egyptians did not borrow from each other but obtained their alphabet from a common source, these characters having originated in the same hieroglyphics. The Maya alphabet is a survival of this. "And it must be remembered that these resemblances are found between the only two phonetic systems of alphabet in the world." (2)

The Point within the Circle, so profound in Masonry, is found in this ancient phonetic alphabet produced from the sound language. Inscriptions on monuments in Central America tell of a civilization far anterior to any known in Europe today, for they had belonged to antediluvian times.

It is claimed by John Greaves, an English astronomer, that an Arab tradition states the Pyramid was the tomb of Seth. Ancient structures, such as the Great Pyramid, were geometrically reduced to a pyramidal form which the Atlanteans and Egyptians realized in their Cosmic System. Josephus declares that the Patriarch Seth was the inventor of the pillars upon which in sacred characters was carved that peculiar Wisdom concerning the heavenly bodies, and that when the world was to be destroyed by water or fire these pillars would not be lost. This legend maintains that they were brought from the land of Siriad, where they remain today. He also affirms that these two Pillars of Seth were erected before the Atlantean Flood. Upon them the rules for astronomy were engraved. They had been preserved down to his time. (Josephus was born A.D. 37.) These were the celebrated Atlantean antediluvian columns or stelae containing the lore of the ancient world reputed to have been carved before the Great Flood.

(1) - DONNELLY, Ignatius; ATLANTIS, THE ANTEDILUVIAN WORLD, Page 217.
(2) - Ibid; page 232.

Siriad, from whence these pillars were said to have been brought, represented the Solstices, and in this instance Siriad was the abode of the Sun. "Numerically the entire scheme of the pillars leads to the Sun's orbit at its center and explains why the Arabs called the innermost rhombus of the Pyramid the tomb of Seth." (1)

Plato tells us that "the people of Atlantis engraved their laws upon columns of bronze and plates of gold;" and Manetho says, in a passage taken from an Egyptian legend, that Hermes, aware of the impending Deluge (meaning the destruction of Atlantis) inscribed his laws, giving the principles of all knowledge, in hieroglyphics and sacred characters, on pillars of stone, stelae or tablets. After the Deluge a second or reincarnated Hermes, known as the Egyptian Taht -- called At-hothes, showing his Atlantean origin -- translated these hieroglyphics into the vulgar tongue; and so we recognize how primitive man, in his effort to perpetuate the knowledge of these hieroglyphs, furnishes a solution to the legends which have come to us. The first Hermes "was the intelligence of the Word of God." Taht was one of his incarnations. It is probable that symbolical copies of the primitive records had been placed in the most sacred corner of a temple in Egypt. An Egyptian tradition of these pillars in the third and fourth centuries mentions so-called fragments of Hermes, but the knowledge given in these fragments has been greatly colored by the Judaizing Christian writers. These pillars, whether of Seth, Hermes or others, symbolized the magical or celestial tradition of universal law. Ancient names coming through from antiquity, such as Hermes, Seth, Taht, Tat, Set, are all generic, one and the same, a name given to Atlantian Initiates who were called Sons of the Son of the Dragon.

"The Secret Wisdom teaches that the arts, sciences, theology and philosophy of every nation which preceded the last universally known deluge had been recorded ideographically from the primitive oral record of the Fourth Race, and that these were the inheritance of the latter from the early Third Root Race before the allegorical fall."

Hermes, known as the God of Wisdom, is the Divine Ancestor and progenitor of the early men of the Third Race. He was reputed in one of his incarnations to be the forefather of Israel.

Legends of the pillars of marble and brick have been perpetuated in the mysteries of Masonry as its legitimate precursor. They are known to the world at large and have come down in an unbroken continuity through tradition, symbol, allegory and emblem.

In the Chaldean legend the god Ea ordered that Divine learning should be inscribed on tables of terra cotta which were to be buried in the City of the Sun at Sippara. In the version of Nerosis, Chronus appeared to him (Xisuthros) in a vision and warned him of a flood which would destroy mankind and enjoined him to write a history of the beginning, procedure and conclusion of all things and to bury it in the City of the Sun at Sippara.

"The people of Atlantis, having thus seen their country destroyed, section by section, and judging that their own time must inevitably come, must have lived in constant terror, partly explaining the origin of primeval relig-

---

(1) - THE CANON

ion and the hold it had upon the minds of men; and this condition of things may furnish a solution to the legends which have come down to us of their efforts to perpetuate their learning on pillars, and also may be an explanation of that other legend of the Tower of Babel ... common to both continents, and in which they sought to build a tower high enough to escape the Deluge. All the legends of the preservation of a record prove that the united voice of antiquity taught that the antediluvians had advanced so far in civilization as to possess an alphabet and a system of writing; a conclusion which ... finds confirmation in the original identity of the alphabetical signs used in the old world and the new." (1)

Similar legends are extant about books. It was a belief among ancient nations that the art of writing was known to the antediluvians -- that is, before the Great Flood. Legends abound concerning these sacred writings which were to be preserved from destruction by fire or water. The Druids believed that their books, "the books of Pherylit" and the "writings of Pridian," were more ancient than the Flood. "Ceridwen consults them before she prepares the mysterious cauldron which shadows out the awful catastrophe of the Deluge."(2)

The first Avatar of Vishnu incarnated as a fish and after the Deluge he recovered the Holy Books -- which had been lost -- from the bottom of the ocean.

Berosus tells us that Oannes, sometimes represented as a fish, before the Deluge wrote concerning the generation of man. Hebrew commentators write of the Book of Precepts given to Adam (Adam meaning the first), received by a company of angels -- the stars. The Hebrews, as well as Josephus and Suidas, preserve a tradition that the Ad-ami (which surely must mean the people of Ad, or Atlantis) possessed the art of writing before the Deluge. The Egyptians claimed that Anubis (Hermes) had written annals before the Deluge. The Chinese have a tradition of a first people who wrote a book teaching the arts of life. The Goths always had known of letters, and one named LeGrand tells us that before the Deluge or soon afterwards "there were found the acts of great men engraved in letters on large stones." Pliny, Strabo, and many others speak of these lost books that were written before the Flood. The Atlanteans preserved their Ancient Wisdom on substances incapable of destruction, and variously named, that their great civilization might be known for all time. And so this ancient knowledge has come down to the present and confirms the belief that an alphabet was derived from an antediluvian world; and that world was Atlantis.

"If the Spirit of which the universe is but an expression -- of whose frame the stars are the infinite molecules -- can be supposed ever to interfere with the laws of matter and reach down into the doings of man, would it not be to save from the wreck and waste of time the most sublime fruit of the civilization of the drowned Atlantis -- a belief in the one, only, just God, the father of all life, the imposer of all moral obligation?" (3)

---

(1) - DONNELLY, Ignatius - ATLANTIS, THE ANTEDILUVIAN WORLD, page 128.
(2) - FABER'S PAGAN IDOLATRY, pages 150-151.
(3) - DONNELLY, Ignatius - ATLANTIS, THE ANTEDILUVIAN WORLD, page 213.

Chapter II

EGYPT

> "Before thou canst address Ra thou
> must be able to proceed skyward and
> kneel among the Stars."
> - "The Book of the Dead."

ANCIENT LEGENDS held truths; Ancient Wisdom was truth verified; symbolism was the expression of primitive man's thought under the guidance of natural law when individual authorship was unknown. Necessity was the inventor; type, as a pattern, was the first model; and doing was earlier than saying; so, the dumb drama came first; signs entered into the second phase -- which language it was necessary to learn, as ignorance was considered deadly. Egypt was the interpreter of antiquity. In her sign language we find the origin of mythology, symbology and numbers.

Indescribable charm surrounded primitive man's spiritual life, difficult for us to grasp today. He studied the "Book of God" -- the heavens -- which held the wisdom of all that was, is, and will forever be. His vision carried him far beyond the material world; discouragement never hindered his search; he could not rest, and did not, hoping that in spirit he would find a vision of hidden love. He merged the outer with the inner marvels of life, just as the true Mason today should seek the doctrine of eternal truths.

Priestly astronomers in those days were the mystery-teachers of the heavens; they knew the laws of motion and of life; they searched the soul for the indwelling Deity, and sought through spiritual powers to understand the relation between man and heaven. Ages before religion had intervened, primordial man, divinely inspired, had reverenced unseen powers, which was proceded by a recognition of those powers in nature. To him that which seemed to be of the greatest simplicity became the most profound when spiritually interpreted.

From the standpoint of the genuine evolutionist we get the truths relative to Beginnings. Almost a lifetime is needed to unlearn the falsities introduced into legendary lore. The evolutionist begins in time and he alone is freed from the untruths generally accepted by the modern theologian in his interpretation of primordial cause.

The civilization of Egypt in its first appearance was of the highest order, showing that she must have drawn her power from a civilization greater than her own. Egypt's very beginning seems to have been mature, as if the country had never known youth, presupposing that her people represented myriad centuries. As all roads lead to Rome, the seeker may find that all roads lead to Atlantis.

Egypt did not claim that her system of hieroglyphics was her own, but that it was "the language of the gods." The art of writing was said to have been given by Taht, an incarnation of Hermes; and legends state that among the gods Hermes was known mystically as the son of Zeus and Maia; and Maia was the daughter of Atlas -- hence Atlantean.

Egypt's religion was developed from mythology and was the most profound and perhaps the most spiritual ever known. Her celestial mythology was later called the "Word of God" -- showing how great it was. In the hidden side of the Egyptian Mysteries relics of the ancient past were found; and what was brought over should be studied by every Mason today. In their celestial mythology they acknowledged but one God -- Ptah -- whom they endowed with the attributes of all the gods collectively. Ptah was known as the father of all the later Fathers, and was called THE GREAT ARCHITECT OF THE UNIVERSE. In the solar regime he was known as Amen-Ra, who symbolized the hidden sun. He was endowed with the same attributes as Ptah who had been the first Great Father hundreds of thousands of years before; and symbolically Amen-Ra was said to be born out of a cycle of a new era.

The Egyptians enacted a very spiritual ceremony relative to this god, which is of greatest interest to all Freemasons. It was named "The Building of the Temple of Amen-Ra." Its Ritual, perhaps one of the most magnificent ever known, was given with a majesty, splendor and beauty very difficult for words to describe.

The Temple of Amen-Ra was composed of seven officers and thirty-three members, which constituted a Lodge. Through their knowledge of how to work the Ritual, the officers and members in opening their Lodge were enabled to build a thought-form of the god Amen-Ra. Amen means the hidden light, and Ra, the dawn, or the Sun, coming out of the darkness to become light. When Ra, the Sun, with his ship sailed through the sky he carried Amen-Ra and the others with him. His boat was attached by a rope or cable to the Pole-Star. One end of the cable was fastened to the Pole, the other end to the boat of Ra (the Sun) which was cable-towed around the ecliptic, symbolizing the Sun going through the twelve signs of the zodiac. Finally there were seven ropes, cables or powers, each representing one of the Seven Great Stars of the Fraternity, now symbolically used in Masonic Rituals.

The Temple of Amen-Ra practically corresponds to the building of the Temple of Solomon in Masonry. The closing of the Lodge, or the ending of the Ritual, worked cosmically, and each of the forty members was enabled, through his understanding of Light, to evolve a thought-form. Each carried away with him a portion of this sacred Light, which not only blessed the surrounding country but the whole universe as well. True initiation was attained through the knowledge of Cosmic law. An understanding of the Temple of Amen-Ra, its Ritual and thought-form, enabled the earnest candidate to unfold the centers within himself, giving him what the mystics called "the mind of Hermes," thus showing how Hermes incarnated the God-Mind, representing the opening of the Lodge; and its closing would be the Sermon on the Common Mind which is given in Hermetic books and teachings.

"The Book of the Dead" states that "before thou canst address Ra thou must be able to proceed skyward and kneel among the stars." During the Roman period of Julius, owing to the degeneracy of the Priests of Amen-Ra, ancient esoteric and spiritual lore ceased for a time. The mysterious light which illuminated the temples of Egypt was said by the Priests to be a reflection of the Central Spiritual Sun. It is this same light which illuminates those strange mystical temples said to surround the world. Manly Hall states in his great book, MASONIC, HERMETIC, QUABBALISTIC, ROSICRUCIAN, SYMBOLICAL PHILOSOPHY, (page LIII) "This weird light seen ten thousand miles beneath the surface of the earth by I AM, THE MAN, in that remarkable Masonic allegory ETIDORPHA (Aphrodite spelled backwards) may well refer to the mysterious midnight sun of the ancient rites."

In times of great moment, when Egyptian Pharoahs needed greater strength and vigilance, they wore the tail of a lioness, thereby completing the positive and negative forces of life. This symbol of a double power is with us today, though rarely understood. The long feminine garment of a woman is worn by Priests, ministers, professors and others. In Masonry it indicates the power of man to march forward in the first ranks, heralding a new civilization, or a new consciousness, which is foretold in this age by bringing out of the past centuries the profound and Sacred Wisdom of old.

The Ritual of "The Book of the Dead" was pre-eminently a book of knowledge or wisdom containing the gnosis of the Mysteries, which was the science known by all Mystery-teachers. "To possess knowledge was to be the master of divine powers and magical works. This Book of the Dead in life became the Book of Life in death." (1)

It is the oldest known of all religious writings, a key to the Divine Mysteries. Eschatology was founded in the mould of mythology, and can only be unraveled through mythology. All primordial types of mythology were universal. The difference between the two constituted the Lesser and the Greater Mysteries -- the Greater, perfected in the Egyptian religion, were eschatological and to be read in the Ritual as the Mysteries or Amenta; the Lesser were partly sociological and similar to the ceremonial Rites of Totemism. (2)

Amenta was the "threshold of the other world, the secret solid Earth of Eternity" which was opened by Ptah and his Pygmies. The earth of eternity was for the human soul evolved on earth. After its life on earth came resurrection in Amenta. Amenta was the generating sphere where disembodied souls waited between lives. It was also the meeting place of the Sun and Moon, from whence came the newborn Sun or son, "the Ever Coming Son." Through mastery of the sign language and its wisdom one could complete the passage of Amenta; otherwise ignorance precluded any knowledge of how the next world could be reached. (3) Horus, of the Greater Mysteries in the religious legend, suffered, died, and was buried in Amenta, and arose in the glories of the East.

---

(1) - MASSEY, Gerald, - ANCIENT EGYPT, THE LIGHT OF THE WORLD.
(2) - Aborigines of the world have the same Totemic ceremonies and hieroglyphics, the same signs and many words that belonged to Egypt. Life, birth, regeneration, as well as the life to come, belong to the earliest stellar age of Egypt, brought over by the ancient Priests of Atlantis.
(3) - THE FRATERNITY OF THE BUILDERS -- the Seven, with Ptah (mentioned in the making of Amenta); the Seven Old, Old Ones; "the Seven Patriarchs of Genesis, who lived such enormous lengths of time;" the Seven Giants of celestial stature, who were "humanized as magnified non-natural men and then transferred to earth;" the Seven Rulers of the world; the Seven Lords and Masters of Eternity; the Seven Never-Setting Stars, keepers of the World's Great Year, who are to arise and "help to establish the new heaven and rejuvenate the earth," -- all are Sons of Light, all show how marvelous is the heritage of THE FRATERNITY OF THE BUILDERS (who have become the Seven Officers in Masonic Lodges today).

The Ritual opens with the resurrection from the earth of Amenta into the earth of eternity. The earth of eternity for the human soul evolved on earth, the final resurrection from the tomb of the underworld, was into the heaven of eternity. The "Resurrection in the ritual is coming forth to day, whether <u>from</u> the life on earth or <u>to</u> the life attainable in the heaven of eternity." The first resurrection in Amenta was an ascension from the tomb by means of a secret doorway. There were twelve sacred or secret doors in this passage through Amenta: The first -- the Door of the Secret Mystery -- was difficult to enter; only a life of purity on earth gave strength to open it. But the exit, which led to the land of Eternal Life, was easy. Horus was the door of darkness -- "The Way," -- Master of the Word of Power, the Door of the Good Shepherd. The funeral valley -- the Open Sesame of many legends -- was the Valley of Death in the West, having its resurrection in the East. There were ten great Mysteries of Amenta, celebrated on ten different nights.

The Ritual of "The Book of the Dead" is carved in stone in the Great Pyramid of Egypt as an everlasting monument. The Ritual of the Resurrection was their Book of Life. "It was a revelation made by Ra, the Holy Spirit" and given to Horus who is said to have talked with his Father in Heaven. It was Horus who spoke as the Word of God to those living on earth as the "Sayer of the Sayings," as well as to the "breathless ones in Hades." Horus personates the WORD in his first coming, and in the second coming he is the WORD MADE TRUE.

"One of the most beautiful ideas of the Egyptians was that of representing the Eternal Father by the Ever Coming Son, as in the child Horus who was the type of eternal youth as an external child. This was the child of a mother who was the Eternal Virgin. ... The doctrines of the Incarnation, the Virgin birth, the Resurrection, the Father-God who is identical with his own son, and others believed to be specifically Christian, were Egyptian, ages and ages before the present era began." (1)

This Ritual contains a true account in symbolic language of how the spirit, after leaving the body and before reaching the Grand Lodge above, learns, by passing through many difficulties and trials met with in Amenta, to obey the principles of Truth, Justice and Morality, which belong to this life; for Truth and Justice were placed in the scales of perfect poise, so powerful it could be turned with a feather. An understanding of the Ritual given in this great book would develop the inner meaning of the Masonic Ritual today. The true Mason, coming from darkness into the Light of a new consciousness, learns that the soul must be born anew before it can be initiated into things Divine. In the old order of the Mysteries profanation of any secret was unpardonable. These secrets were of the Creator, and their meanings were for Initiates only. The entire ceremony concerning the passage of the candidate from the eighteenth to the thirtieth degree is the same as that given in the Egyptian Ritual of Death, Judgment, and its ultimates, when the WORD is necessary before the candidate can pass the Door.

The entire body of an Egyptian temple formed a definite and coordinated system of worship based upon astronomy, which conveyed the belief that a worthy life on earth enabled one to attain the higher planes. The

---
(1) - CHURCHWARD, Albert - SIGNS AND SYMBOLS OF PRIMORDIAL MAN,- Page 397

Great Pyramid was a Masonic Temple, and is known as such today. Ascent of its slopes was made possible. It remains for students of the Great Mysteries of life to trace to its center the "triadic and tetratic" nature of this monument.

The Great Pyramid from its entrance to its innermost shrine was oriented North and South, showing its tremendous age. It was built near the center of the land surface of the world, -- not without great meaning. It is the greatest Temple of Initiation in the world, and still remains a "mute teacher of the Mysteries of Creation." The sole entrance to the Pyramid was through a gate in the North, which imaged a concealed door, secretly hung, which only Initiates knew how to open. This entrance was high above the ground and was called the "Gate of the Great God." It is thought by some to have been built by Atlantean Priests who escaped in boats from over the sea.

Within the Pyramid there are three great chambers which are of significance to Masons. The one above the King's Chamber was called a symbol of the brain. It contains an open sarcophagus, used, esoterically speaking, for the death of the lower man -- his liberation into a higher consciousness. A similar coffin was always used in the Ancient Mysteries and is today, symbolically.

The chamber below the King's, known as the Queen's, was thought to be a symbol of the heart, under the guidance of the Christ Spirit. The third and lowest room, called the Pit, was beneath the surface of the earth, or the generative point. Together the three rooms represented a triad of the Spirit. At the top of the Pyramid is a large flat stone about thirty feet square called "The True Stone which is the head of all corners missing." The Pyramid was "The Secret House." Egyptians of old called it "The Light." A diagram of the interior of the Pyramid would allow the candidate of Masonry to follow the initiation of the old postulant from the mysterious darkness into the brilliancy of light, for the building of Masonry today is reaching towards the light.

From the "Book of the Master of the Secret House" we learn that "the Master of the Secret Scroll" (the Secret Wisdom) was "in the secret chambers of the House which bore the mystic title of 'The Light;' and in order to follow his instruction" the Postulant was to begin by looking towards the heavens to try to understand how the "earthly sphere is itself a member of the starry host;" and that "the God of the Universe is in the light above the firmament and His symbols are upon the earth." And so "we may watch the course of the postulant accepted by the 'Master of the Secret,' as he is inducted, chamber by chamber, into the hidden places of the Egyptian Ritual." (1)

To the Egyptian of old, to have mastered the knowledge of the Secret House, "The Light," "was to have mastered the secrets of the tomb." The postulant experienced neither terror nor fear, for each step was towards his Creator; he was coming into the Light -- seeking the Light of Immortality. Through these mystic chambers of the Pyramid passed the Enlightened Ones of antiquity. The Pyramid was the place of "the womb of the mysteries; those who entered the portals as men came forth as gods." (2)

---

(1) ADAMS, Marsham - THE BOOK OF THE MASTER, Pages 24, 147.
(2) HALL, Manly P.

The religious ceremonies of Egypt, so highly venerated in Masonry, contained the Mysteries of antiquity. It was in "the starry groups of heaven they imaged forth the supernal powers and spirits which the holy departed met with on his progress through the heights as he mounted from the earth to the Great Lodge above" and stood "face to face and eye to eye with 'Him who knew the Depths.'" (1)

When the postulant emerged and rose triumphant from the darkness, he found himself before the sacred portals behind which the Egyptians believed sat the "Eternal Wisdom." Like the postulant of old, may the candidate of today, after his many trials, find himself before "The Gateway of the gods" built so mysteriously by those ancient Masons whose interwoven secrets are still to be read by the conqueror of these trials; and when the portals are opened may he hear the old, old message, "Come! Come in peace!"

Worship of Light, or worship of the Sun as light, was absorbed into the Egyptian Mysteries, as it is in the Masonic Ritual. Secret schools of the Mysteries were divided into two groups, forming the Greater and the Lesser Mysteries. The Greater held the Master Key to the sacred symbolic drama, whose secrets were inviolate; the Lesser Mysteries were for the profane. In one of their initiatory ceremonies the candidate searching for Light entered unclothed, wearing a chain of robes about his neck. He was blindfolded and given a password. Then he began a circumambulation of the Lodge, which was always taken with the left foot first(2) symbolizing the destruction of the serpent -- that Giant Serpent who hides in the dark and then comes forth to war against the light. This enabled him to put all evil thoughts from his life so that his senses could be restored to the fullness of an eternal beauty before starting on his great journey.

It has been written that when the destruction of the serpent had been accomplished its "body was to be cut in pieces and burnt to ashes, and that those ashes were to be scattered over the face of the earth and water by the four winds of heaven." And if a candidate turned back or in any way violated his obligation, "his throat was cut and his head chopped off after the heart had been torn out." After the initiation he was presented to the Master, and a grip or token was given him with the word Maat-Heru, which signified "One whose voice must be obeyed." With this Word of Power he was allowed to pass through the Valley of Death. This was a primitive way of passing through the underworld.

A candidate had always to endure twelve trials, known as "Twelve Tortures," and to make the ascent of a ladder with seven steps representing the seven degrees of initiation. His wanderings were through darkness, his courage and fortitude were tested to the full. He was told in true Masonic form to control his passions, "never to either desire or seek revenge, to honor his parents above all, to respect old age and those weaker than himself," and that he must always remember his hour of death and resurrection into an imperishable new body. Purity and chastity were urged, as immorality might be punishable by death. Ennobling lessons in morality were always given, as

---
(1) - ADAMS, Marsham - THE BOOK OF THE MASTER, page 191
(2) - Origin of, and reason for the left foot first is given in the PAPYRUS of NESIAMSU, most important in Masonry.

perfection awaited the candidate at the end of his long journey. If he proved himself worthy, he was given the sacred name LAO, and taught the "Priestly dance of the Circle," -- a dance following the course of the Sun and the Moon. He had passed through the gate of death or darkness into the Light, which belonged to all Mysteries, just as it is given in Masonry today when the candidate impersonates the figurative prototype of H. A.

It is the same death, burial and resurrection belonging to all ancient Mysteries, originating with the "Dying God" -- the Sun setting in the West and rising in the East. How very few seem to know the true and beautiful eschatology when performing Rites and Ceremonies in the Lodges! Resurrection of the dead and life everlasting were fully believed in, but when this belief became corrupt, those unfamiliar with the hieratic character of archaic times had mistaken ideas. Too frequently the Egyptologists claimed many gods instead of the attributes and powers of the One God represented by Ptah, the Father of all the Fathers, and called THE GREAT ARCHITECT OF THE UNIVERSE.

Dynastic Egyptians held to the creed that man had a body; within this body, a soul; and within the soul, a spirit; that the body belonged entirely to the earth, and the soul and spirit to heaven; and that the spirit, after detachment, had to join the GREAT ARCHITECT before it could return to the soul; and when the soul entered the body it folded its wings and resigned itself to a long imprisonment. What we call death liberated the soul which had many dangers and trials to encounter before the spirit was released so that it could return and regain its "Mansion of Bliss," -- the home of THE GREAT ARCHITECT OF THE UNIVERSE.

The Ritual states that the spirit had to become detached from the soul before the Judgment of the Soul in this Divine Order could take place. When the spirit had been justified, the regeneration of the soul followed. In their creed the holy dead were finally united, soul with soul, in an indissoluble bond. Their teaching of Immortality, Everlasting Life, and Resurrection of the Spiritual Body is the same in the Ritualism of Masonic Lodges today, and taught with the same reverence. The original "Creed of the Egyptians" was always given orally, but so much has been sacrificed through oral tradition, it is practically unknown in its entire purity. Its primordial beginning has become obscured through the mists of vast eras of time.

To the ancient Egyptian the purity of the soul and the body was accepted as a spiritual force, the fire of which penetrated and permeated his whole life. If ever it became sullied, the sacred fire died out. Therefore, the profound inner meaning of the Ritual of the Judgment of the Soul becomes very clear to those who have vision. In this Judgment there were forty-five Assessors present at the weighing of the soul, which took place in the presence of Osiris. The forty-two Assessors corresponded to those principles in nature manifesting in the faculties of the human brain; and when the heart was weighed against the feather it meant, esoterically, that the heart and mind must be brought into equilibrium before the soul could be liberated from the illusion of matter. In a word, "the forty-two Assessors are the forty-two faculties of the human head, and the Ritual explains these Assessors." [1]

"The front and back brain make up the forty-two faculties, -- the hexagram, or six; and these united, just like the six days of creation, form

---

(1) - BLACKDEN, M. W. - THE RITUAL OF THE MYSTERY OF THE JUDGMENT OF THE SOUL.

a seventh; for, the forty-two faculties merged into one, or forty-three, make seven. Hence, it will be plain that the forty-three, as seven, are ready now to receive from the prime seven, unmanifest, that which makes forty-nine. These forty-nine become thirteen (one and three) which is four, or the four elements -- Air, Fire, Water and Earth -- the four quarters of the zodiac, or the instincts of the four sacred animals which, when merged, become BEING or Intuition -- feminine; the dynamic masculine is within; and the instincts of the elements transmuted become Spirit, Soul, Body and Mind, or the 'city built four-square' spoken of in Revelation." (1)

It was in the final degree of initiation that the traditional Esoteric Wisdom of Egypt was taught. The Ritual of the Judgment of the Soul gives two lists of negative assertions: the denial of sin by the Initiate having committed sin; and "the well-known confession in which the 'pure and sinless heart' addresses in turn the forty-two Assessors and denies the sin over which each Assessor presides." (2)

The heart was the central stronghold of Being, that part of man which did not sin on its own initiative "but only by reason of its connection with the man whose being it moulded." The first denial consisted of "thirty-six assertions of freedom from the physical actions of sin." The forty-two of the "negative confession" dealt with these sins which were considered spiritual and mental. The opening of the Doors was of the greatest spiritual significance, the candidate having to answer the symbolical meaning of each Door before it opened. Judgment followed; and when finished, if the candidate was found worthy and requested further advancement, he was obliged to recapitulate the symbols of his tuition up to that period.

In his method of teaching, the ancient Priest used symbolical geography as an analogy. That the whole might be more readily understood, countries symbolized the Lodges; mountains, the cities; and rivers were made to symbolize the furniture of the Lodges; and through this teaching the "country's mystic history was made emblematic of the true initiation of the soul." On completion of the Initiatory Ceremony "the Leader recites a prayer on behalf of the New Brother, looking forward from the Ceremony that is now over to the goal of that path of which it forms the Gateway, from the Symbol enacted in the earthly lodge to those great realities which it will be found to symbolize when the initiate enters the Grand Lodge above and stands before the Judgment Seat of THE GREAT ARCHITECT OF THE UNIVERSE." (3)

In the Egyptian astronomical myth the two first-born of the Great Mother were Sut (Saturn) and Horus (The Sun). They were the two oldest types of elemental powers representing Darkness and Light. They became non-human ancestors. Horus was a Great Spirit, a Divine body in heaven, who sought and vanquished Sut. This battle, as the struggle between Darkness and Light -- a war that has waged ever since the beginning of the world -- is the first battle ever recorded. Shu (Mars) became the reconciler.

Horus and Sut were the founders of North and South in heaven. This was the earliest orientation establishing the two Poles, or Pillars of Heaven.

---
(1) - WIGGS, George W.
(2) - BLACKDEN, M. W. - THE RITUAL OF THE MYSTERY OF THE JUDGMENT OF THE SOUL.
(3) - Ibid.

These two Pillars were found at the entrance to Amenta, Solomon's Temple, et cetera. This heaven raised on two pillars by Sut and Horus, was followed by a heaven of three -- in three divisions -- which was upraised by Shu, and preceded the one built by Ptah on a square or four-fold basis, creating the four cardinal points of the world. The twelve signs of the zodiac symbolized a heaven raised on a foundation that was twelve-fold. The number twelve is frequently found among all ancient peoples, and especially in Jewish and Christian writings, where appear the twelve Apostles, Patriarchs, Tribes, Prophets, or a twelve-fold Deity relating to the Duodecimo -- the Dodecahedron.

Shu, as the equinoxial power, with Sut and Horus, completed the first triad; the two pillars with the line across formed the first triad in heaven which was primordial. Numerous copies of this primal figure, though evolved hundreds of thousands of years ago, have been handed down through the ages as prototypes under different names. The definition of Sut, Shu and Horus, in the Egyptian, is identical with the L. A. B., as demonstrated in the Royal Arch Chapter in Masonry.

The meaning of this earliest triangle is known to Masonic members of the thirty-third degree, and their jewel shows the apex resting upon the cross above the crown supported by the double-headed eagle holding the sword in his claws. In this same myth Shu stands on the Pyramid of Seven Steps with the apex of the triangle resting on them; thus he first lifted up the heavens from the earth in the form of a triangle. This was known as the Ladder, or Staircase of Shu, and was famous throughout Egypt. In the Ritual of the Egyptians two sets of names were given to the seven steps known as the Seven Primordial Powers. The first set comprised attributes of Horus; and the second set is known to all Brothers of the thirtieth degree. When Light became triumphant, the apex of this triangle represented the Pole of the North -- Light. In the oldest papyri and on the oldest monuments, the original triangle was given with the apex down, signifying darkness.

"Shu followed with a new foundation in the Equinox which was double -- East and West." This new foundation of a much later period was given in the Ritual when the orientation was East and West. Shu, standing on the equinox, formed the Royal Arch (celestial) Cantanarian. The Royal Arch Degree has, also, two interlaced triangles surrounded by a circle, in the center of which is a triple Tau.

In Egypt Isis was a prototype of the Great Mother. There are keys to the Secret Doctrine which were symbolically expressed by this "Virgin Isis" veiled as she is always found. Initiates alone can read her secret, so filled with wisdom; but many today aspire to enter her presence, hoping that her veil might be lifted or removed and that they might stand face to face with all the Divine realities of nature which she represents. But to Isis, dwelling behind her veil, to lift that veil would mean a passing from the realm of reality into that of Immortality; and before the veil can be lifted one must be born into Immortality.

Knowledge of the Immortality that lies behind this veil of Isis, which is hidden in the great Wisdom of the Ages, is the aspiration of all Masons bounded by Brotherhood. In his GENIUS OF MASONRY, page 94, Samuel Knapp states: "Behind the veil of Isis I have long thought was concealed our

Masonic birth; I now fully believe it. There was the cradle of Masonry; no matter by what name it is called; no matter by whom it was enjoyed."

Isis often uses the Sun and the Moon, together with the seven planets and the twelve signs of the Zodiac, to give forth her radiating powers in nature, suggesting fulfillment of the whole by being heavenly directed. She wears many symbolical ornaments for the purification of all that may be connected with life. She carries the systrum in her hand with which she strikes the keynote of nature. At times the systrum interchanges with an olive branch, an ear or corn, a sheaf of wheat, or a bunch of grapes -- all symbolical of nature's nutrition; for she is Mother Nature and has been so represented in the zodiacal sign of Virgo, the Virgin. As the Virgin she has been immortalized throughout the ancient world. A sheaf of wheat often exchanges with a young sun-god, to symbolize a new manifestation. The girdle of Isis was held together by four golden plates in the form of a square, symbolizing the essence of the four Elements, or the world of Elementals.

Many myths and legends are found concerning this truly great Mother. The Cult of Isis is still kept alive in some Masonic Lodges. Plato states that the "First Cause of all things is communicated to those who approach the Temple of Isis with prudence and sanctity." Knowledge of a First Cause or Universal Nature is the aim of all the Mysteries.

Isis has been wooed by all philosophers; all ancient peoples believed in her Divine purity and to them she represented the mysteries of motherhood -- the most apparent proof of nature's "Omniscient wisdom of God's overshadowing powers." At times Isis is seen standing between the two pillars on the porch of King Solomon's Temple. These pillars, important in Masonic Lodges, represent "production through polarity," suggesting to all Brothers how Wisdom may be attained through equilibrium. To the modern seeker Isis has become the epitome of the Great Unknown. She has become immortalized as the World Mother, and there is nothing quite so great, so beautiful, as this Divine World Mother and all that she symbolizes. No greater homage has ever been given to another except that given to the Creator. She was the first born, the most Divine, the very Soul of the World; she is Mother Nature, or Woman as the Universal Mother. The Feast of Lights in honor of Isis, portraying in scenic representation death and its subsequent restoration to life -- called "The Mysteries of the Night or of the Dying God" -- belongs to the Master's Degree.

Chapter III
DRUIDS, ELEMENTALS, STONEHENGE

> So backward, always backward we
> must go, into those great gardens of
> the past whose flowers need the quiet
> between the bud and the blossom to
> bring again into manifestation the
> old Mysteries holding the Wisdom of
> the Ages, belonging to the illusive
> lands of Long Ago.
> -- E. V. S.

THERE can be no doubt about the Atlantean Priests having in time entered Druidic countries, taking with them their Mysteries which closely followed in detail those of Egypt. Their close proximity to the lost Atlantis may account for their Sun Worship. They practiced the purest eschatological doctrine which had been perfected in Egypt. Their temples of great stones arranged in circular form were generally oriented East and West, showing the later solar origin, as well as practice of the solar doctrine.

An article on the Druidic Creed states that "it was unlawful to build temples to the gods or to worship them within walls and under roofs." Their ceremonies and religious rites were held in open spaces, often upon great eminences within full view of the heavens to which their reverence was directed. Ceremonies were also held in the deepest recesses of forests or in groves which became their sacred places, watered by consecrated fountains or rivers, and surrounded by ditches or mounds. The middle of each grove contained a circular area enclosed by one, two, or three rows of stones set perpendicularly in the earth. Within these enclosures were altars of sacrifice and inextinguishable fires. The three enclosed circles represented the Star, Lunar and Solar periods of time. Druidic laws reckoned each and every one of the circles or cycles of time.

These places of worship and sacrifice were unlike any pattern belonging to other nations. Sacrifices in Atlantis were of fruit and flowers; Druids of Gaul and Britain used human sacrifices; the Irish, like the Atlanteans, were more merciful. Druids often planted their own trees, especially the spreading oak which was the one most favored and held in highest veneration.

Druidic religion can be read on their dolmens and in the trees of the forests whose sanctuaries held secrets unknown to us. They had faith in the protection of the Genii who overshadowed their trees and stones. In their attainment of knowledge they used both stone and tree as teacher. What they taught was Time. One form of their Time-keeping was called "preserving the fire." The end of an era was looked upon as a time of purification, the cleansing of the earth with its attendant corruptions by the waters of the Deluge. It was said that "preserving the fire" was the natural antithesis of being overwhelmed by the Flood.

The Druids' cures for various conditions were made through magnetism or magnetized metals, the mistletoe, and serpents' eggs, because of their astral qualities. Genius, inspiration and serenity were said to dwell in the magical cauldron of their goddess Ceridwen. The mistletoe is parasitic. It contains a peculiar fruit which was put into this cauldron and used for cures and prophecies. The magic properties of the mistletoe were well known to them; and it is prophesied that some day this spongy growth will be recognized by medical science.

Mistletoe and acorns were used for adornment in their armorial bearings. They worshipped Deity through the oak upon which the mistletoe grew; and when aspects among the stars fulfilled certain conditions the mistletoe was cut from the tree with a golden sickle consecrated for the purpose, and in falling, was received in a white cloth that it might not become polluted by vibrations from the earth. They were instructed concerning the creation of the world, the laws of nature, the occult properties of medicine, the celestial world of magic, and the science of equilibrium -- the latter taught as the true and absolute science of nature.

Magic was the science of Abraham, Orpheus, Confucius, Zoroaster, Solomon, and other great philosophers whose magical doctrines they claimed were those engraved on stone by Hermes. These doctrines are said to have been unveiled by Moses, -- being, in a sense, the WORD revealed. "Magic is spiritual wisdom, nature the material ally, pupil and servant of the magician," and, as a science, to abuse it is to lose it, and also destroy oneself.

The first observers of stars were the Wise Men known as the Magi -- hence the word "magic" which signifies a perfect knowledge of the works of God. Ancient Magi journeyed far to attain knowledge of the stars, and all antiquity regarded them with great affection. They did not worship the stars but followed them as messengers. As astrologers they knew the science of the stars to be the fountain-head of all great doctrines.

"Magical science is the absolute science of equilibrium; it is essentially religious. It presided at the formation of dogma in the antique world, and has been the nursing-mother of all civilization." The Great Work is the attainment of a middle point wherein equilibrating forces dwell. To find this point will give a true knowledge of the Kingdom of Heaven. The science of equilibrium is the key to the occult sciences. Harmony proceeds from the analogy of opposites, just as light equilibrates between shadow and brightness. Study of the Holy Kabala will help wonderfully in the understanding of equilibrium.

Magicians were all conscious of the powers in the deep places of their natures and understood eternal justice -- which may be understood in studying the Seal of Solomon, his Key and his Ring, which were tokens of a supreme royalty. The Seal synthesized both Key and Ring. The Key guards against deviations in relation to occult forces; magical forces are in the Ring, either for darkness or light. The Keys are the talismans of the seventy-two names and convey the Mysteries of the twenty-two paths that are reproduced in the Tarot.

In the fall of the angels, among the two hundred who took upon themselves wives, it is understood that magic of the stars connected with enchantments and the marvels found in the properties of roots and trees were taught. One of the angels taught the secrets of sorcery; another one, the mysteries of the stars; one, the manifestation of signs; and another, the motions of the Moon. These angels were the Sons of God or the Initiates of Magic; but when the harmonies of nature were disturbed, the positive and negative poles of equilibrium became confused. Symbolically this was the profanation of the Tree of Knowledge which had become separated from the Tree of Life, even as it is indicated by Enoch in the Fall of the Angels.

"In all ages God has made known His wonders and when to judge the Quick and the Dead, for there will be signs of His coming by the falling of the stars and the darkening of the Sun and the Moon and by a deep astonishment which will be cast upon mortals." All this we are watching today; for cataclysms are needed to efface degeneracy with its lust for gold which threatens the world. The sanctuary must be kept closed, else the depths of sin will continue to prevail.

The Druids also symbolized Deity under the form of a mighty serpent, as an emblem of Eternal Time. The serpent is the mesmerist or the magician of the animal world. The earliest ideas of magical power were evolved from it. Its fascinating and magnetic power over man is well known. Magnetism is the alphabet of magic; everything in nature is magic; and to attain magical powers was one of the chief aims of Ancient Religions.

The serpent pierced by an arrow is well known as an image of the union between Spirit and Light, also Will and Light. Kabalistically it represents the letter Aleph which is equilibrated unity, Material and Spiritual, Breath and Logos. A lamb bearing a cross has practically the same significance. "The union of the two is the balance, the Great Arcanum, the Great Work, the equilibrium of Jachin and Boaz." (1)

Druids had profound faith in the protection of Elementals. Veneration was given these invisible beings and offerings were made to them. All great religions of the world believed in their existence. Amenta was given by the Egyptians as their celestial birthplace. All philosophers know that the fall of Spirit into Matter is the cause or origin of all our griefs. Spirit-Matter manifests in the four occult Elements and in the Elementals belonging to them. Of these very little is known by man today. "All the substance matter of the physical plane comes into form first on interior planes and is then consolidated by the Elemental Beings which form the constituents of each Element. There is no dead matter, it is all consciously alive." (Anonymous).

Elementals are the Spirits of Nature -- unusual beings of an ethereal order dwelling in Fire, Earth, Air and Water. They are intermediate agents between gods and men; they were called the "Children of the Philosophers." They fill the world with conscious beings; and have always been known and referred to in occult writings. According to some ancient teachings

---

(1) - LEVI, Eliphas - THE HISTORY OF MAGIC, page 411.

these Nature, or Elemental, Spirits were evolved by the ceaseless motion inherent in Astral Light. (1)   They are, in a certain sense, the builders of matter, and are the first self-conscious forms of each Element created from its Astral counterpart, which manifests to us as Fire, Earth, Air and Water.

Study of the Elementals belongs to Masonry through its esoteric and mystical knowledge. Both in Masonry and in the Kabala much may be learned of them. The Kabala is the most sacred book of the Hebrews and difficult to fathom, but tradition tells us that it "has been transmitted from Adam and Abraham by a continuous train of Initiates to the spiritual head of the Hebrew race today." (1)   Its Inner Wisdom is unknown except to a very few who have had it orally from Hierophant or Disciple.

Fire is represented by the Salamanders as Astral Ether and motion in all things of life. These Elementals of Fire correspond to touch, and their function is in building, destroying, and regenerating the substance on their plane of life. Salamanders live in the South and belong to the zodiacal sign Leo (Fire). They are composed of the most subtle portions of the sphere of Fire; they live in the air, are organized under the action of Universal Fire -- that fire inherent in every motion of nature. As Universal Fire it is the Light of the Logos. They have been seen as balls of fire rolling over the hillside, and as crawling creatures or tongues of flame roving across the field, and as such, have been seen in homes. A spark of fire cannot be lighted without them; they are the most dynamic of the Elementals; they love volcanic regions; they hover around the altar fires in the temples, and they underlie the Astral plane of man.

Earth is represented by the Gnomes as Atomic Ether. They belong to the highest phase of crystallization, keeping in form the matter on their plane of life. Their mission, like that of the others, is to manifest on earth that which is already created in the Astral. They dwell in the North, among creative energies, and are of the finest particles of earth; they work among flowers and trees, and rocks -- which they pass through, as they do walls of stone, exactly as we mortals find no obstacle in passing through air. They have not a spiritual soul, yet they have been known to seek union with men that they might receive the germ of Immortality. All these Nature-Spirits are formed from their own etheric substance; the Gnomes, through what is called the humidity of the earth -- the only substance in which they can function.

The earth is filled to the center with these little people of the Elements; they work with all crystallized substances, but their special corner of creation belongs to the North. In the literature of mysticism they are said to govern the treasures of the earth, the hidden things, so that if one wishes for material treasures, he must gain the friendship of

---

(1) - "Astral Light has been called magnetized electricity. The Terrestrial Mercury to whom sacrifices were ordained by Diviners is no other than the Astral Light personified. It is the fluid genius of the earth, fatal for those who arouse it without knowing how to direct it. It is the focus of physical life and the magnetized receptacle of death."
(2) - DUDLEY, L. -- COMTE DE GABALIS.

these little people. They are very friendly and will either reveal or conceal. They play a very great part in man's development. They really seek beautiful nature, and we hear of them working among the coral reefs under the sea. They also create in darkness, where the rays of the Sun do not penetrate. Their zodiacal sign is Taurus (Earth).

Air is represented by the Sylphs as Mental Ether, memory and reason. The Elementals of Air correspond to sound. They are self-conscious forms created primarily from the constituents of the gasses in the air which they endeavor to combine so that the lower creations may receive the Breath of Life. Sylphs are composed of the purest atoms of air, and, as they live on air, are perhaps closer to human beings than are other Elementals. They are kindly disposed towards man, and are often known as Storm Angels, and Fairies; they are found on the mountain-tops and are the Children of Light who live in the East and come under the zodiacal sign Aquarius (Air) which is the symbol of Light. Like the air, they are whimsical and changeable; they are often heard in the wind. In the present Age of Aquarius many facts concerning these Sylphs, now concealed, will be unearthed and gathered scientifically.

Water is represented by the Nymphs as Humidic Ether, the Water of Life, or the Mother. Elementals of Water correspond to taste; they would absorb the "mothering of the substance of their plane of life." Water is also a builder, as well as a destroyer, and being a symbol of change, affects whatever change is symbolized. Nymphs are of the subtlest essence of water and, like the Gnomes, seem to have homes. The Salamanders and the Sylphs are the wanderers. The Nymphs are very kindly disposed towards man and, again like the Gnomes, yearn to become united with him that they may thereby become Immortal. Poetically we hear of the Nymphs sitting by the water; and poets have draped them in flimsy robes of great beauty. They serve man with a spirit of love and kindness. The power of the West wind is power to them; they love the rain; they live in the West, and their zodiacal sign is Scorpio (Water).

The last and fifth (Ether) is Akasha, or Spirit, Divine Fire; and Spirit is limitless life in which there is no rest; it is the ever-radiant pushing force.

When storms, thunder and lightning rage, it means that the Sylphs and Salamanders are at war. When tidal waves and floods are in combat, the Sylphs and Nymphs are at war. When earthquakes and landslides trouble the world, then the Salamanders and Gnomes are at war.

Each atom of man's body is a self-conscious entity, for living within our bodies is this strange race of beings. Our every movement is due to these astral-psychic Elementals. The work of the Neophyte is to try to understand, control, and use the Elementals according to the Divine plan, no other, within himself; to recognize them with the same thoughtfulness and consideration that would be given human beings; and in a surprising way, they will respond. Love them and understand them; do not ignore them, for they **are** conscious and are able to receive and to understand. The realization that these Elemental Lives are conscious and do respond to consciousness indicates a step along the road of evolution. One must look within, train the mind to become conscious, focus these Beings, and concentrate on power to direct the Will that is within. Thus one would see beneath the surface into the interior worlds. The Arabians taught that with aid from the Elementals, the Nature-Spirits, it was possible to gain entrance to the ethereal world inhabited by them.

The Children of Nature are all builders of everything connected with Fire, Earth, Air and Water; and in man, they operate in his body just as they work within and without all nature. They can readily put one in touch with the currents of life. They were used by the Magus of old, by the Alchemist in his laboratory, and the Occultist knew their secrets. If man would concentrate upon them today, he, too, would learn the secrets of hidden nature. The building of great temples, the swinging of colossal stones can be occultly explained; the destruction of nations, and wars, dreams, et cetera, are all filled with the activities of these little creatures of nature. Their work is endless. Earthquakes, tornadoes, volcanic action, fiery phenomena in heaven and upon earth, cyclones, men and nature, construction and destruction, war between capital and labor, men and nations, -- all are due to the Elementals. This battle between the forces is fully alive today between the Brotherhood of Light, and the Powers of Darkness; but those who follow the Light will come into the promise of Spiritual revelation.

These Nature-Spirits hold a place between man and spirit; but man lives in the exterior world, whereas they live in both the interior and exterior worlds. Men have their leaders or those in authority; the bees and the ants have their queen, but the omnipotence of God is not limited to the care of man, for under His care come also these Nature-Children. They live out their own destiny, just as man does. "The Eternal Wisdom of the existence of all things is without time, without beginning, and without end. Things that are considered to be impossible will be accomplished." (1)

The four Elements are intertwined with the four corners of the world, from which is evolved the Occult Wisdom of the world; and without the vital powers of the Ether which the Elementals represent, our temple building throughout the ages could not have continued. In evolution our consciousness passes through these four Elements; and when we learn the mystery of the vital powers of Ether and of crystallization, we learn the first lesson in the control of human nature. The basis of all life is behind these material Elements; and how alive they are! These Elemental builders have at times appeared to the human eye. Angels are invisible to us, yet they have appeared to those with spiritual sight. We invoke these Spirits through our litanies. Is not the Wisdom of God unfathomable!

In the Ritual of Masonry the Elements of Fire, Earth, Air and Water are symbolically given the candidate during his initiation; they represent a benediction to the four ethers, making consciousness possible, and through consciousness, redemption and regeneration. When the Bishop raises his two fingers, symbolical of Fire and Air, and lowers his other two, symbolical of Earth and Water, the thumb becomes Spirit, as the fifth finger. It is the same benediction referred to above.

Man is the instrument through which the elementary world is acting. Man and the Elementals belong to the Divine order of things; and in this period of Light, that which had seemed incredible is now becoming manifest. Wisdom is not created by man; it comes to him whose mind is pure and whose heart is open to receive it. Spiritual regeneration is accomplished by that which exists within, for there resides the Wisdom of God. Besides these living inhabitants of the Elements, other groups are known as Ghosts, Spectres and passing Shadows. Many books referring to these Elementals would be of deep interest to those who desire to know more of the works of THE GREAT ARCHITECT OF THE UNIVERSE, never forgetting that an invisible universe is within the visible.

Druidism was openly sustained in England but when this open worship had been prohibited by Canute, who reigned from 1015 to 1036, their Rites were concealed under the title of Freemasonry. They formed Lodges, making use of the craft of Masonry to cover their mystical ceremonies. In the Eleventh Century, under Canute, a law was passed forbidding all subjects to worship the God of the Gentiles, or the gods of the heathen -- meaning the Sun, Moon, fire, fountains, stone, trees, or wood of any kind. Druidism was openly practised in France for a hundred years after the edict of Canute had prohibited its worship in England. In 1140 it was reduced to a regular religious body in France. It is of interest to know that at the time of the Anglo Saxon rule, two-thirds of the people, many of them from other nations as well as Britain, were slaves; and, unfortunately for them, they were not admitted into Freemasonry. They were an uncultured, rude people, ignorant, unskilled, and, as it were, untamed under law and government. They were intemperate, riotous in character, and are said, even in the time of Canute, to have sold their children and kindred to foreigners. Unhappy men were sold in the market like cattle. It was through conquest that these people began to attain the rudiments of art and to correct their rough, immoral ways.

The Druids' religion was deep-seated and profound, retaining a belief in One God; their philosophies were co-eval with those of Egypt, Persia, Chaldea, India and other nations widely separated, showing that religious expression had come from one and the same source -- Atlantis. Their religion was sublime in its precepts and purity, beautiful in its teachings, divinely inspiring because of celestial making. The planet Mercury was reverenced as a supreme god under the similitude of a stone-cube. Before the decadence of Druidism their teachings were inspired. The Druids were called "'Men of the Oak Tree' (in Sanscrit the word dru means timber) and were said to stand as mediators between gods and man." They had great power over the people.

In Druidic ceremonies candidates were arranged according to merit, in the order of Three, Five and Seven, and were led nine times around their sanctuary, going from East to West. They had three distinct schools or degrees of instruction, similar to the Blue Lodge in Masonry. On the hill of Ked three great steps had been cut, all facing the East -- sunrise. "On these three tiers or steps of gigantic heavenward strides we may conjecture the Druids stood in their triple ranks at sunrise and on gala days, in front of a stone temple crowning the hill of Ked towards which these steps ascended." (1)

Their colors were given in the Egyptian way. The color Blue, for harmony, was assigned to the highest step; White, for purity, to the second step; and Green, for learning, to the lowest. These three are the chord of color found on the Druidic glains. Those robed in sky-blue were the Bards who had to memorize the twenty thousand verses of Druidic sacred poetry; they

---

(1) - MASSEY, Gerald - A BOOK OF THE BEGINNINGS, Vol. I, Page 429

were the teachers of the candidates awaiting admission to their doctrines. There was a chief or Arch-Druid in every nation, and to become an Arch-Priest or Arch-Druid six successive degrees were needed; then, by ballot, he was elected by the most eminent of the Druids. In common with those of all ancient mystery schools, their teachings were double; A simple moral code was taught the people in general; the esoteric doctrine belonged to the Initiated Priests. The neophyte had to be under the tongue of good report, that he might impart the unwritten words, as nothing was ever to be committed to writing, their wisdom being too sacred. Many trials, temptations and proofs of strength and courage were required before one could enter the degrees representing their Rites.

As a supreme test of courage the candidates were sent to sea in frail open boats. Many never returned. Few ever passed the Third Degree. Their initiations were given in caves, as they had a belief that Enoch had deposited his invaluable secrets at the bottom of deep caverns. All orifices were first consecrated with holy oil. The candidate became symbolical of their Sun-god and was either buried or confined in a coffin for three days, which was to represent a mystical death followed by resurrection. Mysteries celebrated by Druidesses were for the great God Hu, in commemoration of the Deluge.

Some candidates had to pass through an avenue of wild beasts. Those who survived were immersed in water and were afterwards brought into brilliant light -- a ceremony that is also found in Central America, where the candidate passes his last night before initiation in the cage of a wild beast. If he succeeded in taming the beast, all was well; otherwise he went back into a mystical darkness and death. These ceremonies must be interpreted mystically and esoterically.

Druids were firm believers in reincarnation, and at dawn on the twenty-fifth of December they celebrated the birth of their Sun-god, also his resurrection -- which is similar to our Easter celebration. They had their Virgin and Child, as well as the Tau, or three-quarter Cross.

Druids were noted for their golden ornaments -- a remnant or memory of the City of the Golden Gates of Atlantis. Their Priests were known as wearers of the golden chain. Gold represented nobility. In their ceremonies they wore white surplices, carried wands, and around the neck was worn an ornament encased in gold, called the Druidic Egg. Much gold was always used. No one was allowed to enter a sacred recess unless he carried a chain with him as a token of his belief in God. Ancient Britains carried these chains in their religious Rites. Its archetype is the cable-tow, or tow-rope, worn at certain times around the neck of a candidate in Masonry. Its true import symbolizes a belief in God not always known. White was always worn at the time of sacrifice. Priests of Osiris wore white during their sacred ceremonies. It was the white badge of innocence, purity and virtue. This same white emblem of purity and innocence belonged to the Aborigines of America.

Stonehenge represented a rude and most primitive form or architecture for a sacred place of Divine Worship, and, though now known as a Druidic temple, it shows the work of a race far earlier than the Druids. These stones are relics of the Atlanteans, the Giants who lived a million years ago. Had there been no Giants, there never would have been a Stonehenge. Pillars of stone in circular form creating this temple are of prodigious weight, and upon these standing pillars others were placed, forming, as it were, a circle in the air, adding a strange grandeur and solemnity to the whole.

The name "Stonehenge" is Kaer-Sidi, known mystically as the Seat of Sidi, or the Seven. Sidi is Saturn. The outer stones of the circles are thirty in number -- the number of years belonging to the cycle of Saturn. Ark, in Egyptian, signifies the number thirty; and in Hindu, Arki is the name of the planet Saturn; thus, Stonehenge or Kaer-Sidi is the Ark of Saturn. Stonehenge was a temple to the Sun, Moon and Stars. The Gauls and Britains paid homage to the Sun and the Moon in circular temples, which were of the same construction and usually contiguous. "Stonhenge was one of the most perfect and archaically precious memorials of the deluges of time, and the typology of the Ark extant on the surface of our earth." (1) It remains today a wonder belonging to antiquity.

"The solar system was organized by forces operating inward from the great ring of the Saturnian sphere; and since the beginnings of all things were under the control of Saturn, the most reasonable inference is that the first forms of worship were dedicated to him and his peculiar symbol -- the stone. Thus the intrinsic nature of Saturn is synonymous with that spiritual rock which is the enduring foundation of the Solar Temple, and has its antitype, or lower octave, in that terrestrial rock -- the planet Earth -- which sustains upon its jagged surface the divinely versified genera of mundane life." (2)

Sut or Saturn, in Egyptian, means a stone -- a stone became his especial type. He was called stone-head, or stone-arm, in their Ritual, and is alluded to by a Hebrew writer as the wielder of the "hammer of the whole world." Emblematically he holds a sanctified place in Masonry.

Men are known to have first worshipped stones; after that came the worship of other men, followed by the worship of spirits. "Throughout the world the first object of idolatry seems to have been a plain unwrought stone placed in the ground as an emblem of the generative or preservative powers of nature." (3)

Earliest stones, without carving, were symbolical and antedated all knowledge of tools. This earliest worship of stones survives in the stability given to Deity by men, from primeval times to the present day. The Christian faith has its Rock of Refuge upon which its church is founded. Jacob's pillow was a stone which he set up and annointed with oil. Then there was the stone of David; the Rock of Moriah; the Rock of Ages; the white stone of Revelation which John refers to; the White Carnelian (chalcedony) that is so mysteriously known it requires a Hermetic student or an Adept to interpret the great legend which is engraved upon it. It belongs to the legend of many lands, and, often bestowed with peculiar properties, it has been called the "Stone of Initiation" upon which a word is engraved which is given to the candidate when he has passed the trials of his initiation and become a full Brother.

The Books of Job and Revelation speak of this mysterious stone revealing the history of the initiations of both John and Job. A Mason of high

---
(1) - MASSEY, Gerald - THE NATURAL GENESIS, Vol. II, page 259.
(2) - HALL, Manly -- MASONIC, HERMETIC, QABBALISTIC AND ROSICRUCIAN
               SYMBOLICAL PHILOSOPHY, Page XCVII.
(3) - HIGGINS, Godfrey, - THE CELTIC DRUIDS.

degree knows very well the meaning of the seventeenth verse of Chapter Two in Revelation: "To him that overcometh will I give to eat of the hidden manna, and will give him a white stone, and in the stone a new name given which no man knoweth saving he that receiveth it." "The stone which the builders rejected became the head stone of the corner, because it contained the number 231, the measure of the earth, the sun, and the universe." (1)

The aboriginal Australians and others still carry a marked sacred stone called the "Churinga," used in ceremonies of that name. It is a hard white stone symbolizing Spirit. "The Stone of the Wise" was the soul. The foundation stone belonging to all the great and magnificent edifices was generally laid in the northeast corner. In ancient times this stone had a mysterious influence. It was thought to be about a foot square and "solid and angular." The stone was also a sign of transformation from childhood to manhood.

The precious stone that has figured in so many legends is the wonderful Light of the Spirit which opens the eye of the mind -- shown only to the worthy. "The Philosopher's Stone" of the Kabala is the secret of the transmutation of the baser metals into gold, which is the great Wisdom of the union of the Divine consciousness with the lower one of man -- over the supreme goal of all Initiates. The stone in symbolism is far more ancient than that of alchemy or the Philosopher's Stone. An eye was often engraved on a single stone, signifying sleepless vigilance.

The building of Solomon's Temple esoterically was necessary in order to understand the sacred Wisdom of the Ages. This is the opening of the "Eye of Wisdom" in each Mason; and this Eye, in its final development, is "the City of God;" the sanctuary is the image within. In a "Saying of Jesus" claimed to be ten thousand years old, it is stated: "Raise the stone and there thou shalt find me; cleave the wood and there am I." In the Egyptian Ritual it says - "shall find the Word of God." How truly has it been written: "We cannot pass into the cave dwellings of the human mind in that far-off past as high-sniffing. We shall have to crawl on hands and knees at times to enter, as very lowly explorers, _if_ we penetrate at all." But from stones of the far-off past we may erect steps for the future by building in beauty and majesty.

"Builder" should be, and is, the true name of the Mason today. "Masonry has changed greatly since the Eighteenth Century, from the one-time secret fraternities in the days of the sacred name, A U M, of the Brahmans, who had their grip and password. . . . when spiritual peoples and Adepts of all countries were Brothers." But Ancient Rites of true Brotherhood are again appearing and will penetrate into much which has been concealed in the night of the far-off past, and from which the Great Stone will be lifted. Under it lies the sacred Wisdom of the past.

The first Builders or Masons on earth of which we have any knowledge are the Cyclops, carvers of those massive statues in stone; and, though few in number, they belonged to the later Lemurian age. As Builders they were called "Sons of Light," whose descendants have become the Builders of the Temple of Humanity today, and whose services should spread outward through the radiations of the three names of the Sun in one, or, Sol-om-on. It was through the genius and wisdom of this great Builder that the Temple built without the sound of hammer or any iron tool was created.

---
(1) - THE CANON.

Archaic records show that Initiates of ancient races, moving from one land to another, had supervision over the building of menhirs, dolmens, and colossal zodiacs in stone, which were in certain places so that they might serve as sepulchers for generations to come. Colossal monuments of unhewn stone are found throughout Asia, Europe, America and Africa, in rows or groups, and by the peoples of those countries are known as "Druidic Stones," "Devil Altars," "Great Tombs," and also as "The Demons of Lanka."

Who built them? It is positively known that nearly all the Giants perished in the great Atlantean Flood. These archaic stones, as tombs, being gigantic, must have contained giants; but Cyclopian structures were not all intended for tombs or sepulchers. Also, "they are not Druidical, but Universal. Nor did the Druids build them, for they were only heirs to the Cyclopian lore left to them by generations of Mighty Builders (Masons) and Magicians, both good and bad." (1)

This alone would prove that the Masons, or a Masonic Brotherhood, whose origin may always be found in the Seven Great Stars -- THE FRATERNITY OF THE BUILDERS -- were the first to have become known. In every mythology Giants play an important part, mythology being the ancient way of stating facts. "The Atlanteans of the middle period were called Great Dragons, and the first symbol of their tribal deities, when the 'gods' and the Divine Dynasties had forsaken them, was that of a giant serpent." (2)

In the Mysteries the Universal Life was personified in the Dragon of the heavens, seen with its wings stretching across the sky, with light shining from its body. "Druidic bards united in celebrating the Dragon; and this Dragon was the leader in the mystic dance when Alpha Draconis was the Pole Star."

In the Trans-Himalayas, at a height of 16,000 or 17,000 feet, there are groups of menhirs. Their origin is unknown to the Tibetans who say that "they are the Doring-Long Stones; this is an ancient sacred place." These rows of stones are vertical, finished with a circle having three high stones in the center, and dried-up river beds surround them. These oddly arranged temples of menhirs must have been brought from the shores of the ocean.

"When in one's hand one holds an end of an enchanted cord at Carnac, is it not a joy to find its beginning in the Trans-Himalayas? ... But I rejoice in the fact that on the heights of the Trans-Himalayas I have seen the embodiment of Carnac."(3) Professor Roerich writes that "legends of the Tibetans are filled with stories of these old menhirs and dolmens whose origin is unknown." So, backwards, always backwards, we must go, into those great gardens of the past, whose flowers need the quiet between the bud and the blossom to bring again into manifestation the old Mysteries holding the Wisdom of the Ages belonging to the illusive lands of that long ago.

The British stone-men, known as menhirs, were built to keep track of the deluges of time. Stones of the Deluge are known to be memorials of the Cycles of Time. Druids retained their chronology by stones of observation.

---

(1) - BLAVATSKY, H. P. - THE SECRET DOCTRINE, VOL. II, Page 754.
(2) - IBID., Page 756.
(3) - ROERICH, Nicholas - SHAMBHALA, Page 221.

The circle of stones at Stonehenge is related to the Cycles of a particular time. The one placed in the center was called the Observation Stone -- proving it to be of ancient astronomical origin.

The stones forming the inner ring of Druidic temples were green, holding as deep a mystery as the Grail Cup -- a symbol of the creative forces of nature, as well as of the human race slowly learning the mystery of creation. The Grail reveals again the Ancient Wisdom and the ever-living and ever-searched-for Truth. Perfect chastity was a necessary condition in order that one might obtain a sight of this wonderful Cup. Some see in this a variation of the Masonic Legend of the Lost Word, sought by the Brethren of the Craft. It belongs to an ancient nature-myth which has slowly, or rather, strangely, crept into the Christian religion. In a very profound and sacred way, its meaning is significant of the Great Mother. Its color is green and it relates to the planet Venus, holding the mystery of generation; and the color of the Islamic faith, to which it also relates, is green. Their Sabbath is Friday; and Friday is the day of Venus.

Legends of a chalice or cup apparently cover the entire world. Among them there is the "Chalice of Salvation" which is to be rediscovered when the time of Shambhala arrives; and "Great is the Chalice of Solomon, made from a precious stone," but the inscription upon it cannot be read nor can it be explained. "Similar wonders were related to us by educated Bruiats and Mongols. They spoke of a mysterious light which shines above the Khotan Stupa; about the reappearance of the lost Chalice of Buddha. They also spoke of the miraculous stone from a distant star, which is appearing in different localities before the Great Advent. The Great Timur, it is said, temporarily possessed the stone. The stone is usually brought by completely unsuspecting strangers. In the same way, at certain times, it has disappeared, to be again discovered some time later in an entirely different country. The greater portion of this stone remains in Shambhala, while part of it is circulating throughout the Earth, retaining its magnetic link with the main Stone." (1)

Near Khotan a Buddhist stupa is identified with a legend stating that "when the time of Shambhala arrives a mysterious light will shine from it." Many say that this light has already been seen.

The people of all Oriental countries hold in great reverence the most sacred name "Shambhala," which, to the Oriental mind, represents a virile vibratory thought that through Shambhala a rebirth of the spirit will come. Shambhala is known among all these countries as a "Sacred White City" which is high above the clouds, where the Great Mother of the World resides; and legend tells us it is here in this Sacred City that the Great White Lodge of Brotherhood meets to arrange the affairs of the world.

The Orientals seem to feel intuitively that the time draws near for the privilege of worshipping at the Gates of this Holy City, when they will see the Great White Brotherhood sitting in silence amidst the great circle of the zodiac. Then the veil of Isis will be lifted. There are many watchers at the Gate of this Holy City today, for "the greatest missions are assigned from Shambhala, but on the earth they must be carried out by human hands under human

---
(1) - ROERICH, Nicholas -- HEART OF ASIA, Page 144.

conditions ... and you must know that these missions are often executed against the greatest difficulties, which must be conquered by spiritual power and devotion." (1)

Meru is the prototype of all sacred mountains, whether we refer to Moriah, Olympus, or Asgard. Shambhala is a pattern of all heavenly cities as she rises up on the opening Lotus, the mysterious Lotus Blossom on the crest of the Pole. "Shambhala itself is the Holy Place, where the earthly world links itself with the highest state of consciousness. ... Certain indications put this place in the extreme North, explaining that the rays of Aurora Borealis are the rays of the invisible Shambhala. ... The ancient name of Shambhala is Chang-Shambhala, and this means the Northern Shambhala. The origin of this name is explained as follows: The Teaching originally was manifested in India, to which everything emanating from beyond the Himalayas is naturally North. North of Benares is a village, Shambhala, connected with the legend of Maitreya. Hence it is apparent why the Trans-Himalayan Shambhala is called Northern Shambhala." (1)

All legends and writings of this Holy City give its location in symbolic language difficult for the uninitiated to understand. Her mighty energies, her tremendous forces are sweeping over the world today.

This Sacred City is claimed to be the center of the Universal religion which had come to earth long ago when the first part of its surface had become solid enough to support life. The shifting of the axis of the earth alters the position of the Poles; and, due to this, some of these Orientals have located Shambhala in Mongolia.

Mystically, Shambhala in man is his spiritual consciousness which is reaching towards the Infinite, just as the Cosmic Fires when set in motion begin their ascent in man, and the seven holy shrines (Chakras) are encountered on the way, -- a difficult way, beset with trials of the flesh as well as of the spirit. Near the end of this journey there is a "Sacred Desert" where mystically the Lotus blooms, and from its etherealized aroma rises the "Sacred White City." It is the mounting of the Ladder of the Masonic Brotherhood, their "Ladder of Becoming," leading upward as it leads inward. The Sacred Desert is connected with the lower world by the Silver Cord which should not be loosed if the Pilgrim on the Way is to become a Pillar, or one of the Columns in his Lodge, where thought-forms are created whose forces penetrate into the outer world -- forces thought to be even greater than those given through the officers of the Lodge.

The Wise Men of the Eastern countries have reserved many strange traditions, and among them those of Alchemy. It was a knowledge possessed by the different schools of the Magi. The Elixir of Life was to the Alchemist the fuel that furnished the Spirit of Fire that changed base metal into gold, which may be accomplished by man himself in transmuting the desires of the lower world-consciousness into the higher, by filling his own lamp and lighting his own spiritual flame. Thus he may find the Philosopher's Stone, the stone found by beautifying the truing of his rough ashlar. Every man or woman who attains makes it easier for the rest of humanity to follow on the way to the goal of perfection.

---

(1) - ROERICH, Nicholas -- HEART OF ASIA, Page 160.

Alchemists of old sought the secrets of nature in this way. They used Salt, Sulphur and Mercury in their work. Salt was of the material Earth, Sulphur was of the spiritual Fire, while Mercury was the messenger between, whose color they claimed was purple -- the blending of the blue of the spirit with the red of the body. The blending of gold and silver in all alchemical enterprises did not mean the blending of dead metals but the living qualities of the human life. To the Alchemist the mind was as the Sun -- gold; and the heart was as the Moon - silver; and through the strength and power of the Sun and the beauty and intuitive qualities of the Moon, a union of Strength and Beauty was created, and those added to Wisdom formed a triangle of tremendous vibratory power which has become an integral part of Masonry today, where Justice, Mercy and Brotherhood combined become the great triadic signals for the future.

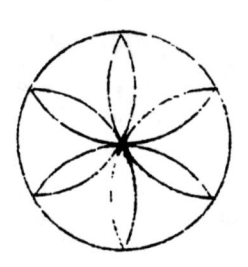

CHAPTER IV

THE MOTHER

> The Rose has always been the symbol of the harmonies of being, of beauty, life and love.
>
> And when in quest of the inviolate Rose, open your casement window towards the Infinite.
>
> E.V.S.

WOMAN is in reality the Transmuter, the Alchemist, the Great Mother of life; she creates, transforms; and the call today is for woman to bring into manifestation all her latent possibilities so that she may express freely. Looking over the world today, Humanity requires the Mother to lift it above its materialism and attendant immoralities, to upraise it, as the world through its changing conditions is in process of creative activity and creative evolution, pronounced everywhere. From this evolution man has been unable to fulfill his mission -- to rise to the requirements of this change. This mission belongs to woman.

Going back into that far-away past, the most ancient system placed the feminine first. As Gerald Massey says: "The Mother fulfilled the ideal of primitive man as the Woman of infinite capacity. Fortunately Providence placed the Mother first and secured her on the side of procreant nature, for the perpetuation of the race." [1] "She became the first of all the gods when she reigned as the Great Mother of the World, Mother of the Fields of Heaven, and Mother of the first ruling Deity -- her son, the Ever Coming Son."

Knowledge of this first Mother and Child is traced through endless ages down to one of the Great Cycles, or the Precession of the Equinoxes, which began about the Thirteenth Century, B.C. A difficulty in reckoning time was due to the equinox being "determined in the lesser year by the recurrence of equal day and night," but "the position of the equinox has to be made out according to the processional year, not the lesser year." [2]

In some cases these Great Cycles, or the Precessions of the Equinoxes, are said to be completed in about 25,920 years, a reckoning which belongs to ancient times. This 25,920-year period formed the basis of nearly every occult Cycle. It is the supreme number in the entire Science of Cycles, and belongs to the ancient Egyptian measurement. Astronomers today among themselves are not in exact accord as to the accuracy of these Time-Cycles; but occult chronology of Egypt can scarcely be denied.

The Child, in ancient myths, was known as Horus. He was always the Ever Coming Son, the Sun, or Child of the Virgin, who appeared at the beginning of all Sidereal Cycles, thereby becoming symbolically the ruler of each in turn.

---

[1] - MASSEY, Gerald - ANCIENT EGYPT: THE LIGHT OF THE WORLD.
[2] - Ibid.

Each of these Cycles represented about 2160 years. "To know Horus in his forms of manifestation was the secret power; to understand Horus in all his names, all his places, conferred the Crown of Illumination."(1)

During the Cycle, figuring about the Thirteenth Century, B.C., lasting through its sidereal period, the constellation Virgo appeared in the heavens rising above the horizon and ushering in the Cycle of the Virgin and the Child. In the Egyptian representation of this constellation she holds an ear of corn in her hand, the grain symbolizing the ovum of the Mother. This Cycle was distinctly Feminine in vibratory action and was the Feminizing of the Universal Vibration. The woman became stronger than the man and so ruled during this period of 2160 years. Amazon women were under this cycle.

About this time, 13,500 years B.C., a band of men and women belonging to a South Indian empire which then existed, came by way of Ceylon into Egypt. The ruling race in Egypt in those days was the Cro-Magnon. Broca, the great brain specialist, noted that the brain content of the skulls of these women surpassed that of the average man of today. Types of the Cro-Magnons "bear witness to the presence of an African stock in the same region in which we find the dolmens and other megalithic monuments erroneously attributed to the Celts."(2)

As the Precession of the Equinoxes receded to the constellation Leo, vibrations took place in the universe which reversed the feminine power and awakened the masculine. Due to this change of polarity in the heavens, the power of man dominated that of woman. When the change from the Matriarchal to the Patriarchal took place, the father took to his bed instead of the mother at the birth of a child, assuming to be its parent. He was careful in every way regarding his food that the child might be kept well. He had his doctor, nurse, and friends in to see him. This very ancient custom, called COUVADE, sprang into activity when the change from the female to the male was ushered in through cyclic law and the child took the name of the father instead of the mother.

It symbolically belonged to the most diverse races in the world, yet its origin seems to have been lost. It was an attempt to individualize the ancestral spirit, which was then believed in before it was personally recognized. In many instances, forty days of fasting and suffering took place -- which custom seems to have been perpetuated. Couvade goes back to this Cycle of the Virgin Mother and Child, followed by the individualization of the father. This conversion, transforming the father into the child, was religiously given; it was a primeval illustration of attaining eternal life. The two characters, the pubescent male and the little child, together with the mother, represent the Trinity in Unity which has become a theological mystery. These strange old Rites, though dimly seen through the mists of ages, steal silently along the path that divides time and eternity.

As the Precession receded, the sign Cancer became dominant in the universal vibration and this was called the Cycle of Physical Motherhood when the "Mother Principle was relegated to the position of nourishing the young, and it was at that time that the woman, through Evolutionary Law, was relegated to the position of Motherhood alone."(3)

---

(1) - CHURCHWARD, Albert - SIGNS AND SYMBOLS OF PRIMORDIAL MAN, Page 197.
(2) - Ibid., page 135
(3) - RALEIGH, A. B. - WOMAN AND SUPER-WOMAN, Page 15

When the Cycle of Gemini -- the next in zodiacal order -- was ushered in, it produced a period when the feminine aspect became a purely material one, the vibrations being very strong on the lower planes. At this time man became stronger in every way than woman, which almost gave credence to the thought prevalent at the time that woman's nature was soulless. It was Natural Evolution, for which man was not responsible.

This again was followed by the Cycle of Taurus, when the woman or Feminine Force receded to a lower state of degradation by the Evolutionary Forces of Nature and was reduced to powerful development of Passion and Desire. This deterioration or waning of Feminine Intelligence resulted in man's domination and caused him to look upon woman as the slave of his desires.

When the Cycle of Aries arrived, the vibrations represented the highest development of the Masculine Principle, and Woman was further degraded. But after five Masculine Cycles, the constellation Pisces rose upon the horizon, -- "the Cycle of the Child, in a certain mystical sense; and from that time forth we see the Mother Principle in Nature awakening;" but the woman, as wife, though mother, gave power still to the masculine. [1] It ushered in the age of our Christian manifestation, and the position of the wife received greater honor.

The Piscian Cycle was one of many unbalanced conditions that often aided and abetted evil; yet the previous Cycle was over-severe and cruel. But in the on-rushing Aquarian Cycle, woman will again come into her own through the entering in of Light, which will bring back her spirit of Wisdom, awakening it out of its long slumber, when she will begin to catch glimpses of those precious gems that have been hidden away for ages, "for the Future is in the Past and the Past is in the Future."

We have now come to this, our last Cycle for the time being, as we enter, or are within, the constellation Aquarius, the Waterman. In the planisphere of Egypt this constellation is symbolically given as a Divine Figure pouring from an urn a double stream of water, representing Light and Love, and within the urn are thirteen large stars. Anciently thirteen was the symbol of the Mother. Water is the great Feminizing Principle, the Feminine Spirit in Nature; and these "two streams are the Heavenly Waters of the Great Mother, and the Earthly Waters of the Earth Mother." [2]

This Cycle is very pronounced as "Feminine" and brings this Principle into full manifestation. "On all of the Planes of the Manifest Universe the Feminine Vibration is being awakened and aroused to action." [3] It is the Cycle of a New Birth.

The Great Seal of the United States is a profound esoteric occult symbol, filled with Masonic symbology, bearing many signatures of the Mysteries, and showing the leadership in things spiritual. Originally the eagle on the Great Seal of the United States was a conventionalized phoenix, and the phoenix was a symbol denoting spiritual achievement and victory, especially esoterically through the Great Work. The phoenix was also the symbol of immortality, as it rises reborn from its own flames. It is said that when building its nest it used sprigs of acacia.

---

[1] - RALEIGH, A. S. -- WOMAN AND SUPER-WOMAN, Page 16.
[2] - Ibid, pages 16 - 17.
[3] - Ibid., page 17

The significance of the number thirteen, so apparent in the Seal, peculiarly coincides with the present Feminine Cycle of the world -- thirteen being the number of stars in the urn of the Waterman who ushers in this Woman's Age; and in this constellation of the Seal, the number thirteen of the Great Mother is given. Is it not strikingly significant that just at this period, for the first time in its history, the United States uses the diagram of the Great Seal to decorate its paper currency?

The sacred emblem of ancient Initiates was a group of thirteen stars which, in the constellation of the Great Seal is given above the head of the eagle surrounded by clouds. These stars form a hexagram, and each star a pentagram -- all include a central star. The former was a symbol of God, the Macrocosm; the latter, a symbol of man, the Microcosm. The union of the two triangles in this way would give spiritual humanity and humanity incarnated on earth.

Consider these stars as twelve plus one, and we have the Zodiac with the Sun at its center. The motto "E Pluribus Unum" contains thirteen letters, as does the inscription "Annuit Coeptis." In the right claw of the eagle are thirteen leaves and thirteen berries; in the left is a sheaf of thirteen arrows. On the reverse side the unfinished pyramid is symbolical of a Tracing Board; above it is the All-Seeing Eye; the face of the pyramid has seventy-two stones arranged in rows of thirteen. Our Seal is filled with much that is enlightening spiritually, and shows the material advancement of our country.

Our Aquarian Age will be one of fulfillment. Many parallels may be drawn from the Scriptures which will prove this to be true. It will be the one period in the long Cycles when humanity will have the advantage of the true Light of Wisdom and Understanding. It has been stated that from the Golden Age of a previous time ancient brethren saw clearly through the future as well as through the past and "made every effort to leave Permanent Memorials and Landmarks for the guidance of Humanity which would arise during the twilight and dark periods that must inevitably follow High Noon." (1) During this period Humanity will have the Tree of Life and Wisdom and Understanding; but after this, when the Capricornian Cycle enters, the light may decline for a long period.

The Emerald Tablet reminds us that "Therefore am I called Thrice Great Hermes, having the Three Parts of the philosophy of the whole world. That which I have written is consummated concerning the operation of the Sun. . . . The Three Parts of the philosophy of the whole world, the Three Supernals, now directly exert their influence upon the Earth" (our incoming cycle or revival age) "through the Channels of Wisdom, Love and Power, and that in very Truth 'That which is above is as that which is below, and that which is below is as that which is above, for performing the miracle of the One Thing,' which One Thing is the One Thought of the Supreme and Concealed Father, as manifested in the Ever-Coming Son." (2)

As woman becomes a stronger power she will dominate the earth during her Cycle; for the woman becomes the Positive Pole of Nature and the Positive Pole of Humanity. It is apparent today that woman has begun to free herself from the dominance of man; and also, that man is gradually accepting this --

---

(1) -- FRATER ACHAD, THE EGYPTIAN REVIVAL, Page 116
(2) -- Ibid., Pages 119 - 120.

obedience reversed. Women is becoming Militant, as Feminine Will and Intelligence grow stronger. It is a curious incident that as the universe itself becomes more and more Feminine, man necessarily becomes more Feminine, sharing the "Moulding Principle in Evolution which will be stronger in the woman." Obedience demanded by woman will be given by man. It is Nature, it is Evolution, and this trend in Evolution will be with us for the next twenty-one centuries. Nothing can stand in its way, nothing can prevent, for it is so decreed in the heavens.

Woman's strongest interest is seen in Universal Motherhood and a great sphere of action. Her slumbering soul of the past is breaking through the veil and will ignite and destroy the old conventional woman. Out of the ashes will arise in triumph the woman of the future. She will demand and she will receive. She is the great Moulding Force through which all things come; and as the Mother of souls, rather than of bodies, she is to bring forth a Super-Humanity -- a new type; and, as Super-Mother she may bring forth Super-Men -- man and woman co-equal, made possible through Creative Evolution. Through the joining of these two forces the affairs of the world will be run as wisely as were those of the gods; for during this period man will learn more clearly the true spirit of Wisdom and Understanding -- to a degree beyond that which was possible during the past Masculine Cycles.

This Universal Mother will not only be active on the plane where the Fairies, the Elementals, are born, but on the physical, where in prototype she performs the same function as she perpetually gives birth to other lives. For the "woman's body and soul are the Vase of Art in which is created and gestated, and from which is born innumerable beings, each one designed in the course of time to become a god. Thus it is she who in reality evolves the Universe."[1]

She is therefore the true Alchemist, and her body is the "Vase of Art." The mystical Mother is not the physical mother, who is her prototype on earth. In this aeon we shall recognize the Great Mother of heaven and discover the secret of the lost Father. If the welfare of the people is to be considered and advanced, Mother-love must play a great part. The home of the Mother in our incoming era will be the home of the world. The entire world will be changed, due to her moral instincts and her creative faculties.

Space was called "Mother" before cosmic activity, the first awakening; and descent was always recognized through the female. We learn through biology that the female was first, fundamental, and that in the beginning the male was only an assistant to the female. The first caress of unification must come from the Mother -- womanhood being the bridge of ultimate unification. The Mother is the beauty of the world; for did not all begin with the Great Mother of the World? Mother-love explains all religions. Creeds are but paths on which one travels in seeking the Supreme. The Mother-Spirit, pertaining to holy and spiritual life, is the symbol of that which is sacred and divine and destined to be a leading force in human affairs. The geometrical and symbolical figure upon which Masonic Lodges are built is the oblong square, which is a symbol of Mother.

Birth of a Christ is the result of Law and Evolution and this Law and Evolution are continuous. Thus it is that every Christ-child must come

---

(1) - RALEIGH, A. S. - WOMAN AND SUPER-WOMAN, Page 92.

into the world; and women have ever been the mothers of the Saviours of the world.

The region of the mystic is in the universe of the human soul. Much history has been made out of mysticism. "The province of mysticism, although parallel to occultism, transcends and surpasses the latter." (1) The true mystic is one who knows that all symbols are registered in the heart, and that long ago as an occultist from the outside he contacted cosmic principles and registered their symbols in his heart -- the heart being Love, or the Great Mother. The mystic unfolds the path of true Brotherhood in its ideal of service, which lies at the foundation of all mysticism.

To be a mystic it is necessary to know Christ. The occultist sacrifices all things to knowledge and the understanding of man; he aspires to the active science of life. The mystic would sacrifice all things, even knowledge if he could, to goodness. He follows the path of devotion; and the Mother's path is that of mysticism and devotion. The finding of Christ is through the inward way -- in the soul of everyone who finds Christ at all, for peace and rest abide in those inward depths of the soul.

It was through the study of the stars conjoined with ancient prophecies that the search for Christ was born. Every prophet in every age and nation has taught this great truth; and through comparative study of this truth came the consciousness of Christ.

The Mother of God, as the Mother of Saviors, belongs to divers peoples in remotest ages and in common with all that has evolved out of mysticism and the Ancient Mysteries. The tendency today is to recognize the Motherhood of God, a tendency which grows stronger and stronger. It is so decreed. When the soul begins to worship it is as a little child -- the little child that clings to its mother's breast, unconsciously recognizing motherhood before fatherhood. The cry for Mother echoes throughout the entire world, filling it with love. As long as the Motherhood of God was understood, woman was honored and had her rightful place; but when God ceased to be worshipped as Mother, then came her ruin.

The beginning of mythology -- that ancient way of stating facts -- was with the Great Mother, the Virgin Mother and her Child. It was the first Immaculate Conception -- a primitive way of understanding creation. It was universal, and has survived in the Virgin and Child of Rome. In this ancient form of belief the son preceded the fatherhood. This first son was named Sut, who later became known as Sothis, -- our well-beloved Sothis who guarded the portal of the illimitiable heavens, the Harbinger of the Dawn who is so prominent in Masonry as the Blazing Star, and who finally yielded his starship to become known as the planet Saturn. This Great Mother in the Kabalistic interpretation was Nuit -- Lady of the starry heavens or the Star Universe. The worship of Nuit was not only pre-dynastic but seems to have been eternal, for "The Infinitely Great is Nuit, the Mother of the Stars, the Infinitely Small, ... the Innermost Essential Self of All, the Flame that burns in the heart of every man, and in the core of every Star." (2)

---
(1) - KINGSFORD, Anna.
(2) - FRATER ACHAD, - THE EGYPTIAN REVIVAL, Page 34.

Both are invisible to the mind and senses. "Every atom in our body is itself a little solar system, so are we in the Body of the Mother of Heaven, and She is energized by the Invisible Point which is Not, yet which is the Life of All." (1)

In this great Star Universe wherein every being is a star, when man recognizes that every atom is a star and absorbs the true idea of this sphere, then, and not till then, will come knowledge and understanding of "The Throne of the Great Mother" -- the Great Mother who holds the Universe in her arms. The entire solar system evolves around the Central Sun leading to Infinity; and the search for Infinity proves Infinity. There is no limit to consciousness in the Here and the Now. "The Light shineth in the Darkness, but the Darkness comprehendeth it not, for the Children of Time as yet do not know the mystery of the Here and Now."

> "There is no now, nor then, no here, nor there,
> To those who walk accompanied by Thee,
> The end becomes the point from which we rose,
> The all submerged in one, unfettered, free.
>
> Oh, let Thy children, calling from their star,
> Catch from Thy downward gaze the spark Divine;
> Kindle the beacon fires that, mounting high,
> Guide to Thy feet our souls from near and far."
> -- C. Elphinstone Klots.

"There is a realm where the rainbow never fades, where the stars will be spread out before us like islands that slumber in the ocean. Why is it that all the stars which hold their festivals around the midnight throne are set above the grasp of our limited faculties, forever mocking us with their unapproachable glory?" (2)

Night is the daytime of the soul; night is the Great Mother, that molding force, feminine, intuitive, which alone can give expression to thought. Daylight and the sun create the Masculine dynamic energy; but the kindling of the Divine spark in life is said to come in the night and into the silence of the soul when, through dissolution of the natural or human, the Divine is liberated that it may be free to manifest. When daylight comes, the vision of the night is thrown into surface-consciousness. True light is equilibrated and concealed in the darkness, which becomes the Wisdom of the Mother. It is in the silence that thoughts and desires are at rest; and then, through the Divine harmonies within, heavenly messages are sent down through the angels, for the material must be crucified if the spiritual is to be resurrected and live. Therefore those who are among the liberated should sustain those still in bondage, help to free them from the yoke of worldly passions which Masonry teaches how to subdue -- passions overcome by a manifestation of God in man. The great mission of the soul is to educate the body and mind, always expressing from within.

The Masonic student will find that the Great Thought of God and His Designs are traced upon His Tracing Board, always prominent in the Lodge, that thereby the soul may discover that which it seems to have lost through material

---

(1) - FRATER ACHAD -- THE EGYPTIAN REVIVAL, Page 23.
(2) - PRENTICE, George D. -- MAN'S HIGHER DESTINY.

thinking. "The soul is not a thing of which man may say, it has been or it is to be, or it is to be hereafter; for it is a thing without birth; it is pre-existent, changeless, eternal, and is not to be destroyed with the mortal frame."

Accept and receive at the portals of the Inner Life. These portals are open, attracting the beautiful, but one does not always know how to approach beauty, unless the human heart is throbbing with infinite love towards the Great Mother. "In the presence of great beauty the soul is stilled, for God never seems very far from that which is beautiful."

The form of our Government of the United States was borrowed from the Iroquois Indians, or Six Nations, who were governed by Mother Rule, and "the world became indebted to the Mother Rule for its full conception of inherent rights, natural equality of conditions, and the establishment of a civilized government upon this basis." (1)

The Mother had authority over all religious ceremonies and festivals. Only mothers could elect the President. Women and men sat together in Congress. To the Iroquois, this earth was the "Mighty Mother." They honored women as the spirit of their plants, corn, et cetera. "The Bright and Morning Star of the Pale Face was called their 'Star Woman.'" Women were a great power among the clans everywhere. The Iroquois had their League of Nations and a League to Enforce Peace, which they called "The Great Peace;" and over their League to Enforce Peace they put a great woman whom they called "The Mother of Nations." Disputed questions among them for final adjustment were referred to the Council of Matrons, who elected their chiefs of the nation or tribes and held power in the event of war; and descent fell from this line of the mother blood. "The Confederation of the Thirteen American Colonies, accomplished in 1774, was patterned after the model of the Iroquois Confederacy."

Tradition states that the Great Eagle of the Iroquois was their symbol of power, "which the Six Nations called Don-Yon-Do, -- the Golden Eagle of the far-away heavens, and the Head Chief of all the birds. Don-Yon-Do won this distinction by her strength, acute sight, and extraordinary powers of flight." (2)

It becomes interesting to know that "the American Eagle is a female bird (the female being the larger and the more progressive of the species). Her dominant characteristic is a portentous ferocity of ideas. Her element is strength. ... She is proud; and although she swoops down on the lowlands for her prey, she flies to the highest mountain top to devour it. The strong rays of the Sun cannot blind her, and her heart throbs to the skies. By her strong wing and swiftness -- denoting aspiration -- she rises higher than all other birds, and is therefore the first in dignity. ... The Eagle is wise, and does not answer every call. She knows her power and waits."(3)

"It is prophesied through Frater O.M., in the 'Vision and the Voice' 8th Aethyr, 'UNTO HIM THAT UNDERSTANDETH AT LAST do I deliver the secrets of truth in such wise that the least of the little children of the light may run to the knees of the mother and be brought to understand." (4)

---

(1) -- PENFOLD, Saxby Vouler, - THE MARRIAGE OF TWO NATIONS, Page 67.
(2) -- Ibid., Page 68.
(3) -- Ibid., Pages 67 - 68
(4) -- FRATER ACHAD, Q. B. L., or THE BRIDE'S RECEPTION, page 105

Light is the only instrument for the Spirit. It is a creative power and belongs to the Masonic field of labor. "It is spirit and life; it is the synthesis of colors, the accord of shadows, the harmony of forms; and its vibrations are living mathematics."(1)

The privilege of service is the highest to which one can aspire. All true children of Light -- Masons -- should help, and earnestly desire to help, Humanity. "As long as we go forward we travel with the Ever Coming Son, who is, after all, our destiny, since He is within each of us as the True Urge of our Being. This, then, is the Secret of the Way of the Tao; step boldly out on the Path of Destiny, having aligned the personal with the Divine Will. ... Keep ahead of the urge from behind, and it will not fret us." (Those who wilfully avoid the Divine Plan will meet with the Great Avenger, who) "still drives ahead in His Chariot, and millions will feel his force and Fire, until the Race recognizes that it must right about face and cheer the Conquering Hero on. Then we shall have Peace and Rejoicing and the Stern Warrior" -- who is again the Great Mother -- "will seem as the Gentlest Child." (2)

The Holy Mother of all ages "was born in the womb of space, impregnated in space by God, the Father, protected by God, as Mother, and God the Child is Himself the seed that was so sowed."

Euthymius, the monk, in the first part of the Twelfth Century, wrote of a certain doctrine concerning the Paulicians: "They say that as many among them as are inhabited by the Holy Ghost are mothers of God, ... and called as such, because they conceive the Word of God and carry it within."(3)

There is a very charming story in mystical symbolism of the unfolding of a myth about Vishnu the Supreme, and Lakshmi, the Beautiful, of the way in which Vishnu discovered her lying naked in the heart of a rose and of how they became united. Remember that Vishnu and Lakshmi both represent cosmic powers, two different poles of the Universal Spirit, or the electric and magnetic sides of the Spirit; and out of this comes the story, far-reaching in symbolism.

The finding of Lakshmi in a way reflects a certain Rite in Masonry. Vishnu is the masculine dynamic energy of the spiritual plane, and Lakshmi the feminine static substance. One could not exist without the other. In nature, Vishnu was the Life side, and Lakshmi the Form side. Vishnu corresponds to the Christ of the Christians and to Hiram Abiff of Masonry, and Lakshmi corresponds to the Mary of the Christians. The father in symbolism corresponds to the energies in nature; but it was the feminine that supplied what is called "the dust of the earth," which is primordial or spiritual substance and belongs to the Mother.

Matter as substance, and energy can never be separated as one is merged into the other. Thus the Vishnu energy and the Lakshmi substance became the makers of life and form, representing the manifestation of all life, for a spiritual type of humanity is thus born. So Vishnu discovers Lakshmi lying in the heart of a rose, the rose having one hundred eight petals, and every petal was a symbol of love. The rose is a symbol of life,

---
(1) - LEVI, Eliphas, - THE HISTORY OF MAGIC, Page 286.
(2) - FRATER ACHAD, - THE EGYPTIAN REVIVAL, Pages 96-97
(3) - MAYER, Francis, - THE GLOVES OF A MASON -- The Word, Vol 25, Page 141

the color of Prana -- and Prana is a life-principle. In this universal life-principle Lakshmi was found, its vitality thus making the rose a symbol of the cosmic life forces -- that life, fire, or force in nature without which the individual form would die.

The Hindu rosary has one hundred eight beads. In all the great religions of the world, past or present, there is always the worship of the Feminine Principle, and all great religions use the rosary. Kabalistic Wisdom, identical with esoteric Masonry, helps in the understanding of the one hundred eight. The number "one hundred" Kabalistically represents the letter "Qoph," which means the uniting of the Elements; it is the head or something moving. And the number eight is the letter "Cheth," which means balance -- the balance between attraction and repulsion. "Cheth" is also the union of the destructive and constructive forces in nature harmoniously blended. "Qoph" is also the back of the skull, which means the vital center and the seat of the family, hence the maternal force. Therefore, one hundred eight means the seat of maternity, enclosing all the universe within her arms, as by a fence. (1) (Qoph-fence).

Lakshmi, with the infant incarnation on her bosom, is the Holy Spirit who bears the Messiah in her arms; she was known as the God-Mother, and always as a beautiful Virgin, robed, crowned, and of flashing loveliness and light.

The very first universal idea was feminine -- the source of all beginning. It has always proceeded from the dark which was the creative birthplace. When we find Vishnu symbolized as the guide of the Sun, it is stated that at his smile Lakshmi arises from the darkness bearing her chalice of nectar "and before her radiant beauty all evil spirits of the night disperse and a new cosmic energy is manifest in the world." (2)

The rosary with one hundred and eight beads -- one bead for each petal of the rose -- was formed to direct Lakshmi's order of worship; and when an Oriental holds a rosary in his hands and concentrates in prayer on the beads, the petals of the rose are symbolized in the beads. Hindus, Buddhists, Christians, even Mahommedans who have their houris, perpetuate the feminine element in the rosary. With the Sufis, this element is in "The Beloved," their feminine side of Allah, whom they always mention as such. "The Beloved" is also the Virgin Sophia among the Christian mystics, and Isis in the Egyptian ceremonial -- all leading back to the Universal Mother of the World.

The Mother of Jesus, Mary, was the Rose of the World -- partaker of a Divine nature, and key to all cosmic meaning. She was the mystic rose of many petals; and "out of the virginal heart of Mary sprang the very Tree of Life" which, bearing its beautiful flowers, is reaching towards the highest heavens. It is said that all living things that tend toward God are gathered in her heart. It was within this mystic rose that Dante saw Eve sitting at the feet of Mary, healed and made radiant -- Mary, the humble maid who was the Perfect Way towards the Divine Idea. Every grace that comes from Christ is through the Mystical Mother, and in all the mysteries of the Divine Life this Mother is invoked and glorified. To ignore Mary, the Mother, separates man from his soul.

---

(1) - RALEIGH, A. S. - LAKSHMI
(2) - ROERICH, Nicholas

In the Divine Comedy Beatrice recalls to Dante the beautiful garden blossoming under the rays of Christ. We perceive here "The Rose in which the Divine Word made itself flesh," for in this beautiful garden, blossoming under the rays of Christ, grew nothing but roses and lilies. "It is sufficient that in the Magistery there are but two degrees; the White and Red. Again, by adding to these the green of the foliage we have the tricolor" (White, Red and Green) "symbolizing not only the three cardinal virtues of theologians, Faith, Hope and Charity, but also the three cardinal virtues of a Mason," a reason why the colors, Red, White and Green are used "in the decorations of certain Chapters." (1)

The Rose, as has been stated, has a preservative vital principle in nature. Among flowers the Lotus of India and the Rose of the Rosicrucians are of the greatest importance, signifying the maternal creative mystery. Flowers are symbolized in the Chakras or Whirling Wheels of the Hindus. Their names are given to the sacred ganglion of the spine; and the unfolding or awakening of these are keys of the greatest symbolical significance in Masonry, as in allegory or symbolism.

The Rosicrucians have placed the Rose on their Cross as a symbol of crucifixion, of destruction, for the Divine Life to come forth, "that the Rose of the Spirit may blossom when the human rose has been crucified; ... the human ceases that the Divine may spring forth;" (2) and so the rose has been made a symbol of the crucifixion in order that the Divine may manifest through transmutation.

"The litany of the Virgin Mary has its place in all religions of the world." Was not the Great Mother symbolized in her spiritually? But far earlier than the worship of Mary a "litany was used in praise of the Virgin Sophia as the Divine Feminine." So "the Rosary was not at first the symbol of the worship of Mary . . . but of the worship of the Divine Feminine;"(3) and in time the Divine Feminine became associated with the Church, and the Church became the "Bride of Christ." The Roman Catholics speak of the church as "The Holy Mother."

Going very far back into that wonderful past, it was the Divine Feminine that was used in the service of praise as the feminine aspect of God. Mary symbolized in the rosary "is used to aid in concentrating the mind on this Divine Feminine aspect." (4) Time has created many misunderstandings of that Universal Great Mother, whether as Lakshmi, Sophia, Mary, or other Virgins of mythical renown, for "the symbol has taken the place of the spirit symbolized." (5)

The Rose has always been the symbol of the harmonies of being, beauty, life and love; and when in quest of this inviolate Rose, open your casement window towards the Infinite. Eternal Wisdom leads by way of the cross and the grave to the atmosphere of Reality. In the Zohar it is stated:- "the community of Israel was symbolized by a Rose; it was the secret name the Rose-Croix gave to their Fraternity." Therefore we may read that Adam sent

---
(1) - MEYER, Francois, - THE GLOVES OF A MASON -- THE WORD, Vol.25, page 141.
(2) - RALEIGH, A. S. - LAKSHMI, page 31.
(3) - Ibid., Page 27.
(4) - Ibid., page 31.
(5) - Ibid.

roses from the Garden of Eden. The Rosy Cross has its origin then in the heavens. The Rosicrucians had their mystic teachings from the Atlantean Priests. They are today a mystery; their society as true a mystery as of old.

In India today the advent of the coming Lakshmi is filling the Oriental heart with joy. They know that when she arises from the darkness "before her radiant beauty all evil spirits of night will disappear," and that she will bring with her her Seven Veils of Peace from which will radiate joy and happiness. She is ever embroidering new and beautiful designs on these Veils as she invokes creative fire, that the energies of the spirit may inspire with light and love all hearts below; she is ever rekindling the fires of purification that purity, simplicity and fearlessness may come to her beloved people. Many are hailing the coming of this Great Mother as the element of fire abounds in the world today. It will release many precious treasures of heaven, as well as of earth, which are to be inwardly revealed and revered.

This Mother of Happiness endlessly embroiders and weaves great beauty in her Seven Veils, which the wicked Siva Tandava urges her to destroy, desiring to bring death and destruction into the world through evil; but the Blessed Goddess kindles new fires and answers, "I will not destroy my Veils but will embroider new designs that will be most beautiful, precious and powerful, and in them there will be sacred emblems of the Bird of Flame, . . . and I will give healing herbs to the drooping wayfarer, whom I shall guard with my loving prayers and invocations." "I will evoke from the abyss the greatest creative fires. And with a rampart of flame will I safeguard the luminous strivings of the spirit." (1)

Great teachers travel toward the mountain, for on the height is the Supreme who stands witness to the Great Reality; and in the splendor of great heights may be found the smile of Vishnu at the coming forth of the Great Mother -- Lakshmi, the Beautiful. In far distant lands, beyond the highest mountains, out in space, is a great silence, watching and guarding the world. It is a sacred place where TRUTH alone dwells; and TRUTH has ever been the symbol of the Great Mother -- the first of all creations, the first Great Builder, the first Great Mason the world has ever known, who presided over those Seven Great Stars -- THE FRATERNITY OF THE BUILDERS -- her Sons of Light; and as her Sons of Light they are prototyped in the seven officers of all Masonic Lodges today. As the Great Mother Builder she remains, and ever will remain, the Worshipful Master of all Masons in the World, known as her Sons of Light.

> The emerald buds of opening leaves and flowers,
> The golden gleaming sun, the gentle breeze,
> Soft fleecy clouds the mountain tops concealing.
>   'Tis Mother smiling.
>
> Sound of clear water down the hillside falling,
> Pure note of Robin and in early dawn
> Thrillingly sweet, the voice of lark uprising,
>   'Tis Mother singing.

---

(1) - ROERICH, Nicholas -- SHAMBHALA, page 105.

Crash of the thunder, gloom of summers lightning,
Roar of the wind through forest temples dim,
Metals and stones sound their reverberations;
                'Tis Mother chanting.

Death with his heavy tread nears us with sable wand;
Feet, falteringly, firmly, tread the dim-lit way,
Attachment, space and time assume their own proportions;
                'Tis Mother teaching.

But at one call all hearts and hands are lifted;
The AUM of stone and man rings true and clear;
Flowers, birds and beasts their answering notes assemble.
                'Tis Mother calling.

Then in life's evening, in the sweetest moment,
When flowers close their eyes and robin's note is still,
When man and lesser man sink into sleep, forgetting,
                'Tis Mother loving.

                          -- C. E. Klots

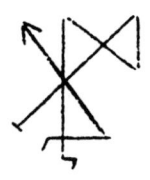

CHAPTER V

VISHNU, THE ZODIAC, THE CHERUBIM

>"One comes, One undelaying,
>Before whom the hierarchies of heaven bend --
>One comes in unutterable majesty;
>Across the pitiful borders of our night.
>One rides,
>On a White Horse; One takes His lordly way,
>One who keeps the divine appointment
>   with the ages,
>One undelaying, swiftly, swiftly, . . .
>Mark how the lamps of the East burn bright,
>Mark how the night is aflame
>   with His footsteps,
>How the whole earth is full of His coming!"
>   -- Mary Siegrist.

VISHNU was known as the active principle of the universe, a personified principle of Divine Knowledge, Universal Intelligence, identified with Time. He is said to be all that is and all that is not. In the Vedic text he is said to stride through the seven regions of the Universe in Three Steps -- referring to the spheres of man and the region of the earth. These Three Steps do not belong to the Hidden Scriptures alone. Cosmically they mean Fire, Lightning, and the Sun, "as having been taken in the earth, atmosphere, and the sky." Astronomically they symbolize the Sun rising, the Sun at noon, and the Sun setting. Esoterically they are emblematic "of Spirit, Soul and Body (MAN), of the circle transformed into Spirit; the Soul of the World, and its Body (or Earth)." All simply explained and with authority in sacred books. The circle (Boundless Space) was always a symbol of the Unknown -- "Limitless Time in Eternity." From the circle issues the radiant Light, the Universal Sun.

"The three strides relate metaphysically to the descent of Spirit into matter, of the Logos falling as a ray into Spirit, then into the Soul, and finally into the human physical form of man, in which it becomes LIFE."(1) Thus we see him striding through the seven regions of the universe in THREE STEPS.

When Vishnu dreams, during the interval between his creations, he is supported by the serpent with seven heads on the waters of the abyss. "Water was permanent first, the Tree of Life figured at the point of commencement, and round this Tree twined the starry dragon or serpent with its seven leaves," emblematic of the Great Mother and her FRATERNITY OF THE BUILDERS.

The greatest of all serpents is the Sun. Each planetary spirit, as a ray of light, is also symbolized as a serpent. Lightning, or the Light,

---
(1) - BLAVATSKY, H. P. -- THE SECRET DOCTRINE, VOL. I, Footnote #160, bottom of page 113.

travels in zig-zag movement (which is also that of the serpent); hence, duality coming from unity. This explains why the serpent travels in a zig-zag manner, as does the lightning.

All Vishnu's incarnations are emblematic of the Sun passing through the twelve signs of the zodiac, assuming their figures and performing their astrological functions. Avatars of Vishnu are said to have come from the "White Island;" and according to Thibetan tradition, the White Island lies in a locality which cannot be destroyed by fire or water. "Vishnu is an expression of the universe, and the spiritual realization of divinity."

The traditional account of the ten Avatars of Vishnu is a portrayal of the development of Humanity and a prophecy of the future which can be read in the zodiac. It marks the physiological development of the foetus. By a careful study of this an evolutionary doctrine is revealed through different stages of physical life, subtly concealed behind curious emblems. His ten incarnations correspond numerically to the ten spheres of the Kabala in which the Universal Spirit incarnates during involution and evolution. He has already come into objective manifestation nine times, called the Avatars of the Great Savior. The tenth is awaited, when it is said he will judge the world and the soul of every creature.

On the last day, when the world is to be consumed by fire or purification, the Sun and Moon will lose their light and a new heaven and earth will appear. His nine appearances have been for the sake of saving humanity. Each incarnation corresponds to and shows the changes taking place in the human embryo before its entrance into the world. Scientists claim that all life on our planet comes out of water, the human embryo being enveloped in water through its early stages. These nine months of prenatal incarnations have been used in symbolism for many ages. Proof is sufficiently given of evolution through the growth of the human embryo.

At the end of our present age of darkness, iron, misery, and sorrow, Vishnu will appear as the Kalki Avatar -- the Messiah, on a white horse, with a great sword in his hand -- to bring about a rule of righteousness, to create a New World; and in establishing righteousness he will lead the people onto paths of truth, when the love instinct will incarnate in its highest aspect as the pure impersonal love of the soul. It is also said that he descends for the purpose of overcoming the body, freeing it from the necessity of reincarnation, or establishing it for the purpose of immortality. The horse is symbolical of the envelope of the spirit of evil.

Kalki "symbolizes a time when humanity or an individual will have so perfected its body that the mind may, in that incarnation, complete its cycle of incarnations by becoming actually immortal." Lakshmi, the Beautiful, incarnates at this time, being spiritually related to Vishnu who appears as Kalki, merging electric and magnetic forces in individual incarnations. It is said, also, that he will return in his proper form, leading the white horse of the Last Judgment -- the dread steed with its forefoot raised; when the left foot is put down, it is said that the world will be torn to atoms. This is the "Fire Horse" champing at its bit. It is a time of great manifestation of the Spirit under the guidance of Vishnu, the Father, and Lakshmi, the Mother -- the Mother who is always supreme.

"The entire life of man is the living of his zodiac. He has his period of manifestation and he has his period of rest, according to the signs of the zodiac. His body is fashioned according to the laws of the zodiac; he is born according to the zodiac; his body is built up, strengthened and developed according to the zodiac; he reaches adolescence, is educated, and reaches maturity according to the zodiac; he is related to his family and his country according to the zodiac; develops his mind according to the zodiac; performs his duties and his calling according to the zodiac; and he dies according to the zodiac. The elements of which his body is composed are dissipated according to the zodiac; his life is separated from his desires according to the zodiac; ... he enjoys the period of rest -- called heaven or devachan -- according to the zodiac. The period of rest being at an end, he leaves his sphere of rest to come into contact with the emotions of the world, according to the zodiac. He selects his parents, who are to prepare his body which he is to inhabit, according to the zodiac; he contacts the parents according to the zodiac; makes connection with the foetus, and transforms his desires and tendencies of thought to the foetus which is being prepared for him, all according to the zodiac. At birth he transfers a portion of himself into the new-born physical body according to the zodiac; and he reincarnates, dependent on the degree of development of the body, all according to the zodiac." (1)

From the signs of the zodiac the body is built and divided into three quaternaries representing the three worlds, each acting for its own purpose from the human or divine to become the archetypes of the next manifestation. These three worlds are cosmic or archetypal, psychic or procreative, and physical or mundane. The archetypal directs the plan, the procreative obeys it, and the physical plans its use. From one quaternary to another the zodiac calls us onward. Each quaternary consists of the elements, Fire, Earth, Air and Water. Triangles, hexads, pentads, signs, figures, all are differentiated aspects of the One Eternal Changeless Consciousness.

The circle of the zodiac divided by a horizontal line, from Cancer to Capricorn, creates a duad, the upper part representing the unmanifest and the lower part the manifest. Symbolized as columns they were used to denote birth and death -- the extremes of physical life. Cancer, as breath, was the sign of involution; evolution came through Capricorn, when individuality had been attained. With this came the astronomical forces which underlie all the ritualism of Masonry.

"The Soul, as it descends from the one and indivisible source of its being, in order to be united to the body, passes through the Milky Way into the zodiac at the intersection of the two in Cancer and Capricorn, called the 'Gates of the Sun,' because the two solstices are placed in these signs. Through Cancer, or the 'Gate of Man,' the soul descends upon earth, which is its spiritual death. Through Capricorn, the 'Gate of the Gods,' it re-ascends to heaven, its new birth taking place upon its release from the body." (Within the Milky Way, which suggests a circular form, are the same creative elements that are in man and in the zodiac. Every soul, as it journeys towards earth, has to pass the planets, each one being of the substance of Divine Light.) "As soon as the soul has left Cancer and the Milky Way, it begins to lose its divine nature, and arriving at Leo enters upon the first phase of its future

---
(1) -- PERCIVAL, W. H. - THE ZODIAC. "THE WORD," VOL. IV, page 324.

condition here below. During its downward progress the soul, at first a <u>sphere</u> in form, is elongated into a <u>cone</u>, and now begins to feel the influence of Matter, so that it joins the body intoxicated and stupified by this novel draught.... The Soul thus descending, as it passes through each sphere, receives successive coatings, as it were, of a luminous body, and is furnished with the several faculties which it has to exercise during its probation upon earth. Accordingly, in Saturn it is supplied with reason and intelligence; in Jupiter, with the power of action; in Mars, with the irascible principle; in the Sun, with sensation and speculation; in Venus, with the appetites; in Mercury, with the power of declaring and expressing its thoughts; in the Moon, with the faculty of generating and augmenting the body." (1)

As the planets contain all the elements that constitute "the Inner Man, the Genii, their rulers, exercise their tyranny over it through such agencies as long as the soul is subjected to them during its imprisonment in the body."(2)

"The history of life and death and the promise of immortality are written in the zodiac."(3) When man grew wise, he realized that the only way to understand the zodiac was to relate it to his own body, learning through this "that the human soul comes from the unknown, and slumbers and dreams itself into the known." (4) Completing the path of the zodiac he passed consciously through Infinite Consciousness.

Hailing from different nations and uniting themselves into a Universal Brotherhood, having at heart the interests of Humanity, a few wise men have attained Divine Knowledge and Wisdom. These wise men have passed through the human stage. Their disciples are permitted to go out into the world as messengers and teachers, to give knowledge and explanation of the various signs of the zodiac, at the same time preserving the Wisdom in its inner meaning, which was only given to the few who could understand.

Each sign of the zodiac represents a part of the body which is really an occult center, the constellation or sign being similar in function and appearance to that center. Ages before the advent of history, the ancients found in the zodiac the creative principle of all things; it was their great wheel of rebirth and necessity; and to them man himself was a part of the great universe, having insight into the Hidden Wisdom revealed in the Sun, Moon and Stars of heaven.

Man, similar to the zodiac, is circular before he enters the physical world; but, it was necessary for him to break through that circle into his present state. "He is a broken and extended circle, - or a circle extended into a straight line." But man may again become a conscious circle or sphere by following the path of his occult spiritual zodiac, which is the circular regenerative zodiac of immortality, showing him how certain signs may be changed from the physical to the Divine.

---

(1) -- MACROBIUS, Somn. Scip., 1. 12.
(2) -- KING, C. W. -- THE GNOSTICS, Page 45
(3) -- PERCIVAL, W. H. -- THE ZODIAC, - "THE WORD," VOL. III, page 2.
(4) -- Ibid.

"The circular zodiac, which is the occult spiritual zodiac," is still within man, awaiting thought to bring into manifestation what has become atrophied; but when the "spiritual ascends towards the head by way of the spine it enters the soul centers there and shows the way via generation of the spiritual life. ... Along the spine man raises procreative functions to spiritual power. Thus he builds a bridge from the physical to the spiritual world, across the psychic world." (1) It is the law according to which everything comes into existence, remains for a time, then passes out of existence to re-appear with that which is in accord with the zodiac.

A foetus is one of the most important, wonderful and solemn things in our physical world, created through the highest spiritual powers. "In its development it brings with it the powers and potentialities of the past as suggestions and possibilities of the future. The foetus is the link between the visible physical world and the invisible astral world." (2) For any departure from the sanctity of this spiritual force, full payment will be exacted through tremendous Karmic power. The creation of the world with its forces, elements, kingdoms and creatures, is repeated in the building of the foetus. "The pentagon, or five-pointed star, is a symbol of man. With the point downward it signifies birth into the world by means of procreation. This pointing downward represents the foetus with its head pointing downward -- the manner in which it comes into the world." (3)

If one can see the plan of the zodiac, the path is not difficult to follow, -- the exoteric as well as the abstract principles are not difficult to solve. It is a "plan according to which universes and men come into existence from the unknown, pass through their periods of development, and return into the unknown." (4) There is also the path of the soul leading from the unknown through the known and into the infinite within and beyond. Through the soul centers in the head there radiates the light of the soul giving illumination to the mind that it may contact the "relationship existing between each 'I' and 'thou,' and by which the human being is transformed into that Divine principle, a Christ." (5)

The cosmos is unfolded through the zodiac and gives an understanding not alone of how Spirit, Soul, Mind and Body evolve, but of the transmutation on the lower plane of Fire, Earth, Air and Water. The zodiac belongs to the Infinitely Great as well as to the Infinitely Small; it belongs to all that has being; everything in existence comes in through the zodiac, just as it invariably passes out through the zodiac; the atom, the molecule, stone, plant, animal, the cell in man, his body and each organ of his body, all are known to have their own zodiac.

In primordial times animals typified the signs of the zodiac and were reverenced as symbols only. The word "zodiac" is from "zodion" and is resolved into the diminutive "zoon" -- an animal. Symbolically and esoterically every sign or planet affords a key to the inner laws of nature. The twelve signs of

---

(1) - PERCIVAL, W. H.   THE ZODIAC.   "The Word"   Vol. 3, page 193
(2) - Ibid   Vol. 4, page 257
(3) - Ibid   Vol. 4, page 257
(4) - Ibid   Vol. 3, page 65
(5) - Ibid   Vol. 4, page 324

the zodiac were called the sacred animals or genii of the zodiac. They are the starry skirt of the Milky Way through which the earth moves in its passage around the sun. These twelve animals are archetypes, each having a particular vibratory motion, force and color. They find expression through the twelve months, manifesting as the four seasons; spring, summer, autumn and winter; or Fire, Earth, Air and Water, the four elements out of which all things are built. The archetypes produce types, such as the animals which they represent -- the Bull, the Lion, the Eagle and the Man, the sacred Cherubim; or, on a lower plane, all the species of mineral, vegetable and animal life.

"The twelve senses have their correspondence in the twelve Disciples, or the twelve signs of the zodiac in the head. These, when merged, make the thirteenth or Christ consciousness; but there is something even above this, for the Christ must TURN HIS KINGDOM OVER TO THE FATHER. The Disciples are only glyphs for the twelve brain-centers which manifest as the sacred animals. Assimilating or taking on the characteristics of the sacred animals belongs to the dramas of ancient mysteries. Primitive performers clothed themselves as animals, acting the part of the animal they symbolized." (1)

In French Masonry the candidate as the Loveteau is said to enter as a young wolf, to guide through the darkness. In the Mysteries of Egypt, Isis wears the head of a wolf, guide of the Sun through the darkness of night. He was her guardian, helping her in her search through the underworld. This wolf may be seen in the Denderah planisphere of the heavens computed to be 87,000 years old, and at the place of the Vernal Equinox, which was at that time the place of commencement.

Images of serpents, bulls and other things, both animate and inanimate, were symbolized as types only, and as attributes of the Great God whom Egyptians called The Great Architect of Heaven. Through signs, symbols and ceremonies the soul and spirit were prepared here for the future and for that which man had to encounter and pass through after his material body had ceased to exist. It was one of the earliest natural customs preserved in a symbolical phase even after links of the old chain had been lost. In Egypt no one with any physical disability could be consecrated; even animals, if in any way deformed, were never used in either symbolical worship or for sacrifice. This was also rigidly adhered to in the sacerdotal order of the Levites, and belongs not only to the institutions of the Egyptians and the Jews but to the Freemasons of today as well.

Our Bible frequently mentions the offering of animals for sacrifice. They are merely representations of the zoa, the little animals representing the zodiac. Each sign signifies an animal instinct relating to that of man. We have the sacrifice of the Lamb, or Ram, typifying the sign Aries; or that of the Bull, belonging to the sign Taurus -- the Bull representing the virility of life, relating to the instincts or desires within men. King Solomon, when finishing his temple, offered bulls for sacrifice. Similar sacrifices belong to all ancient mysteries whose interpretations are found in the celestial signs of the zodiac. Pythatoras claimed the soul passed through the bodies of various animals before attaining perfection -- meaning the twelve signs of the Zodiac. Heaven, earth and nature were given similar attributes and these were later introduced into the arts and sciences. Our human arts are but imitations of nature. Everywhere fragments are found coming from that past; and though

---

(1) - WIGGS, George W.

the good has been mingled with much that was evil, there has ever remained a silver thread of ancient spiritual thought. Nothing is ever lost. Signs and symbols had practically the same meaning over the entire world, and all were of celestial making.

"An inspiration comes with the study of this Wisdom, giving an understanding of the opening of the planets and zodiac within oneself, and showing how the twelve Disciples and the sacred animals are but the involutions of the Central Spiritual Sun, making the periphery of the circle in which the sacred animals function, or the human head in which the twelve senses are to be transmuted; and in being merged through evolution or centripetal force, may carry back to the center of both the cerebrum and cerebellum, or the back and front brain, into the center brain, so that in becoming Bi-une (male and female merged) the One Will can function in us, so that the Thinker thinks us; but before this takes place, one must be able to gain retrospection, or to read the past in his own subjective, which will also, when read, help him to know the future. When instinct is transmuted to reason and merged back into intuition it contacts the Spirit of Truth and can express itself in Love and Wisdom, or, become Bi-une within oneself so that one may become the instrument which the Great Architect of the Universe, and even the Master below, can use." (1)

The Cherubim
The Four Holy Animals of the Zodiac. "The Christian form symbolically representing St. Matthew, St. Mark, St. Luke and St. John. Brought on from the old Eschatology of the Egyptians and represented throughout the world."
-- Albert Churchward.

In Masonry much importance is placed on the Cherubim, constituting a great mystery very sacred in Speculative Masonry today. They are in the armorial ensignia of the Royal Arch Degree of the American Rite, where four veils of different colors are given, and to each belongs a banner, for the purpose of emphasizing their mystical importance, -- of intense interest if properly understood in relation to their manifestations in nature. Egypt, India, Britain, China, Japan, Persia, Greece and others have used them symbolically, representing that which would be of supreme interest to each nation.

Enoch, who represented the Wisdom of the Fourth Race, the Atlantean, in his double type or dual nature of man -- spiritual and material -- has been placed in the center of the astrological cross within the six-pointed star of Solomon, together with the four sacred animal signs of the zodiac which, when given with wings, were called the Cherubim.

----

(1) WIGGS, George W.

A holy animal, as a Cherub, is found in the arch placed over the eastern gate of Eden as a token of the Divine Presence. Cherubim were found at the gates of Egyptian temples. They are in the temple of Solomon, in the sanctum sanctorum, standing on each side of the cube, their wings forming a seat over the Ark. They are portrayed in cathedrals, churches and Pagan temples, each with its emblem. They are borne upon the insignia of the great fraternal societies of the world, and are used in the Roman Catholic Testament to preface the Gospels, representing the Evangelists. It is claimed that all faces are to be traced to the types of these four sacred animals, and the animal nature representing the instincts in the human that must be overcome before man can rise into the sphere of Light.

The Cherubim were primarily the four animals that represented the four points of the compass in the making of the zodiac. They were called the "Holy and Sacred Ones of the Great Circle," and were adored almost over the entire world -- were even worshipped by the Gentiles. The Aquarian sign, as the Angel or Man, was often pictured surrounded with wings and carrying a flaming sword. "The flaming sword turning every way may be understood to signify the perpetual motion of the Cherubim." (1) Aquarius, as the Man, is the light-bringer, finding polarity in the woman; and in this double role of masculine-feminine, will liberate the new energy which presages the opening of a new consciousness.

The Cherubim are not only represented in the four fixed signs of the zodiac, given in the form of the four sacred animals, but represent the four sacred elements -- Fire, Earth, Air and Water. They accompany the four Evangelists and prefix their respective gospels. Matthew comes under Aquarius, the Man; Mark, under the sign Leo, the Lion; Luke, under the sign Taurus, the Bull; and John, under the sign Scorpio, as the Eagle. Corresponding to the sacred elements we have Cosmic Fire, Cosmic Strength, Cosmic Spirit, and these three become Air, or Cosmic Spirituality. Cosmic Spirituality is a positive force and transcends everything. It is all-pervading. Spirit is indivisible and is at the core of every individual life. Cosmic Energy is eternally young. It is the open sesame to the Spiritual World. Among the tribes of Israel, Judah comes under Leo, the Lion, Fire; Ephraim, under Taurus, the Bull -- Earth; Dan, under Scorpio, the Eagle -- Water or Spirit; and Reuben, under Aquarius -- Air. They were on the insignia of the banners of the children of Israel which were placed at the four corners of the world.

A Hebrew word for "Cherub" signifies a bull; and the Angel with the head of a Bull is the image of a very obscure symbolism. The Cherub as the Angel or Soul of the earth, in ancient Mysteries, was always given as the figure of a bull, -- obscure but understandable. In the Mythraic Mysteries the Master of Light plunges his sword into the flanks of a bull of the earth, and the drops of blood that follow represent the setting free of life. The sword, as the Blazing Sword, came to be known as the Light which man seemed to have forgotten how to direct; but when he had controlled its forces, then knowledge was given of magical work in all its purity, for he had become the Conqueror of the Flaming Sword. Anciently, sacrifices of blood, even to the testing and eating of flesh and heart of great heroes, were thought to give an inner strength and Light. In some countries the people would eat part of a serpent and drink its blood in the hope of awakening the inner voice whereby sacred knowledge might be

---

(1) - PHILO, Judeas

obtaines. Wagner makes Siegfried drink of the dragon's blood that he might hear the voice of Nature, the song of the birds, the rustle of the trees. It was a very old habit to cut into the flesh and draw blood and pass it between two comrades so as to make of them brothers. Grape joice was poured upon the altars in temples at Heliopolis, symbolizing the blood of enemies who had fought against her people.

It was an ancient belief that blood was full of Astral Fire and Life; and in the mysteries of blood, the Priests of Baal made incisions in their flesh, that through the blood drawn the Fire from Heaven might be brought down. Blood that had been spilled was thought to fill the air with cries of vengeance or mercy, or with angels or demons, and, being full of Astral Light, that it would increase the images in the brain during sleep, the globules being either sympathetic or antipathetic.

Astral Light was the instrument of dreams. Many legends are filled with knowledge of the "three drops of blood" as restoration of vision; for light, its counterpart, is found in all the Mysteries of the ancient world, three being a remarkable and ineffable number, as well as conserving many virtues. In the Persian myth, Rustam, the Hercules of Persia, conquers and obtains the three drops of blood from the heart of the White Giant, with which to restore the sight of the blind Cai-Caus. Today at divine altars it is symbolically given as a sacrifice for the washing away of sins that the consciousness may open on higher planes. It became a part of the Kabalistic Ritual that through this sacrifice inner Light might be given, in the hope that perhaps in some unknown way it would be for redemptive purposes. This symbolic sacrifice of blood trails along the path down to the present time through modern Ritual, though softened and glorified, and is deeply revered.

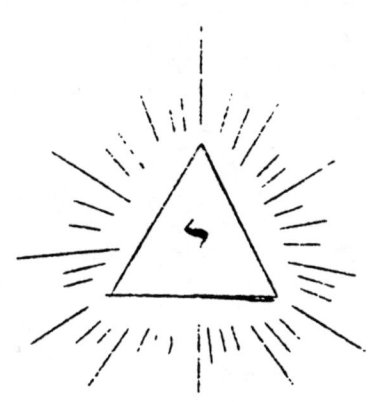

CHAPTER VI

THE MYSTERIES

<blockquote>
All ages are slowly moving up
this Ladder of the Stars -- the
Mighty "Altar Stairs" from the depths
to the heights of a victorious end.
- E. V. S.
</blockquote>

MYSTERIES were universally sacred. Divine in their message, but never historical, they were the common property of all countries, guided by an astronomical orrery overhead which taught the celestial myth illustrated in allegory independent of time or place. Mysteries were the great educational centers of the ancient world established in every civilized nation of antiquity for the cultivation of the sciences, the bettering of man's moral nature, and the development of his mental faculties with an understanding of the laws governing the material and spiritual worlds, thereby bringing man closer to Deity. Mysteries always held a message for fallen man, bringing him nearer to his God.

Egypt's secret doctrine of Life, Death and Immortality was the foundation of them all, as well as of all established religions throughout the world. The wisest of all ancient peoples spoke of the Mysteries with commendation. Plato himself states that "He who is purified through them at his death will find his habitation 'with the gods.'" The Book of Job is a perfect representation of an ancient initiation, including the trials preceding the ceremonies. In those early ages the neophyte was a man of profound learning and unimpeachable character. He had to face death and triumph over all limitations of the flesh. Even death was met heroically as a reward for failure. Today very few could stand the tests of the neophyte of those olden days, when disciples gladly paid with their lives for the Master's word of hope, or died of a broken heart at his rebuke. Through the Mysteries were taught the noblest aims of life and the worthiest means of obtaining them.

Both the Lesser and the Greater Mysteries were always given under all possible circumspection, the veil of secrecy being impenetrable. Many of the Lesser Mysteries discoursed upon the pre-natal epoch of man "when consciousness in its nine-day period (embryonic months) was descending into its world of illusion and assuming its veil of unreality." The Greater Mysteries were for spiritual regeneration, an uplifting method of liberating the higher nature from the bondage of materialism. Very few attained to the Greater; all could be initiated into the Lesser. Originally all mysteries were spiritual; but when they passed from the Initiates they became materialized and degraded. "The Greater obscurely intimated, by mystic and splendid visions, the felicity of the soul, both here and hereafter, when purified from the defilement of a material nature and constantly elevated to the realities of intellectual vision." (1) Four years were generally necessary for instruction in the Lesser Mysteries be-

---
(1) - TAYLOR, Thomas.

fore admission to the Greater; and there was a time when the Entered Apprentice had to serve seven years in his grade before advancement.

Spiritual unfoldment came for disciples who had passed the highest degrees, which are practically unknown today. It is presumed they were taught in the Brahmanic Mysteries. An Initiate, on reaching Nirvana, sees an inferno below and the mountains of the gods above -- the gods who were the "Keepers of the Vale of Tears." It was thought that the gods themselves would punish any revealer of the sacred secrets; and not only would the revealer be punished, but those who listened; and to the more indiscreet, capital punishment was meted out with merciless severity. When degeneracy of the Mysteries crept in, it was principally through the physical side, but the inner spiritual meaning of every symbol, sign and allegory held, as it does today, its mystical import, powerful enough to pierce the mental and reach the higher consciousness.

The doctrine of a future state had its origin in the Mysteries. It underlies all Rituals, and has come to us today without most of the degeneracy which befell those ancient Rites. The Mystery of birth and death was a solemnly accepted fact held in spotless purity, being a Mystery connected with the Creator; hence those emblems representing generation and regeneration and the new life. It is at the end of all cycles that corruption creeps in, resulting in degeneracy. It can also be found in the ending of the cycle today; yet the undercurrent retains the ancient spiritual teaching.

Many of the old Fathers derided the Mysteries, failing to grasp their import, and gave them the name Paganistic, losing sight of that which was behind the name and the Ritual of the Pagan which was the Word of God. During the Third Century, when the followers of Christ were severely tried by the fires of persecution, secrets of the Mysteries were most strictly observed. All Mysteries, by reason of their nature and constitution, should be faithfully concealed.

Voltaire tells us "The truly grand tragedies, the imposing and terrible representations, were the Sacred Mysteries, which were celebrated in the greatest temples of the world, in the presence of the Initiated only. It was there that the habits, the decorations, the machinery, were proper to the subject, and the subject was the present and the future life."

Two fundamental religious doctrines were always taught in all old Mysteries; one was philosophic; the other simple and literal, for those incapable of understanding the deeper Mysteries. The philosophic taught esoterically of the hidden side of nature and the sciences; the exoteric was for the profane. Ancient temples everywhere were ruled over by mystics and philosophic taught esoterically of the hidden side of nature and the sciences; the exoteric was for the profane. Ancient temples everywhere were ruled over by mystics and philosophers deeply learned in the secrets of nature. Strange mystic Rites had initiated these great souls into sacred Fraternities. Many Rites through which they passed were extremely cruel, testing the courage and strength of those remarkable souls through the unfolding of the sacred drama.

Many of the greatest philosophers have spoken in eulogistic phrases of the spiritual unfoldment that awaited a candidate for the Mysteries. This same unfoldment awaits the earnest Mason today, and though clothed and hidden in the folds of a great sanctity, will be revealed to those who have trod the path of unfoldment, recalling the message of old, "Let him approach who is pure from all wickedness, whose soul is not conscious of any evil, and who leads a just and upright life."

"It appears that all the perfection of civilization and all the advancement made in philosophy, science, and art among the Ancients are due to these initiations, which, under the veil of mystery, sought to illustrate the sublimest truths of religion, morality and virtue, and impress them on the hearts of their disciples....the chief object was to teach the doctrine of God, the resurrection of man to Eternal Life, the dignity of the human soul, and to lead the people to see the shadow of the Deity in the beauty, magnificence and splendor of the Universe." (1)

The Mysteries were organized to help struggling humanity towards a high ideal through the awakening of spiritual powers. Mystic ceremonies are found among the lowest forms of savagery, primitive indeed and interwoven with a touch of the Masonic Ritual. Voodoo Rites are practiced today in the West Indies, always with the rhythm of the Voodoo drums, using mystical powers unlawfully, through the astral world, certainly not through the spiritual. Undoubtedly those West Indians are reincarnated Atlanteans who had practiced the black arts -- from a preponderance of which, it is presumed, Atlantis perished.

When degeneracy, passion and fear crept apace in the world, Egypt, Greece, Rome and other countries allowed an overshadowing of the black arts or black magic. Their Priests lost, as it were, the WORD. Little by little their flame flickered away, leaving mighty nations buried beneath the "dead ashes of their own spiritual fire." Yet the true Flame lives eternally; it is the essence of the Spirit; it is Life. Around the Flame other nations arose. There were other worlds to conquer whose people revelled in the spiritual beauty and brightness that had been. Today, by living Truth, the Flame shall be kept burning in the midst of great fraternities. It is the only way.

In all Ancient Mysteries a candidate who aspired to participate in the higher degrees was placed in a coffin or something similar to one, where, during a prescribed time, he remained in loneliness for reflection, to prepare for the great truths that awaited him when delivered from this solemn state of darkness and silence. It was regeneration, or the rising from death to be born into a region of Light -- resurrection after the "deep sleep of death." These changes were all enacted under sacred scenic representation. The candidates were often kept many days and nights in darkness; the time varied in different nations. In Britain, the candidate was kept in darkness nine days and nights; this time was tripled in Greece; while in Persia it extended to fifty days and nights of darkness, fasting and rest. The nine days allotted the candidate for initiation by some nations were symbolical of the nine spheres through which the human soul descends during its process of assuming terrestrial form. Plato placed his candidate in darkness three days and nights to await his resurrection. It was the re-enacting of the fabled death of the Sun, sinking in the West and arising in brightness and glory in the East -- a fable that has proved so profound in conception it has been dedicated to the religions of the entire world.

---

(1) - MACOY, Robert; GENERAL HISTORY OF FREEMASONRY, Page 33

Mystery Rites became universal, innumerable. All taught and confirmed the doctrine of a future state, while some gave greater expression to their religious doctrines. The most noted were Egyptian, Eleusinian, Mithraic, Samothracean, Orphic and Bacchic. Each country retained in secret the doctrine of the One God, Creator and Governor of the Universe, which was tenaciously held by all orders of Priests -- extraordinarily so.

During the Mysteries amazing objects appeared. At times it seemed as though earthquakes were taking place, or tornadoes were spending their fury; and again something would appear as if bathed in resplendent light. Flames would issue from walls, invisible hands extinguishing them. There would be profound obscurity, then dazzling light, thunder and lightning. Calls for help and cries of agony were heard, for the candidates' nerves were to be tried to the utmost, testing his moral and physical courage. All the Twelve Tortures were featured.

Vitruvius describes "the disposition of bronze vases about a room, placed so as to produce certain definite changes in the tone and quality of the human voice. In like manner, each chamber in the Mysteries through which the candidate passed had its own peculiar acoustics; thus, in one chamber the voice of the priest was amplified until his words caused the very room to vibrate, while in another the voice was diminished and softened to such a degree that it sounded like the distant tinkling of silver bells. Again, in some of the passageways the candidate was apparently bereft of the power of speech; for though he shouted at the top of his voice, not even a whisper was audible to his ears. After progressing a few feet, however, he would discover that his softest sigh would be re-echoed a hundred times." [1] And so these wonderful architects built in harmony with the Universal Self.

The great and true object of initiation was sanctity, that the candidate might be able to SEE, and thereby have a concept of Deity -- the Light of all Mysteries. Its object was to enlighten the uncultured, pointing the way to a life of greater worthiness through knowledge given of truth and the principles of a moral life. Originally they were very simple; but time, evolution, made them more rigid. The voice of secrecy became more intense, more complicated. Ancient signs and tokens were given, that Brothers of the Fraternities might be better known to each other. Different degrees were invented which were thought to lead to the inner chamber of life, so that a few of the Initiates might more effectively help candidates to a better understanding of Nature's great and venerable secrets, holding sway over their individual molding powers. They taught of a new life of thought, of virtue, and prepared the candidate for the doctrine of the One Supreme God; taught of death, eternity, immortality and the mysteries after death. In their first institution the Mysteries were most powerful for the promotion of virtue and knowledge, but in time they became horribly subservient to the gratification of the flesh.

In all Mysteries clothing played a most important part, the body being, as it were, the robe of its Spiritual nature and beauty, which brought out its spirituality or its materialism. These adornments suggested virtues of the candidate's accomplishments. Colors also played an important part. White symbolized purity; blue, altruism and integrity; while red meant sacri-

---

[1] -- HALL, Manly P.: MASONIC, HERMETIC, QUABBALISTIC AND ROSICRUCIAN SYMBOLICAL PHILOSOPHY; Page CLXXIV

fice and love. Knowledge of the esoteric value of these colors, coming through from ancient times, enters into Masonic Ritualism today. Insignia, jewels and ornamentations worn by the ancient hierophants symbolized the spiritual energies radiating from the human body. Their philosophies were given in myths and legends, especially those of the Sun, Moon, Stars and Planets. Chemistry of the Soul was often called physical regeneration. A chemistry "which will be new because it is old" is already waiting in the astral for manifestation on earth, to be beneficial to mankind -- one of the many spiritual truths that have been secreted from the profane.

Feasts in ancient times were always of great importance. Early Sabean feasts go back hundreds of thousands of years. They were held for each planet when in the zodiacal sign of its exaltation. Great were feasts among all nations inaugurated during special configurations of the heavens. From these have emerged the sacred calendars of the Ancients. "The famous divisions by seven and by twelve, appertaining to the planets and the signs of the zodiac, are everywhere found in the hierarchal order of the Gods and Angels and the other Ministers that are the depositories of that Divine Force which moves and rules the world." (1)

Astrology was practised by all ancient nations. Egypt's Book of this great science was reverently carried and held during all great religious processions, or feasts, which were usually held during the Equinoxes and Solstices. "It was the Mother Book of all the sciences." It taught the secrets of the stars, how to appeal to the gods, and to learn of the future

Generally speaking, in the processions of these feasts a small chest or ark was carried, which contained different and often strange symbolical devices, but nothing was more commonly found than a van, a child, a serpent, a human head, a flute and a drum. These can all be found on the ancient monuments. The express emblem of life to come partook of the nature of the amulet, or phylactery (small leathern box containing slips inscribed with certain Scriptural passages). Two such boxes are worn by orthodox Jews during prayer, one in the hand and one on the left arm, a charm for protection. The Jews had in their chest or ark a book of the law, a pot of manna (celestial), the rod of Aaron, and a copy of the Pentateuch written in square characters, possibly the same as those in the chest of the Royal Arch Chapter in Masonry, of "ineffable characters" which consisted of right angles in various attitudes, with the addition of the dot. Every Royal Arch Chapter in Masonry is supplied with a similar chest containing testimonials of time past, and a celestial food declared to be manna -- the food upon which the Israelites were supposed to have been fed in the wilderness. It contains also a skull, the figure of a serpent, together with other emblems, their origin being possibly unknown to many Masons.

During certain feasts of the Egyptians the basket and chest symbolized monuments of their progress in husbandry. These were followed by sesame seeds, heads of poppies, pomegranates, cakes, corn, bayberries, branches of fig-trees, salt, wool and, finally, a winnowing van, a child and a serpent. In the feasts of Isis and Eleusis the sacred basket enclosed, among other things, a child and a golden serpent, the van, grain, cakes -- all were there. A basket containing a child and a serpent was carried by young Athenian women. The Ark set up in the wilderness by Moses is similar in all its measurements to the

---

(1) - PIKE, Albert; MORALS AND DOGMA, Page 474.

"Stone Chest" in the King's Chamber in the Great Pyramid. Miniatures of this were carried around the Egyptian temples at Memphis on stated occasions. A chest was carried in all old Rites in which sacred treasures were placed. Sometimes strange and curious things were put within; but the Ark of God contained only what was considered too sacred to be touched by any one save the Priest.

The Ladder was a component part of all Mysteries, and is important in Masonry, where it represents the soul's journey through the world of materiality. In Indian Mysteries a Ladder of Seven Steps led the soul towards perfection. Joseph, referring to the lower step, explains that "this is the House of God, and the Gate of Heaven." There was a gate for each step to reach from earth to heaven. Each gate represented a planet and the metal belonging to it. The last and highest gate was of pure gold, opening the way to the home of Celestial Deities. These gates of metal were gradual in their increasing purity, so that when a candidate reached the summit he was under the protection of the Most High Sun-god. In Egyptian and Hebrew Mysteries the final gate above the seventh belonged to the Celestial Triangle (called Peniel in Genesis) and became the vision of seeing God face to face. The rounds of the ladder were often called the stars of heaven.

"In the Zoroastrian caves of initiation the Sun, Planets and Zodiac were represented overhead in gems of gold. The sun appeared emerging from the back of Taurus." The seven Pleiades in this constellation were made famous in Masonry as the seven steps of the upper end of the sacred Ladder. The ladder was a rhythmical arrangement of the passage of the Sun through the first seven signs of the zodiac, and, arriving at the Autumnal Equinox, brought with it the various fruits of the earth, which in the Ritual were gathered symbolically by the candidate in his ascent of the ladder, beautifully portrayed as he followed the onward march of the Sun.

The seven steps in the Scottish Rite Ritual, in the degree called "Knight of Kadosh," (1) are claimed to have been invented at Lyons, in 1743. In the ceremony of the Knight of the Eagle, and also in that of the Knight of Kadosh, the candidate is not permitted to see the person who initiates him. (2) When the Ark of the Seven and of the Covenant is shown the candidate, it symbolically recalls the Seven Great Stars, THE FRATERNITY OF THE BUILDERS, belonging to the earliest covenant made in heaven, and as the planetary Seven, they are illustrated by the seven steps or seven degrees of ascent. In the Scottish Rite Ritual the ladder with the seven rounds ascends from the red room. Red was the color of the Great Mother. It was also symbolized in the nocturnal Sun. A red cross was placed over the heart of the candidate. Red is sworn to in Masonry.

"Ne plus ultra" is written at the foot of this ladder, which is said to contain the highest Mysteries, or the height of attainment.

---

(1) -- Kadosh or Cadosh, resolved into the Caduceus -- a sacred person (Knight of Kadosh) or, the Black and White Eagle.
(2) -- Presumably this was derived from an ancient custom when the Initiator was never seen nor known, probably following the method of Pythagoras, who stood behind a screen when giving his lessons. In those old times it was thought to be unlawful to reveal the name of the hierophant.

The steps, given in their Hebraic names and briefly sketched, are, with their zodiacal signs:

1st Step	- Isedakah (Righteousness)	zodiacal sign,		Aries.
2nd "	- Shor-laban -- in mythical language,			Taurus.
3rd "	- Mothok (Sweetness)	"	"	Gemini.
4th "	- Emunah (Truth in disguise)	"	"	Cancer.
5th "	- Hamal-saggi (Great labor) - Celestial Lion			Leo.
6th "	- Sabbal (A burden, or patience)	zodiacal sign,		Virgo
7th "	- Gemulah, Binah, Tebunah (Retribution,) (Intelligence, Prudence)	"	"	Libra.

(These were of special importance).

In the Ritual of the Egyptian Aments there were two stages represented by two ladders; one, called the Ladder of Sut, was to reach the horizon from the land of darkness; the Ladder of Horus reached into the land of Light -- a ladder by which Spirits gained Heaven.

Jacob's Ladder was always considered one that ascended from the earth to the Divine Sphere. He saw a ladder set in earth and reaching to heaven, on which souls were ascending and descending; and the topmost round of this Ladder of Jacob was the threshold of the Divine. Strangely, too, Jacob's Ladder has an occult reference to the soles of the foot, -- the organ of locomotion. But long before the vision of Jacob, the ascent of the Paradisical Mount of God by means of a ladder of seven steps was given even in the Ritual of Mexican savages. During the Initiatory ceremonies, as a mode of purification, the candidate wandered through seven dark caverns, each one ending in a narrow orifice creating an entrance to the next in procession. Through these "gates of perfection" the humiliated candidate had to squeeze his body with pain and labor. When he finally reached the summit he was said to have "passed through the transmigration of the spheres, to have accomplished the ascent of the soul, and to merit the favor of the celestial deities." [1]

In the Mysteries it was said that seventy-two aeons or Angels were on this ladder. There were names and powers that emanated from Shemhamphoresch, the separate and Ineffable Deity. Mahomet journeyed at night to heaven on his steed Alborak. Alighting in Jerusalem, he saw a ladder made of golden ropes resting upon Mount Moriah. This he climbed, and entered into the presence of the loving and many-veiled Deity -- analogous to climbing the golden rope of the Kundalini. All nature is symbolical of the mystical ladder, but the magician's golden rope was unseen. The evolution of a soul from the lowest step of the ladder into the presence of the Holy One was the Ladder of the Spirit, rising upwards from the darkness of oblivion into celestial splendor above. In the doctrine of the Kabala, "the Spirit clothes itself to come down, and unclothes itself to go up," and the unending ascent of the ladder begins.

St. John climbed heavenward through the seven churches of Asia and found himself in the presence of the Lord of the Cherubim. The "Great World's Altar Stairs" were the means by which men could climb heavenward. The home of the gods was at the summit. The North Pole was ascended by Seven Steps.

---
(1) - FELLOWS, John; THE MYSTERY OF FREEMASONRY, Page 322.

Many pyramids have been built to commemorate those Seven Steps which were called High Places in Hebrew books. This was the Ladder of the Stars, which enabled one to lose oneself on the heights. All ages are slowly moving up the mighty "Altar Stairs" from the depths to the heights of a victorious end. It is the onward rhthmic march of life or evolution. Those who are ignorant may turn away for a time, but those with vision face this eternal progress with intrepidity. God has not limited the rounds in this great Ladder of Light, for all nature is symbolized in it.

If every Mason accepted what Albert Pike has so profoundly given, there would be no affirmation that Masonry today had been clothed in personalities for "the veil drawn between the high ascent of the Ladder, whose last rung envisioned heaven, or the path to the spiritual mountain that led to the nearness of Infinity, was too tremendous for petty words."

The Greeks fix 1423 B.C. as the date of the Eleusinian Mysteries at Eleusis. Their renown was so great they seemed to swallow up all other Mysteries. At the beginning of the Fifth Century Theodosius almost totally extinguished Pagan theology in the Roman Empire, when the Eleusinian Mysteries suffered a general devastation, yet though stripped of their original splendor and beauty, they were at least secretly observed and continued at Athens until the Eighth Century, when they became beclouded, if not extinguished. They passed into the care of the Arabians and are found depicted on the early Mohammedan monuments.

The Greeks found the greatest happiness in their Mysteries, and Hercules is made to say that he was blessed when he had a sight of them. They ramained in their splendor many years. Their two great corruptions were magic and impurity. Responsibility for this was laid to the crafty Priesthood, though it may have been due to a mistaken cause. They belonged to the greatest of all secret societies. The glorification of life, which was a mystic interpretation of the most precious secrets of nature, was taught by Initiates and Sages as the greatest achievement. The price man paid to enter the Eleusinian Mysteries was the surrender of body, soul and life, "to signify occultly the condition of the unpurified soul, invested with an earthly body and enveloped in a material and physical nature."

It was in these Mysteries that Wisdom was read to the Initiates from a book of stone called Petroma, which was in two parts, fitted closely together. It was the Book of the Great Mother written in stone. When these tablets of stone were presented to be read, thunder and lightning, bellowings and other awful sounds were heard; and at times a radiant light appeared resplendent with fire; then darkness would come, with awful apparitions of a supernatural appearance. "The garments worn by the Initiates were accounted so sacred they were never changed or cast off, but allowed to drop away in rags." (1) the last being consecrated to Persephone.

Moses is similarly presented, with the two stone tablets, at the scene of his Initiation on Sinai; (see Exodus XIX, 16, etc.) "There was thunder and lightnings, and a thick cloud upon the Mount, and the voice of the trumpet was exceeding loud; . . . and Mount Sinai was altogether on a smoke, because

---
(1) - MASSEY, Gerald; A BOOK OF THE BEGINNINGS, Vol. II, Page 204.

the Lord descended upon it in fire." The cloud and the supernatural appearances of the one scene are found in the other. It may be that the clothes which never wore out were simply those of the Initiates which were not to be cast aside till worn to tatters; (See Deut. XXIX, 5): "And I have led you forty years in the wilderness: your clothes are not waxen old upon you, and thy shoe is not waxen old upon thy feet." The enactment of the Ritual in this drama was one of purification, washing and regeneration. It is known that the Eleusinian Mysteries were closed with the Sanscrit words, "Knox Om Pax."

It is said that Mithra was born in a cave at the time of the winter solstice, the twenty-fifth of December. Many Mithraic ceremonies were in imitation of the motions of the heavenly bodies, the candidate being dressed to represent one of the sacred animals symbolical of the signs of the zodiac. One of their caves was adorned with two signs of the zodiac representing the Solstices, Capricorn and Cancer. These were always known as the Gates of the Gods through which the Immortals were ever ascending and descending, symbolical of the ascent and descent of the soul. It was in this degree of their Ritual that a cape was given to the candidate upon which the signs of the zodiac were woven. After this he was hailed as one risen from the dead; he was instructed in the secrets of the Mystics, and was called a Lion. (Initiates were usually called Lions.) A cross was marked upon his forehead, and he was given the Grip of the Lion's Paw.

In their Mysteries the candidate's courage was tested to the fullest within a cave constructed for this purpose. Before final initiation the Twelve Tortures or Trials were undergone -- applicable to the passage of the Sun through the twelve signs of the zodiac, or houses of the zodiac. Abraxas, important in Masonry, has a numerical value of 365. It was also one of the names of Mithra, treated in the same manner and having the same numerical value. After final initiation a small round cake of unleavened bread was given the candidate, emblematic of the solar disk, thereby making it a symbol of celestial bread, or manna.

A cup engraved with mystic symbols was placed upon the altar and the sacrifice of a lamb or bull was made, the blood being sprinkled upon the candidate. Their purification was by water; and they had a confessional. They had, also, seven portals to pass through, each holding a perilous adventure, before being admitted to a gorgeous Sacellum -- a heaven illuminated with a thousand candles reflecting every shade of color, rich gems and amulets copiously adorning the walls. In its finality this was known as the ascension of the ladder. Their Ladder of Seven Steps leading to the summit represented the seven spheres of the planets, each step emblematic of one of the Seven Mysteries which were revealed to the candidate comparable to the Seven Seals, opened one after the other, in the Book of Revelation.

In the accounts of the probationary trials belonging to their Mysteries, when a candidate was eager to become a chief or leader of an army he was known as a Soldier of Mithra. He could not be initiated until he had passed his probationary labors to acquire a certain apathy as well as sanctity. During this ceremony a wreath was given to him on the point of a sword, which was thrown aside with the words: "My only crown is Mithra;" after which he was led into the secrets of the Mithraic Hidden Powers. Their Ritual is filled with references to the birth of the Sun-god, his sacrifice and resurrection.

Their Rites superseded the Mysteries of Bacchus and were the foundation of Gnosticism. Mithraic Rites are similar to many others belonging to the ancient mystery schools. Spiritual life, self control, intelligence and purity were necessary.

The caves of Mithra were said to represent the whole world and the grandeur of man's destiny.

The Persians did not build temples -- they used high hills, inclosures of untrued stones, and caves. Sun and Fire were the emblems of their Deity. Ancient Persian Astrologers made images of gold, silver, wax, wood, earth and stone, under certain constellations, "for the use of which they did also receive much benefit but that it was either by way of enchantment or witchcraft there is no man able to tell."

Voltaire pertinently asks, "Who are these hierophants, the sacred Freemasons who celebrated their ancient mysteries of Samothrace; and when came their gods, Kabiri?"

Samothrace was an island in the Grecian Archipelago, famous in days of old for the Kabiric Mysteries celebrated in its temples; and though but little is known today, these Mysteries were very sacred and profound. They were renowned among all Ancients, through the Seven Never-Setting Stars, the Seven Divine Watchers, the Seven Sailors. The Kabiri, "Children of the Sun," being connected with At-Al-As "the Divine Sun," were said to have brought Light into the world, their generic name being the "Holy Fires," which created the "Seven Localities" of this island.

Noah was called a Great Kabir, evolved from the Kabiri of Samothrace of Titanic tradition. Tubal Cain was a Kabiric instructor. The Deity of Israel was called a Great Kabir. They were all Masons, Sons of Light, belonging to THE FRATERNITY OF THE BUILDERS. They were the children of the Great Mother. Cain is represented by the planet Mars, god of generation and power and of the first shedding of blood. Tubal-Cain was an artificer in brass and iron, and he was one with Vul-cain, the greatest god of the late Egyptians. Their ritualistic drama centers around the Seven Kabiri, and, whether together or separately, they are used in symbology. Similarly we have the legends of Hiram Abiff, Osiris, Bacchus, Adonis and others.

Their Mysteries covered three degrees applicable to the death of the Dying God. The first dramatic representation was the death of one Cashmala by three brothers; the second, the discovery of the mutilated body; and the third -- after much seeking and toiling -- the finding of and rejoicing over his resurrection was looked upon as signifying the salvation of the whole world and similarly given in all Rites of the Dying God.

The Initiate enters the land of the dead for a special purpose -- that he may return a conqueror of death.

These ceremonies are termed by Clement "The sacred Mystery of a brother slain by his brethren." The Kabiric death is a sacred symbol of all antiquity; "Thus the allegory of the self-murdered by the not-Self is perpetuated through the religion of mysticism of all peoples. The _philosophic death_ and the _philosophic resurrection_ also are the Lesser and the Greater

Mysteries respectively." (1) Their Mysteries were held at night, as were those of Isis and others, the object being the consecration of man to the Deity and the promise that he would, through consecration, become pure and just.

The Kabiri were not only called but were the Seven Stars, the Seven Glorious Ones, the Stars of the Constellation that Never Set. They were called the Seven Spirits and were said to be with the Mother before the Throne of Saturn. They were the Sailors who made the first circle or cycle of time as they sailed through the celestial waters around the Pole of Heaven -- the Pole representing the dot or Point Within the Circle. When Ra, the Sun in Amenta, launched his boat with the Seven Kabiri or Sailors, he made his voyage nightly forever around the Pole. The Sailors were assigned to the Seven Stars of the Lesser Bear. According to ancient stellar myth, there were in the course of precession Seven Pole Stars -- Seven Stations of the Pole. Originally these were called the "Seven Glorious Ones." They were later given as the Seven Stars of the Lesser Bear of the Constellation that Never Set. They were the Divine Watchers and Rulers in the Great Year of the World -- starry types of eternal powers, who were also Sons of Light, Masons, children of the Great Mother.

Through the melody of song all things were made beautiful by Orpheus -- creating a worship of beauty; and through this alone he will "live in immortality forever." Orpheus was one of the many Immortals who sacrificed himself that mankind might be taught the Wisdom of the gods. He taught that "Light was the most sublime of all things; it was God, the inaccessible God who envelopes all things in His substance." Light was greatly reverenced by the Ancients as the most beautiful attribute of Divinity. It was claimed that Fire produced Light, but this was the etherealized fire in which they placed the substance of Divinity or the Universal Soul of the World, from whence emanate Light and Life, the Logos or the Word "which lighteth every man that cometh into the world, and giveth life to all beings."

"The ancient symbol of the Orphic Mysteries was a serpent-entwined egg, which signified Cosmos as encircled by the fiery Creative Spirit. The egg also represented the soul of the philosopher, the serpent and the Mysteries. At the time of initiation the shell was broken and man emerged from the embryonic state of physical existence wherein he had remained through the foetal period of philosophic generation." (2)

Orpheus went into hell by the power of his lyre, symbolical of the law by which he humanized and civilized the profane. It was to the music of his seven-stringed lyre and the harmony and beauty of his songs that all Nature bowed in reverence, establishing a country enthralled by the beautiful. But he had first to lose Eurydice. His worship of beauty and his control of passion brought back love; and through his sorrow he became a doctor of souls and bodies. He died the death of all Initiators, proclaiming unity and love. To him the beautiful became the splendor of the true; and this was the foundation of the Orphic Mysteries. He gave poetry, the beauty of all uplifting thought, and the perfection of form to Greece, and perished in that which he refused to join; -- the mysteries of Bacchus. Therefore the Bacchantes dis-

---
(1) - HALL, Manly P.
(2) - BRYANT'S - AN ANALYSIS OF ANCIENT MYTHOLOGY.

mombered him and sacrificed him in their mistaken deified drunkenness. Their orgies were mystical tumults. Under Rome, Bacchus became the god of wine and was represented by wine in the Mysteries; Cores represented bread.

The Mysteries of Bacchus were known as the Orphic, Sabazian, and Dionysiac Mysteries. The secret doctrine of Dionysiac worship claims Orpheus as its founder. The Dionysians taught that the Initiate, by a pure life of asceticism, would become mystically identified with Divine Nature. All these mystic Rites go back to remotest times. Among the Greeks they were only partly attributed to Orpheus, but "Backhos was an Oriental Deity, worshipped in the East, and his orgies were celebrated there long before the Greeks adopted them. In the earliest times he was worshipped in India, Arabia and Bactria." (1)

The rod used in the Mysteries is said to have been the one which Backhos cast to the ground and turned into a serpent. His followers crowned their heads with serpents and carried them around with them, and the Initiates would grasp them with both hands. The cross placed upon the breast of an Initiate after the new birth was accomplished, in both the Bacchic and Eleusinian Mysteries, similarly belongs to all Mysteries. The Rites, given in allegory, have it that Bacchus was torn to pieces by the Titans.

The Sabazian Mysteries were similar to those of Bacchus. Both Sabazius and Bacchus were born at Sabazius, or Sabaoth. In the former there was a presentation of a live snake which was drawn across the breast of the candidate in token of their Mysteries. A golden serpent was a symbol of the Sabazians which represented the annual renovation of the world by the solar power, typified in the casting off of the skin by the serpent. The Jews are said to have borrowed from them the name Sabaoth for their Mysteries and to have adopted it as one of their appelations of their Supreme God. During the time that the Sabazian Mysteries were celebrated in Rome, the cult gained many followers which later influenced the symbolism of Christianity.

In the mysteries of Serapis the candidate had to cross an unbridged chasm, needing magic powers to sustain him, else he would fall and die, or die from suffering due to intense heat from which he had been exposed.

At the time of the Christian Manifestation followers of the Essenes were the only group or Order that taught the Ancient Mysteries in all their original purity; and any idea relating to eternal punishment or an eternal hell was never given, nor did our Great Master teach such doctrine; to the contrary, He emphatically says: "As ye sow so shall ye reap," which is the ancient doctrine of reincarnation that has been taught since the time man appeared upon earth, and holds the same eternal message today. It was the doctrine taught in all sacred mysteries, therefore by the Essenes and by Jesus.

It was required that men should learn the secrets of the Spirit, the Laws of Nature and to know God whom they served with great piety. Garments that had been worn during initiations were looked upon as sacred and reserved as such. All passion and anger was transmuted into Love. Initiates considered their given word as even more powerful than an oath which in their ordinary life was thought superfluous and near to perjury.

---

(1) - PIKE, Albert; MORALS AND DOGMA, - Page 419.

Ancient Wisdom was called the "Mother of Religions" and in the Essenian mysteries it was known that the Great Master Jesus would call Himself the "Son of the Mother" -- or of the "Divine Light" which is the "Bride of God" for the Light of Love would shine within Him.

"The Union of God with the Soul is the principle of all mystic life." The Soul cannot escape the law, it must obey it, and "this becomes the mystery of rebirth and reincarnation."

During the period of the degradation of the Mysteries a book disappeared from the world. It was carried in a sealed and very sacred casket by Initiates into another land, and is known to be in existence today. It teaches the path trod by the old Initiates, and can still be read by those who have fitted themselves to serve the Great Masters and are willing to search until they find it. It is called the Key to Immortality.

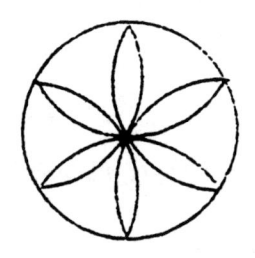

CHAPTER VII
MASONIC, ROSICRUCIAN & KABALISTIC ORDERS
-- INCLUDING THE TAROT --

"O Builders of the Circle of Eternity --
That primal Paradise not built with hands --
Stars of the Mighty Mother, ye builded
 mightily;
Still shines thine Eden, and the
 Rock of Ages stands!"
-- Mary Siegrist.

A SEEKER wearily yet happily treading Nature's Highway will discover that there is but One Great Truth found in her Book of Nature where keys to all secrets are hidden. At the end of the Road symbols and glyphs of the ancient Masonic, Rosicrucian and Kabalistic Orders will be found; there is but one original organization of Mystics all aspecting this One Great Truth, mystically found at the end of this Highway which has existed since the creation of the universe, to end only with time itself.

This One Great Truth belongs primarily to those who have found the Light in the Darkness where the mysteries of God or Nature are preserved for them.

The mysticism of the Rosicrucians is said to be hidden in the far away sanctuary of the clouds; the mysticism of the Kabalists is given in the secret teaching said to be from God in the language of the Angels; the mysticism of the Masonic Order to her Sons of Light is given through the spiritual messages from the ancient Great Mother whose sons they are. All are receptive to this Light, their place of meeting is the Temple of the Holy Spirit pervading the universe but hidden from the eyes of the profane. These Children of Light, whether Rosicrucian, Kabalist or Mason, cannot be consciously made; they grow on the unfolding of Divine Power in the heart. Watchfulness makes them see the Law at work and the importance of Cosmic Power.

Necessary to all seekers of spiritual heights belonging to the Rosicrucian Order is an understanding of the many enigmatical writings of imperishable importance that is given in the Fama Fraternitatis and the Confessio Fraternitatia which contain the original declarations of the Order. Very great occult significance is given to the description of the Vault in which the body of R. C. R. was found, it being a perfect miniature of the universe. On the door of the Vault are Latin characters which, translated, read: "After 120 years I shall open."

The symbolic significance of the Vault to man is most important; its inner meaning represents the human body in which he is to be mystically buried that the Great Light may enter the Darkness and be recognized.

The time of the passing of this Great Father was unknown to the initiates and adepts of this Order. The discovery of the Vault came one hundred and twenty years after his death -- the notable time period previously predicted. Under a circular stone the body of Christian Rosenkrantz was found in perfect condition, with an ever-burning lamp hanging from the ceiling; clasped in one hand was the Arcane of the Order.

The name Rosenkrantz has been given for the re-founder of the Order, the Rosicrucian Fraternity, a name that does not appear in the Fama or Confessio. The initials given as C. R., or C. R. C., or again K. R. K., are only glyphs for Kaph-Resh-Kash. Original members of this Order were never known by name, only by initials given to represent the different states of consciousness that were to be opened in man. The Kaph-Resh-Kaph, K. R. K., or C. R. C. represent a circle and this circle becomes the One Reality, the supreme I AM, the everliving self; Jesus called this One Reality Father.

The initial names given in the old manuscripts bring with them the pronunciation of names connected with the Age Old Wisdom. "Wiser readers we may suppose penetrated the veil of enigmatic language (the magical language of the Kabala and the Tarot) and have perceived that our Father and our Brother R. C. is but a personification of the True Self in man." [1] Truth never fails nor does it ever grow old; in Light, untruths fade away.

Kabalistically the "Tree of Life" with its ten Sephira relates to the universe itself as the first, second and third Logos and corresponds to the three Rosicrucian Orders as the Father, Mother, Son principle.

Accepting the Rosy-Cross as a cube of six squares, each square measuring 9x9, enclosing a rose at its center of five petals, from which radiate twenty-five rays of light, and folding these squares in the form of a cube, "It will exactly enclose the Mystical Rose," which IS the ancient True and Invisible Order, with all its sacred inheritance including the "transcendental mathematics of the universe."

Tracing origins to the heavens, the Rose on the Cross, or the Cross on the Rose, is the four quarters of the zodiac that are to open the twelve centers in man, through the manifestation of the operation of the twelve signs of the Great Circle of Necessity.

We are taught that the practice of initiation alters or modifies the chemistry of the initiate's blood, changing certain areas of the brain which, with the "Strength of the Eagle," leads to clairvoyance. The Masters of the Invisible Order become visible to human eyes when those eyes have "borrowed Strength from the Eagle." (The mysticism of the Eagle, symbol of initiation, is the Spinal Spirit Fire.) Members of this Order cannot be seen by ordinary human eyes, as above explained. "For in the holy communion is the primitive storehouse of the most ancient and original Science of the human race, with the primitive mysteries also of all sciences ..... it is the unique and really illuminated community which is in possession of the keys to all mysteries which know the center and sources of nature and creation ... and include members from more than one world." [2]

---
(1) - CASE, Paul Foster; THE TRUE AND INVISIBLE ROSICRUCIAN ORDER; Page 19.
(2) - ECKGARTSCHAUSEN, N. B.

It is written that God had encompassed them about with His cloud that they may not be beheld with human eyes unless the Spirit of Fire has given them the strength of the Eagle. It is to those alone that the Angels may speak. The one way these are drawn into this Invisible Order is through the Will of God.

The true and bona-fide Rosicrucians and their Fraternity of Initiates and Adepts is one of the most remarkable in the world.

With the incoming of the Aquarian Age, when numerous things will be revealed in its Light, many of this Order are anticipating the revelation of a fundamental Rosicrucian secret that has been promised them.

As the Seer, so will the Rosicrucian observe the rule of silence, wisely enclosing knowledge in the ancient symbols while they test everything in the light of Truth and Reason.

Owing to its antiquity the Kabala has been mystically called the "Emblem of the Soul of the World," or, the Great Mother; also, being the product of Infinite Wisdom, it has been called "The Holy Tongue." Anciently, it was understood that beginnings were founded upon the female, the Genetrix, showing that their Adam, Kadman, as a male, came later. Each word of the Kabala contains within itself a profound mystery, making it possible for man to aspire to the highest contemplation of the Mysteries which were contained in their letters, words and points. These letters or words are also numerals, and contain everything known of a spiritual, mystical nature, forming an important part of Masonic tradition and coming from unfathomable archaic ages.

The Kabala contains a direct approach to old canonical secrets of the Ancient World. Being very obscure it is not easily understood, yet it furnishes the fundamental facts of old esoteric philosophy. Its theology reasons concerning the phenomena of heaven through analogy of human creations and its system, based upon this idea, constituted the Kabalistic Secret Doctrine which was taught orally.

When the Protestants broke with the older church, they declined to acknowledge or teach the unwritten word, bringing about a certain nervous tension between them and Freemasonry concerning a true understanding of the Ancient Wisdom. The Christian equivalent of the word Kabala is Gnosis. "The Christians had their Gnosis, said to have been received from Christ, by whom it was transmitted to the Apostles and successively to the heads of the church."

The doctrine of the Kabala forms a geometrical diagram in which Ten Steps are grouped, according to a progressive scheme, so that emanations of the Spirit of the Elohim issue from the first Step, called Kether, the Crown, passing down through the entire figure until the Tenth is reached. These Ten progressive Steps are the basis of philosophies, religions, and the arts of the world, showing the nearest approach to the direct revelation of traditional science which was never communicated except through myth or symbol. They symbolize a trinity of persons, their work being to transmit the Spirit of Life in the passage from heaven to earth.

The diagram showing the **Ten Steps** is given in the form ascribed by Freemasons to what they call the Double Cube or Cubical Stone. Triangles and squares had their own uses similar to other geometrical symbols. "The Quabalistic Tradition of the last few centuries is that the 'Ten Sephiroth,' or 'Numerical Emanations,' were formed by the 'Lightning Flash' of Creation, while the 'Twenty-two Paths' were produced by the Ascent of the 'Serpent of Wisdom' from Malkuth to Kether." (1)

"The SEPHIROTH were emanated by means of the FLAMING SWORD, or LIGHTNING FLASH, which descended from Kether to Chokmah, which is, in turn, the First Path of the FLAMING SWORD." (2). The Ten Sephiroth are said to have come from Ain-Nothing; for, prior to any manifestation, the Supreme was not. Ain was Pure Spirit, and Suph, Limitless Space; Aur-Light and Ain-Suph-Aur, Limitless Light. Infinite Space and Infinite Light were concentrated upon a central point which is called Kether, the Crown, or the Heights. "From this all else proceeds, very much in the same way that Light may be broken up into the Colors of the Spectrum." (3)

These Ten Sephiroth are Kabalistically called "The Tree of Life." The Tree of Life is a Trinity of Triads, with Malkuth (the Kingdom, or Earth) pendent. The LIGHTNING FLASH connects these Ten Sephiroth. "It is also known as THE FLAMING SWORD, which is united with the idea of THE SERPENT OF WISDOM." (4)

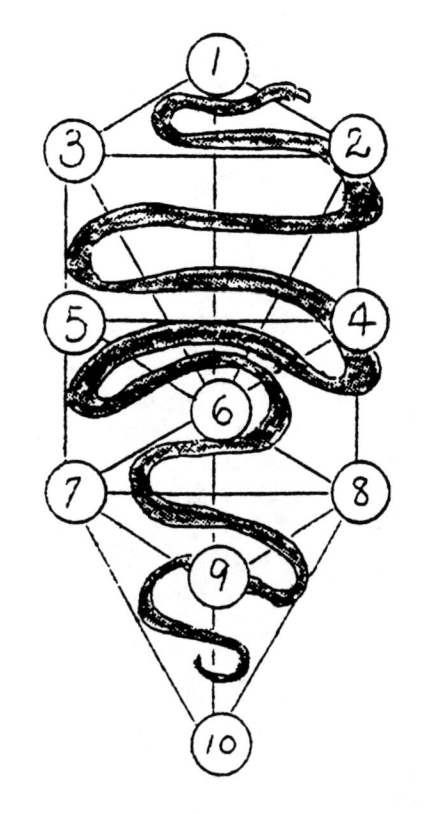

The Ascent of the Serpent of Wisdom, on the Path of the Flaming Sword that had Descended from The Heights.
-- Frater Achad

A great Supernal Triad is formed by KETHER, CHOKMAH, and BINAH, the three highest steps. KETHER, the Crown, was "The SPHERE of the PRIMUM MOBILE," the Point within the Circle; CHOKMAH, Wisdom, The "I AM I" or SELF RECOGNITION, was "The SPHERE of STABILITY;" and BINAH, Understanding; the MOTHER, The Path of the Mystic, was "The SPHERE of REFLECTION AND SELFLESSNESS;" the tenth step, which was below all, MALKUTH, was "The SPHERE of the EARTH," the Depths. (5)

The necessity of retaining knowledge of early beginnings led to a Hidden Wisdom where ancient traditions were preserved. Any revelation of the secrets of this Wisdom was punishable by death. Judaism is responsible for

---

(1) - Frater Achad; THE EGYPTIAN REVIVAL, Preface; pages ix-x
(2) -   "   "   Q. B. L., or THE BRIDE'S RECEPTION; Appendix, page 5.
(3) -   "   "   THE EGYPTIAN REVIVAL, Page 14.
(4) -   "   "   Q. B. L., or THE BRIDE'S RECEPTION; pages 11-12
(5)   "   "   Q. B. L., or THE BRIDE'S RECEPTION.

slashings in the exoteric side of the Masonic Ritual. Esoteric knowledge, through the more ancient Hebrew writings, stands quite alone; and though much has been handed down in tradition, the inner secrets have been kept in silence.

Ancient traditions and commentaries are still preserved in the Kabala; and though a key is now known to be in existence, the Mystic Key was lost in the ages when superstition had crawled in. The Apocalypse is incomprehensible without this Kabalistic Key. A complete knowledge of the Holy Kabala can be acquired only by a Hebrew scholar capable of deciphering the letters, numbers and words. Why wonder, therefore, that their Hidden Wisdom wore a veil? In it are preserved many symbols taken from ancient Masonry. The double triangle, or Seal of Solomon, with the addition of a circle, is the ornament of the Royal Arch Masonic Degree, upon which an inscription called Agla is seven times repeated. This is an image of the four corners of the world united to the heights of heaven and to the depths of earth. The Agla belongs to the Seven Great Stars of the Beginning -- THE FRATERNITY OF THE BUILDERS -- and, curiously, Agla was also the golden calf, at one time a symbol of Divinity worshipped in Israel, reflected in the world today.

Nearly six centuries before the time of Jesus, the Hebrews having become Jews neither spoke nor understood their original tongue. They used the Syrian dialect called Aramaic, made up of several united idioms, Assyrian and Phoenician, not Chaldaic. "We must remember that after the ancient Egyptian language had died out, Aramaic intervened before the earlier Coptic, Moabite or Biblical Hebrew." [1] The Jews also had a Greek mixture of Hebraism called "The Hellenistic tongue." The Septuagint and the New Testament are written in this Hellenistic tongue or language.

The modern Jew is descended from the Pharisees who boasted so haughtily that they possessed the oral law of Moses. They really had only a semblance of his unwritten law. Because of it they were constantly reproached by Jesus. The Jews had their knowledge from older nations than themselves, and during the Babylonian captivity they received their metaphysical and practical tenets. During the days of the Pharisees, the Jews lost the science of the Corner Stone -- the Cubic Stone, or mystically, the Philosophers' Stone; and this was the fundamental stone of the temple which was square at its base and triangular above.

A certain few of the Pharisee savants to whom the sacred traditions had been submitted carried them to the Essenes. It was among the Essenes that the moral law of Moses had been preserved. Moses had his secret doctrine from the Egyptian Priests who had three ways of expressing their thought: "The first was clear and simple; the second, symbolic and figurative; the third, sacred or hieroglyphic. They made use of three kinds of characters, but not of three dialects, as might be imagined. .... Such was the genius of their tongue." [2] But the modern tongues cannot make this distinction.

The principal retreat of the Essenes was in the environs of Alexandria, near the Lake and Mount Moriah. "Mount Moriah had become one of the symbols of Adonhiramite Masonry. The word signifies the reflected Light --

---
[1] - CHURCHWARD, Albert; SIGNS AND SYMBOLS OF PRIMORDIAL MAN, Page 210
[2] - d'Olivet Fabre - THE HEBRAIC TONGUE RESTORED, Part II, page 24.

-- the Splendor." (1)   The Essenes deserved their merited reputation for sanctity and learning, living as anchorites in separate cells, occupied with the study of Nature. The Hebraic Sepher was, according to them, "composed of Spirit and substance: by the substance they understood the material meaning of the Hebraic tongue; by the Spirit, the spiritual meaning lost to the vulgar." (2)   They guarded the traditions and oral laws as secrets of the Sanctuary.

The writings of Moses, to distinguish them in a general way from the Bible, are represented in the Sepher. The Bible holds the material form of the Sepher of Moses, which are well preserved; but those who can see no farther than the material do not even suspect the spiritual that is hidden therein.

The Holy Kabala embodies the True Science, which is embodied also in the Book of Revelation, and concealed in the symbols of the Bible. The Kabala is a revelation of the spiritual, by means of words, letters and numbers. The tenets of the Essenes, the doctrine of Pythagoras, and the Kabala should be studied by all Masonic students in relation to the Bible as the Word of God -- the Omnific Word for every student in the Fraternity.

"The Hebrew contained in the Sepher is the pure idiom of the ancient Egyptians." It may be considered as a transplanted branch. It is the tongue of a religious, thoughtful people "profoundly learned in moral sciences and friend of the Mysteries." The Sepher is a sacred refuge for the Hebrew tongue. Its sublime beauties, its poetic fancies and eloquence rise almost above any other book of the ages. Moses, foreseeing the fate to which this book might be submitted and the false instruction that might follow, had recourse to an oral law given by word of mouth to men whose faithfulness had been tested, and he charged them to submit it in the secret of the sanctuary to other men whose fidelity had also been tested; and so, from age to age, in this way, was it transmitted that it might reach posterity. This oral law is called the Kabala, "from a Hebrew word signifying that which _is_ received and which comes _from elsewhere._" Famous Hebraic books are almost entirely Kabalistic.

Through various distracting troubles the Tribes of Israel became separated. Ten kept the name of Israel, the other two, the name of Judah. Hatred spread rapidly between them; former oaths and obligations were forgotten; and the Sepher was forgotten. Neither of the tribes possessed it, but a long time afterwards it was found at the bottom of an old coffer, heaped above with pieces of money. Which tells its own tale.

The Kabala holds the great and inviolate secrets of Israel; and her Priests, truths that are everlasting. These traditions have always been preserved from the profane. Its doctrine centers among the Great Stars of the North -- THE FRATERNITY OF THE BUILDERS -- who were among the first makers of the Great Circle of Eternity, where Paradise, the Garden of Eden, was formed around the great Rock of Ages -- the Pole. These stars were the Ancient Builders -- Messengers of the Eternal, the Progeny of the Great Mother, the first great Builder or Mason who, in the Egyptian Book of the Dead, was called "The Living Word;" and with her originated the Ancient Wisdom given to her

---
(1) - d'Olivet Fabre -- THE HEBRAIC TONGUE RESTORED, Part II, page 24.
(2) - Ibid.

Builders in Heaven. The basic doctrine of the Kabala is this Great Mother, in whom may be found a key to the formation of the Tree of Life, which is the Kabalistic conception of a creative process.

In the Kabalistic Mysteries the name Jehovah is at times written by grouping together the twenty-four dots relative to the twenty-four powers before the Throne. The True Word of the Masons can be found in this Ineffable Name of Deity, wherein it is concealed. Its pronunciation was the great secret, the secret that contained all the knowledge that might be revealed concerning God. "He who can rightly pronounce it causeth heaven and earth to tremble, for it is the NAME which rusheth through the Universe." The name Jehovah is but a substitute, one of many for the lost Omnific Word. Followers of the Holy Kabala are well aware of this. The Word, belonging as it does to the greatest antiquity, is Bi-Une. Only the High Priest knew this sacred Word, which at his death passed to his successor. So sacred was it that should even a suspicion arise that the least whisper of it had been given, danger of life, or life itself, was the price to be paid.

So priceless was knowledge of the secret doctrine of the Holy Kabala, containing knowledge of the hidden Soul and the Word, that the life of Rabbi Simeon Ben-Ioachi, the compiler of the Zohar -- a great Kabalistic work in which he had incorporated the highest secret knowledge -- became endangered. He fled to the wilderness and lived in a cave for twelve years, surrounded by his most ardent devotees. He is said to have died amid signs and wonders, and "it is recorded he suddenly disappeared while a dazzling light filled the cavern with glory;" and "since the death of Simeon Ben-Ioachi this doctrine remains an inviolate secret to the outer world. Delivered only as a mystery, it was communicated orally 'face to face and mouth to ear.'"

The Holy Kabala can never be made complete, as its most important wisdom was only given orally, and to a very few. It required an initiation into the Mercaba, and that was taught only in the "darkness, in a deserted place and after terrific trials."

Knowledge of the true name of God, and its origin, are among the unsolved enigmas of the world. Veneration of the WORD, with its potent charm of mystery, has come through the long ages of the past, containing the most beautiful of all truths belong to the traditions of a primeval people, and forming the inner teaching of one of the profoundest and deepest of the Atlantean mystery schools. In the old Masonic Orders this Divine Unutterable Word had become a living reality, piercing through corners of the whole world wherever Lodges were held, and, as a living reality, teems with thoughts for the modern world. Masonry is one of the living centers -- one of the mightiest social organizations known -- and through its vital significance one can seek the Lost WORD, that Word of Light -- the Life of all Humanity.

The inner or secret Brotherhood of Initiates became the guardian of this Lost Word, as well as the keepers of the great Inner Mysteries. The finding of either is rewarded beyond any mental estimation.

In the Ineffable Name are the mysterious characters symbolical of the nine names or attributes which Initiates knew belonged to Deity. "These nine names of the Deity were imported into Egypt in the 22nd Century, B. C., and can be discovered upon monuments twice that age by Egyptologists." "In form and under symbols strange to our modern thought, and yet most true and most suggestive, the 'Divine Word' is presented to us as 'The Great Architect of the Universe,' and, at the same time as its source, light and support -- its wisdom, strength and beauty -- lost as a 'word' for men to speak, but immortal as the manifested power, nature, and truth of the unfathomable yet ever-living and true God." (1)

The Seven Great Stars were called the Sons of God, divinities or powers who knew and could impart all the secrets of nature to man and reveal the wonderful but now Lost Word. "The real secret and unpronounceable name -- 'the word that is no word' -- has to be sought in the seven names of the first emanations, or the 'Sons of the Fire,' in the secret Scriptures of all the great nations, and even in the Zohar. ..... This word, composed of seven letters in each tongue, is found embodied in the architectural remains of every grand building in the world; from the Cyclopean remains on Easter Island .... down to the earliest Egyptian pyramids." (2)

In the old Pagan Mysteries this knowledge remained with a few Adepts. "It has been the result of whole milleniums of thought and should be the joint property of Initiates of all nations of the world. Yet so potent is its influence, so widely-spread and so strictly guarded, it could only be retained by the successors of that ancient order of Builders, the first, original Fraternity." (3)

One should go to the land of Mitzraim, in Egypt, to seek this mysterious Word, remembering that there is an Egypt above, as well as an Egypt below, and Mitzraim is up there in the midst of the Seven Great Stars called THE FRATERNITY OF THE BUILDERS.

The Word dwells in God, and esoterically is an objective expression of the concealed Light, a direct reflection of the unknowable upon a plane of universal manifestation on earth, Divine thought acting in matter. The Zohar states that "the Word which discovers unto us the supreme mysteries is generated by the union of Light and Darkness and dwells in the supreme heaven. Creative Fire emerged from the darkness as the keynote of creation." The Supreme is the center of Light, and souls are purified by this Light rising on the wings of a great love. This Creative Word lies in the depths of our being "as stars in the body of Nuit, Mother of Heaven." The Word is always with us; it lives in our soul, and subsists eternally in the heavens, with Christ the counterpart on earth. His Word to us is the gift of spiritual vision. When man has reached real unfoldment he lives from within, and by meditation. In the beginning man had the Word; all things were created by the Word, and out of the living power communicated to man in the Word came the Light of His existence. Ancient philosophy and theology teem with questions on the importance attached to the Lost Word which is so strongly emblazoned in the Hebrew Scriptures and in the Gospels and in the Book of Revelation where, in Chapter XIX, 12, we read: "His eyes were as flames of fire, and on his head were many crowns; and he had a name written, that no man knew but himself, and he was clothed with a vesture dipped in blood; and his name is called 'The Word of God.'"

---

(1) - GARRISON, Rev. J. F.; A CONTRIBUTION TO THE HISTORY OF THE LOST WORD; page 472, from
FORT, George F.; THE EARLY HISTORY AND ANTIQUITIES OF FREEMASONRY.
(2) - BLAVATSKY, H. P.; THE SECRET DOCTRINE, VOLUME I, Page 438-9.
(3) - BLAVATSKY, H. P.

Ancient Egypt's great magical Word of Power was attributed to Isis, the Egyptian prototype of the Great Mother of the World. Her Word of Power in the human sphere was personified in the child Horus. This was the Word that issued from the Great Mother "Out of the Silence." It was made flesh in mortal likeness. The mystical Word of Power from the beginning was female and belonged to the Great Mother who was known as "The Living Word."

AUM was a word of mystical significance and power, still uttered under the form of OM among peoples of Eastern Asia; but its true pronunciation is known only among the glorified Initiates. There are so many corruptions of the name, the true name of God, even that spoken on the Five Points of Fellowship at low breath remains unknown.

The first word spoken in raising the body of Hiram was to be a substitute for the Master Mason's "Lost Word." This was an ancient superstitious custom. The Lost Word in the Royal Arch Chapter is the Logos, the Second Person of the Trinity. In Masonic Mysteries the candidate is made to seek or find this Word, as well as a book containing a record of the Law, and on its plate is the symbol of the double triangle -- the Seal of Solomon.

Postel has written: "The Word has been made man, but the world will be saved when the Word shall have been made woman;" and, "the sublime grandeurs of the spirit of love will be taught by the maternal genius of religion." (1)

The archetype was the first mold or plan of the Universe; creation came at a later period. In the vision of Hermes it is said: "Beholding the Archetype, the Supreme Mind became enamored with Its own thought; so, taking the Word as a mighty hammer, it gouged out caverns in primordial space and cast the form of the spheres, in the Archetypal mold, at the same time sowing in the newly-fashioned bodies the seeds of living things. The darkness below, receiving the hammer of the Word, was fashioned into an orderly universe. The elements separated into strata and each brought forth living creatures. The Supreme Being -- Mind -- male and female -- brought forth the Word, and the Word, suspended between Light and darkness, was delivered of another Mind called the <u>Workman</u>, the <u>Master-Builder</u>, or the <u>Maker</u> of <u>Things</u>." (2)

A name for the Supreme Deity was so elevated in nature that Moses was obliged to throw a veil over it. It is said that the name Jehovah was the rending of that veil; and that when it was rent, one found there the Genetrix called "The Almighty," belonging to the ancient birthplace in the North and to those old celestial allegories long before they were ever supplied to earth. It has been noted that on account of the feminine name of Jehovah it was thought blasphemy to utter the name aloud; hence the sacredness attached to this name which the Rabbins called their mystical Tetragrammaton -- the name of four letters.

The Tetragrammaton was preserved and transmitted by the Essenes and was always communicated in a whisper. The letter Shin was adopted as a mysterious emblem of it; and this letter symbolized the True Fire of the Spirit. To be correct, the name is really composed of three letters, not four, and this

---

(1) - LEVI, Eliphas - THE HISTORY OF MAGIC, Page 337.
(2) - THE VISION OF HERMES.

statement conceals the meaning not meant for the profane. It resolves itself into the three letters J H V, "He who revealed himself as he who was, is and is to come." I A H in Hebrew was called the monogram of the Eternal. Yod is a letter of Fire or flame; He', a letter of Water; and between them was the concealed letter Aleph, Air. A, Aleph, is symbolical of the descent of spirit into terrestrial manifestation. It was the letter of Air, Divine Breath, which was prior to the Word. "A numerical Four and the figure Four are of more importance, however, to the Tetragrammaton than even four different letters." The Ten Steps of the Kabala symbolized in their entirety the four mystic letters, J H V H, the numerical number of which is twenty-six; and this number, the Jews claim, composed the most Sacred Mysteries of the Law.

There is a Gnostic account of the beginning of the world claiming that the Deity uttered a first word of four letters -- ARKE. Ark means to encircle, enclose in a circle; and this first circle is found in the heavens made by the constellation of the Seven Great Stars, called THE FRATERNITY OF THE BUILDERS: and this first word, written in four letters, typifies the four corners of all beginnings.

The root-word of the name "Jew" is IU, or the Son who comes; IU-SUS, or Jesus, the "Ever-Coming One," a name that belongs to all ages. Again, IU was the first Genetrix or Mother before IU became her son, and the name "Jew" can be traced from the Hebrew to their substitute or the name Jehovah -- the Great Mother. The Hebrew J H V H became the mysteriously unutterable name the nature of which could only be communicated to the Initates, whether in Israel or in other countries.

The Jews, neglecting the study of their secret traditions of Widsom given in the Kabala, lost sight of its purpose in their creative plan of the world, leaving it for others to discover. There has always been a universal tradition that the peak of enlightenment for all nations presupposed a decline or downfall. When the precessional Cycle of Pisces was ushered in, called the time of the coming of Jesus, this tradition had faded into the past; but they had the promise of a second coming at the eleventh hour, when the Golden Age that once was and which lies in the future would be renewed for a time -- when sorrows, fleeing from the shadows, would be lost in joy.

"The Hidden Wisdom wore a veil; the same veil that Isis boasted no mortal had lifted from her person was made to cover these writings, together with their interpreters, who stood behind the veil but never lifted it."(1)

The Book of Enoch is a resumé of the main features of the history of the Third, Fourth and Fifth Races, an inspired production of an antediluvian patriarch, and is said to have been "dropped from heaven gradually, in the sense of having been distilled." It is a book of the revolution of the luminaries of heaven and relates to the Stars, Moon and Sun Cycles of time, the Cycle of twenty-four hours, and the Great Cycle of twenty-six thousand years. The reading of this book is of inestimable value to all Masonic students. In no sense is it a book of human history. This great Hebrew Book is said to have been given to man through the angels in Paradise. (Angels were said to be the repeaters of time -- meaning that through the stars

---

(1) - MASSEY, Gerald, A BOOK OF THE BEGINNINGS, Vol. II, Page 178.

knowledge was given.) The history of Israel from its beginning in Genesis is identified with it. "Either the Book of Enoch contains the Hebrew history in allegory, or the celestial allegory IS the Hebrew history." It transforms the Hebrew history into a celestial allegory by the usual modern route. History came after mythology, not mythology after history. "The Book of Enoch certainly contains the same characters as the sacred or secret history of the Jews; and as these belong to the astronomical allegory in the one book, that is good evidence of their being mystical in the other." (1)

The Book of Enoch is a Kabalistic version of a series of events that were astronomical rather than eschatological, verified in phenomena. No matter how ancient it is, no claim has been made nor is there a clue to its origin. "The Messiah Son, the Manifestor of the Ancient of Days, appears in it as the child of the woman -- the SON OF THE WOMAN SITTING ON THE THRONE OF GLORY." (2) This is the Mother who from the beginning existed in secret, and whose name was evoked before the Sun or Constellations were, and could be no other than the Great Primordial Mother and her Son who are so prominently connected with the origin of Masonry -- the same Son who in Jewish history finally became their Lord God of Sabaoth, and the "Blazing Star" in Masonry.

Secrets taught by Enoch that have belonged to the beginning of the world were bound by terrible oaths, and were to be divulged only to those who, after severe trials and long suffering, were found worthy. The secrets have the name of Sacerdotal Art, in which Alchemy, Astrology, Magic, and knowledge of the spirits were included; also, the keys to hieroglyphics. A pretended Book of Enoch which has no value whatsoever has been filled with mystical misinterpretations and published anonymously.

The Book of Enoch refers to the beginning of the ages -- the epoch of the origin of the Zodiac, begun by the Primordial Mother and her Sons, THE FRATERNITY OF THE BUILDERS, from whom we have symbols, emblems for analysis, and the relationship between the stars and man. It can be read through ancient traditions by means of the universal alphabet of symbols -- symbols in correspondence with those of the Hebrew alphabet. Initiations vividly recall that which is fully divulged in visions in many of the chapters of the Book of Enoch. From the eighteenth to the fiftieth chapters are descriptions of the Mysteries of Creation, one of which is the Burning Valley of the Fallen Spirits. It intimates that at the time of the beginning of great deluges, the Spirit of Wisdom departs from the earth. Man has lost many sacred keys -- keys that might have opened the gates to the inner sanctuary -- and has forgotten the meaning of the Kabala and defiled the words of Christ, through his love of and craving for gold.

Ancient Hebrews represented the stars, either altogether or severally, by the letters of the alphabet. In this manner they expressed or distinguished them, as we do in the names of the constellations -- Aries, Taurus, et cetera. They used as many letters or stars as were needed to more perfectly express the nature of the star or constellation; hence, the significance of the names of the stars mentioned in the Bible and not easily understood. When setting up a horoscope, they did it with characters and letters. Astrology of the Hebrews had not lost its luster so long as it was practiced by them; but when the

---
(1) - MASSEY, Gerald; A BOOK OF THE BEGINNINGS, Volume II, Page 226
(2) - MASSEY, Gerald; A BOOK OF THE BEGINNINGS, Volume II, Page 225.

Northern nations began to have knowledge, they very soon invented strange and wild fancies with faults galore.

The originals of the twenty-two letters of the alphabet were derived from the stars. There were three mother letters, twelve simple letters, corresponding to the signs of the zodiac, and seven double letters, one for each of the planets. The fixed stars belonged to their consonants, the planets to the vowels; and, spelled in various ways, future events were foretold. It was a book of symbols analogous to the stars and man.

The beginning of the zodiac belonged to the beginning of the ages. The circle belonged to heaven, followed by the square of the four corners. Wise men of those ancient times had knowledge of the invisible God through things that were visible, and nothing could have been more wonderful than the visible Sun, Moon and Stars, through which they had their knowledge of God. Thus one should cherish all the treasures that come from the stars, for angels guard them, and angels of the Sun and the Moon were often invoked in prayer. Belief in the magic of prayer and the invocation of spirits or the stars finds its place even today in the Ritual of the Christian churches.

Egyptian Priests have in their possession a curiously-engraved emblematic work, called The Tarot, based on the word Rota -- The Way, revealing "The One Way" or the road to immortality, a great part of its symbolism being associated with Masonry. A great field of speculation covers the origin of this work but occult tradition places the date and invention of the Tarot Cards as the year 1200; this was four centuries before the publication of the Rosicrucian Manifesto. Tradition also claims that these Cards were invented by a group of Wise Men whose meeting place was at Fez, Morocco, and that these Wise Men were the Masters who belonged to the Third Order of the Invisible Order of the Rosicrucians. Rosenkranz finished his education at Fez at the age of 22. In occult mathematics 22 is the number of the circle, the conclusion of a cycle of manifestation.

After the burning of the Alexandrian Library, Fez became the intellectual center of the world, its great University and marvellous Library becoming renowned for its cultural learning, excelling in Mathematics, Medicine and Magic. This attracted many people, among them a Brotherhood of highly enlightened man who, having come from all parts of the globe, found some difficulty in agreeing with certain philosophical discussions. It is claimed they developed a device by which their most important philosophies and doctrines could be known. This consisted of a book of pictures which would express ideas instead of words, interpretations of which led towards a path unknown to the profane and "whose combinations would depend upon the occult harmonies of numbers."

This system of numbers, including letters, is given in the Kabala (the secret Wisdom of Israel). To quote from Paul Foster Case, a great exponent and authority on this subject: "The Tarot represents a summary of the Hermetic Sciences, the Quabala, Alchemy, Astrology and Magic [1] with their different divisions. All these Sciences really represent one system of a broad and deep psychological investigation of the nature of man."

---

(1) - "Wise Men of old made a science of life complete and perfect; and they have given it the name Magick."

Freemasonry is a survival of these sciences and their deep psychological system, yet few Masons today are seeking these hidden treasures, though the Great Heads of the Order know.

The Tarot Cards have no exoteric history prior to the Fourteenth Century.

Court de Gebelin, a great Egyptologist, in the year 1872 wrote concerning these Cards, giving credence to their being of Egyptian origin; unfortunately this had led to many false trails.

The Gypsies came from Atlantis into India, and then migrated into Egypt. One legend states that they were a band of Egyptian Priests or their descendants, who, to preserve the secrets of Serapis (a religious worship in Alexandria) fled in a group from that City after the burning of the marvelous Library and the destruction of the Temple. (1 & 2) In the past the Gypsies have used the Tarot Cards in their rituals and for divining purposes, as they are used today. The Gypsies became, and have remained, wanderers of the road, protesting against civilization and dispensing with anything in the form of duty. They assumed the "Law of the Road;" and the cards they carried with them have been known as the "Tarot of the Bohemians." To a certain extent these cards belong to them, although altered through the infidelity or imprudence of some of the Kabalistic Jews. They have keys that correspond to the letters of the Hebrew alphabet and some figures which produce their forms.

Long ago the Gypsies used these cards for ritualistic purposes and for fortune telling. Their example was followed by Charlatans who claimed occult insight to predict the future; they were proscribed in every land and are today looked upon as a debased remnant of the Ancient World, the profaners of the Great Arcana. (3)

An important work called The Emerald Tablet is known as a memorial of Hermes. It is an engraved stone tablet, holding the Wisdom of the Ages, that immutable Law of Equilibrium. Its author, Hermes, has been known as the Emblem of the Word which creates, - that creative Word which reaches throughout the universe.

By tracing his lineage back to beginnings, Hermes is discovered to be the first known Son of the Mother of the World. He has since had many celestial incarnations, becoming identified with many of the great prophets and mystics of the world. His books are claimed to have been written through Divine revelation. Through him the sciences belonging to Masonry have been revealed, especially that of geometry. He has been symbolized in Mercury,

---

(1) - The greatest of tragedies was the burning of the books of Hermes during the Alexandrian conflagration. Volumes that have been saved are supposed to be hidden in the desert, their location known to but a few.

(2) - The burning of the Serapheum, under the edict of Theodosius (called "the good") brought the old era to an end, when the early church, calling itself an enemy of learning, destroyed with a funeral-pyre of four hundred thousand blazing parchment rolls, the Library that held the Wisdom of ten thousand years.

(3) - These cards became the progenitors of the playing cards as we know them today.

the planet nearest the Sun. He is of profound importance to all Masonic scholars, having initiated the Ritual of the Masonic Orders, with their symbols, found in the dawn of creation.

A book of universal sciences, called by the Kabalists "The Key of Solomon, the King," contains a doctrine of transcendental magic, wherein the name Jehovah permutates into twenty-two exemplified names called Shemhamphoresch -- the "Holy Name." This book embodies the primal scriptures from which The Tarot is a deduction; it is modeled on the sidereal astral wheel with its unceasing revolutions and is represented by seventy-two magical circles creating thirty-six talismans. Each of them bears two of the seventy-two names. Their signs are emblematic of their number and that of the four letters of the Tetragrammaton corresponding to them. From this is evolved the four emblematic Tarot suits. It states in this book: "The thirty-six talismans will be a book which will contain all the secrets of nature, and by diverse combinations thou shalt make the Genii and Angels speak." A collection of prayers and evocations are given at the end of "The Key of Solomon, the King." "The Keys of Solomon are religious and rational forces expressed by signs. ..... The Seal is the synthesis of the Keys, and the Ring shows its use. The Ring of Solomon is at once round and square, and represents the mystery of the quadrature of the Circle." (1)

The Ring with its double seal is expressed in one sign, symbolizing the powers of heaven and earth and the laws which rule them either celestially or materially. For those who can reach the depths of their own being and discern "in universal law the instrument of eternal justice, the Seal of Solomon, his Keys and his Ring are tokens of supreme royalty." (2) "The secrets of science are but the laws of life, and in the game of life he who foresees is he who wins." Tradition says that they who possess the "Keys of Solomon" can communicate with spirits of all grades and obtain obedience from all natural forces. These Keys are the hieroglyphical paths reproduced in the Tarot.

Many of the Tarot Cards have definite Masonic symbols. All represent the magical constitution of man, each one a law, a power, an element in nature; while the Ten Sephiroth, or the twenty-two paths or cards corresponding to them, are symbols of the cosmic system which, if revealed through study and meditation, will create a treasure-house of wisdom. The reading of these cards enables one to unravel old hieroglyphics.

Eliphas Levi frankly states that "With no other book than The Tarot, if one knew how to use it, one could acquire in a few years universal knowledge and would be able to speak on all subjects with unequalled learning and inexhaustible eloquence." The interpretations were entrusted to the Hierophants of the Mysteries, which held secrets not to be divulged to the profane, for this wisdom was under cover of that which was mighty. The cards were placed under "The Fool." The progress of The Fool is used in all the cards and, like the hoodwinked candidate, he is ready to take the path through the gates of Divine Wisdom -- gates of purification, therefore of fire -- and so pass those heavenly portals called "The Gateway of the Gods," beyond which sits the Person of "Eternal Wisdom."

---

(1) - LEVI, Eliphas - THE HISTORY OF MAGIC, Page 511.
(2) - LEVI, Eliphas - THE HISTORY OF MAGIC, Page 513.

The mystery of the cards is wrapped up in the symbolism of the unnumbered letter called "The Fool," who is seen passing intrepidly and rhythmically along the "Way of Tao," coming forth undaunted through a Source of Light. The paths of magic and mysticism are united in the "Way of Tao." The O or Zero is symbolical of consciousness, which defies definition; O or Zero is the symbol of the Circle, -- the Circle of Eternity and of very great power.

Court de Gebelin, one of the greatest Egyptologists of his day, assigned Zero to Ain-Suph, the unknowable First Cause, to deceive all who could not pierce the veil of illusion -- all interpretations requiring careful study. Taro means "The Law of the Road," or the Taro-Rota -- a wheel. Its alphabet is preserved in the form of the Tarot cards. Taht is said to have invented letters through the study of the stars, the Fires of Heaven. Similarly all Hebrew letters are composed of tiny flames. The Tarot is a universal alphabet relating to the Kabalistic Tree of Life, and the cards are arranged according to a reformed astrological order. These cards are monumental summaries of all ancient revelation -- keys giving the mystery of the sacred ancient Hieratic Hieroglyphs which contained the Great Secrets of Moses, who enshrined them in his Kabala.

The Tarot has seventy-eight leaves or cards, divided into two sections, called major and minor arcanes. The major has twenty-two symbolical designs from glyphs corresponding to the Hebrew or universal alphabet. Their interpretations belong to their ancient origin. The twenty-two cards of the major arcane correspond to the twenty-two letters of the Hebrew alphabet, or the twenty-two paths which correspond to the Ten Sephiroth, and each letter is connected with a sign of the zodiac and the planets.

"In finding a key to the Book of Revelation with its twenty-two chapters, one may discover how to climb the twenty-two paths or portals of the Tree of Life secreted therein. When meditating and leaning towards the ideal, the idea back of the ideal or the spirit within the symbol may merge the masculine and feminine. When the mystic is coming up the path of consciousness, at a certain stage he calls his disciples, two at a time, as Jesus did, and by so doing opens the positive and the negative, or the masculine and the feminine, within himself. Uniting, they lift him into another state of consciousness which, when understood, enables him to open centers of consciousness within himself. One cannot think himself into consciousness, but it may come THROUGH LIVING THE LIFE and through Grace." (1)

In life there is always the action of the two opposite poles, the two unchangeable laws governing it, the negative and the positive; and whether from the higher Spiritual vibration or from the lower material one, this law controls everything visible or invisible in the universe.

There are fifty-six cards in the minor arcane, forty of which are similar to the small cards of an ordinary pack of playing-cards. There are ten to each suit, numbering from 1 or Ace to 10, corresponding to the Ten

---
(1) - WIGGS, George W.

Sephiroth; but in place of the clubs, hearts, diamonds and spades, the true magical weapons of the Mysteries are given, depicted as Wands, Pentacles, Swords and Cups. Those remaining are the sixteen court cards, four to each suit, - Kings, Queens, Knights and Pages.

The Kabalistic Pentagram or Five-Pointed Star of Unconquered Will.
- Frater Achad

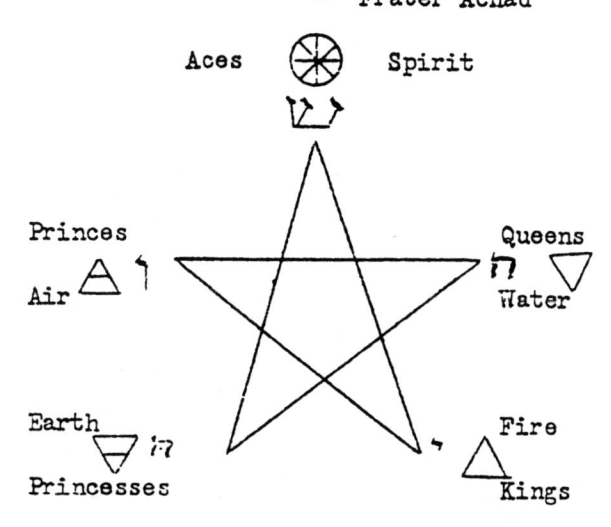

```
           Aces  ⊕  Spirit
                 ש

  Princes              Queens
   Air  △ ו          ה ▽
                        Water


  Earth                 Fire
    ▽ ה            ו  △
  Princesses           Kings
```

י = I	Kings (on Horses)		Fire	Chokmah
ה = H	Queens (Thrones)		Water	Binah
ש = Sh	Aces (Roots)		Spirit	Kether
ו = V	Princes (Chariots)		Air	Tiphereth
ה = H	Princesses (Foot)		Earth	Malkuth

"The PENTAGRAM or FIVE-POINTED STAR of UNCONQUERED WILL and Mystically the letter ש (Shin), which is the HOLY SPIRIT, descends into the God-Man. This process is symbolized in the Tarot by the ACES which correspond to KETHER and SPIRIT being placed at the top of the Pentagram." (1)

The other four are attributed to the Elements, Fire, Earth, Air and Water. Fire belongs to the Kings; Earth to the Princesses; Air to the Princes; and Water, to the Queens. Roots, signifying Spirit, apply to the Aces. Thus the four Elements find their Roots in Spirit. The four kings are represented by the cardinal signs of the zodiac; the queens, by the eight-petalled flower which is always the symbol of Christ, and by the fixed signs of the zodiac; two of the four jacks bear sprigs of acacia, while the others turn their faces away from the symbol of death. The four jacks or princes are represented by the mutable signs of the zodiac.

In the Tarot the four worlds of the Kabalists are under the dominion of the four letters of the Tetragrammaton, the J H V H, as well as the sacred Elements; hence, the worlds are: The Archetypal-Fire, The Material-Earth, The Formative-Air, and The Creative-Water. The magical weapons are also under

---
(1) - FRATER ACHAD, Q. B. L., or THE BRIDE'S RECEPTION, Page 58

the Tetragrammaton and the Elements:

Yod	He´	Vau	He´
Wands	Pentacles	Swords	Cups
Fire	Earth	Air	Water

Noticeably the Last Judgment given as the twentiety letter is represented by the Hebraic letter Shin -- the letter of both Fire and Spirit, meaning regeneration; while the twelfth letter, the Hanged Man, bears a very mysterious teaching; yet every "Way" in this wonderful wheel is a link to both the higher and lower planes -- an endless chain. This Hanged Man is sometimes called "The Redeemer," while the gallows foreshadow the cross and, though dissimilar to the crucifixion, must belong to untold ages as it is given among the most ancient of the cards. It was primarily a symbol of self-sacrifice, or the power of redeeming love.

In one of the cards this man is suspended by one foot, his head and arms forming a triangle, while above, the legs form a cross, and as the body is reversed so that it is reflected in the waters, it symbolically represents the bringing down of light into the subconscious mind of Humanity. His head is surrounded by glory. This Hanged Man has been called, esoterically, the human spirit suspended from heaven by a single thread, "Wisdom, not death, being the reward for voluntary suffering during which the human soul, suspended above the world of illusion and meditating upon its unreality, is rewarded by the achievement of self-realization."

In the myth of The Dying God, of the Odinic Ritual, Odin hangs himself for nine nights on a branch of a large tree and pierces his own side with a sacred spear; and through the experience came his remarkable vision.

Among the easily identified Masonic symbols there was the Master Builder; the Rod that budded; the Pillars where Severity and Mercy were established in Strength; the Chariot of the Sun, or the solar power; the ascension of the Three out of Four in the raising of the flap of the Apron. Solomon is there likened to the Lion with the Key between his teeth; then we have the Seven Sacred Centers; the Cubical Stone; the Blazing Star; the Flaming Sword; the Wheel, in a way, the Eternal Ascent and Descent; the Arcanum of Solomon, Equilibrium; the Coffin; the Trumpet, symbolically giving the Word -- generation or regeneration; Aquarius, the prophecy of the New Aeon; the Cherubim; the Squaring of the Circle; and the Broken Wheel, requiring the three degrees of the Blue Lodge for the Spiritual unfoldment of man that he might become perfect.

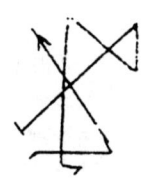

Chapter VIII

THE TABERNACLE, SOLOMON'S TEMPLE, THE TOWER OF BABEL

> There is no greater Temple in the
> Universe than Man.
> — E. V. S.

IT IS WRITTEN that the cosmic Tabernacle, the Tent of Tetragrammaton, or the meeting-place in the desert, was built according to the imagery of Moses on the Mount. "Moreover, thou shalt make the tabernacle with ten curtains. The length of each curtain shall be eight-and-twenty cubits, and the breadth of each curtain four cubits." These ten correspond to the ten divisions of the ark of heaven with its four corners and the twenty-eight measures of the lunar zodiac. Also, ten cubits was the length of each board, made of acacia wood. It not only represented the four cardinal points of the world but the four cosmic Elements, Fire, Earth, Air and Water, in which the genii or angels have their abode. Within the Tabernacle everything had a mystical meaning.

Bazalael, the builder of the Tabernacle, knew and understood the transposition of letters by which heaven and earth were created, and Hermes very appropriately called the zodiac the Great Tent. The solar system was considered a Temple of Initiation, by the passage of the Sun from Cancer (the gate of birth) to Capricorn (the gate of death), the latter being the Great Initiation.

Moses changed the orientation of his tabernacle that it might give as few points as possible when compared with Egyptian temples which, according to Spencer, were entered from the West, the ritualistic utensils and most sacred furniture facing East. "Solomon's temple at Jerusalem, as an exact counterpart of the Mosaic Tabernacle, possessed no entrance at the West, which end was perpetually closed by a wall to exclude the profane from the Sanctun Sanctorum."

The Jew entered his sacred place of worship through the eastern portals. On entering, he advanced by the North Side towards the West, which was the objective point for his worship. When departing, if he retrograded with his face directed West, the South was to the left, showing the Jewish temple was oriented the reverse of a Masonic Lodge. Spencer also observes that "The early churches were not directed towards a particular point of the compass until about the Fourth Century, at which epoch every inconvenience was submitted to in order to secure an exact east and west orientation."

There is always a similitude between sacred edifices and Gothic courts which were generally erected according to the orbit of the Sun. Stellar orientation, used hundred of thousands of years ago, was usually North and South;

solar orientation, East and West, came at a much later period. Stellar myths were universal; they preceded the lunar and the solar, and related to a period of greatest antiquity. The stellar was practiced in the Niolithic age, and there is ample evidence that the people of the Paleolithic age (the little red men) were known in those times. They were found in all parts of the world. Stellar myths remain as pure today as when they originated, but have become evolutionized into the solar.

The Tabernacle was the secret and symbolical school of Moses, erected for the purpose of Divine Initiations. It was patterned, as were all temples, after the temples of Atlantis. Every part, including the enclosure that surrounded it, was a symbol of some Divine truth, therefore very sacred. In miniature it was an abridged image of the universe; "Nature, therefore, was the Tabernacle and man himself its Priest," and the Rituals performed therein were of life and death, with their various problems.

The Tabernacle was divided into three parts, two for the Priests, and accessible to all; but the third was set apart for God or heaven, and was inaccessible to all save the High Priest. The court of the Tabernacle was an area enclosed by linen curtains hanging from brass pillars. The bases of the pillars were of gold, and the capitals of silver, symbolizing both Sun and Moon. Rituals of a sacred nature were held at the time of the new and full Moon. Silver was said to be gold with the gold-ray turned in, -- representing the purified nature of man. At the entrance to the courtyard, East, stood the altar of burnt offerings; a little beyond this, the laver of purification, with a bowl of water above it for lustrations.

The Tabernacle beyond this was in the middle of the court enclosure, the entrance facing East, so that when the sun rose it would send its rays upon it and light the "Holy Place" within. The front of the Tabernacle faced East, the long sides, North and South. The length of the Tabernacle proper was thirty cubits (a cubit being about eighteen inches), and the width ten cubits. In the interior was the "Holy Place," its walls hung with linen embroidered with the faces of cherubs. (Cherub was a name used by the Kabalists to denote a being of the heavenly hierarchy.) Against the walls of this "Holy Place" stood the seven-branched candlestick of pure gold; and on the southern side, near the candles, were many emblems representative of the heavens, the earth, and the fruits of the soil. A table was opposite, on the northern side, with two stacks of showbread upon it, arranged in heaps of six each, -- "the table of shewbread that was always to be set as the oblation in the presence of the Lord." On the table were also two incensories, their belief giving them hope that the vapor or aroma from the showbread, including its soul, might be acceptable to the Lord. The altar of burnt incense was near the center, before the Holy of Holies. This altar was of wood and gold, gold representing its Spiritual nature, and wood its Material nature.

At the entrance to the Tent proper there were seven pillars. Before the door of the Holy of Holies was the veil, hung across four pillars. The four Tabernacle pillars represented the same pillars as those raised at Tyre to the four Elements, facing the four cardinal points, each having one of the four figures from the zodiac upon it. The four pillars with the veil symbolized the Elements necessary to life. None passed through the veil save the High Priest, and he passed through only at stated times. The Holy of Holies held the Ark of the Covenant. The High Priest alone was permitted to carry the Ark.

From Jewish records it is known that the Ark contained the two tablets of stone whose mystery was of arch-celestial import. "The Holy Place ..... symbolized the Mystic Ship, which measured the sun's course, and corresponds to the Naos of a Greek temple, or, to the nave of a Christian church." (The court, the Holy Place, and the Holy of Holies whow that "thus the mystic triad, the ancient emblem of God, invisibly ordered the proportions of this sacred Tent." (1)

The veil was of four different colors: white, blue, crimson and purple. The banners bore the images of the Bull (Taurus), the Lion (Leo), the Man, (Aquarius), and the Eagle (Scorpio). These are the original fixed signs of the zodiac appropriately assigned to the banners. We are told by Philo that "the priestly dress in its whole is a copy and representation of the world; and the parts are a representation of the world." (2)

The shewbread typified the twelve months of the year; the candlestick, the signs of the zodiac through which the seven planets run their course -- the seven lights. The candlestick was a symbol of heaven; the altar of incense, with its offerings, an emblem of earth. As Clement Alexander says: "The golden lamp conveys another enigma as a symbol of the Christ." The whole Tabernacle was an image of man and the universe.

In the Royal Arch Chapter of Masonry there are four veils of different colors and their four banners bear the messages of the Bull, Lion, the Eagle and Man, similar to those in the Tabernacle.

The blazing altar of burnt offerings in the court was an altar of sacrifice. Altars of incense or burnt offerings date from the time of primordial man, as we find him emerging from the Lemurian continent, when the Sun was accepted as the great Spirit-Fire of the Universe. Fires upon altars were regarded as messengers rising from the earth to the Sun, and those who comprehended the meaning of the Spirit of the Law worshipped before altars of Nature, for upon them the Spirit of Fire was forever found burning.

Primitive men made fires in honor of the Sun and the Moon -- the Great Lights. These they kindled by way of returning thanks to God for His great gift. When looking up to the stars they prayed to the angels, who they knew had been placed there by God. They testified the same thing to God which God had testified to them in the Great Lights -- the Sun and Moon. These Wise Men of earliest days had knowledge of the invisible God by those things which were visible. They were the Sons of Fire, or the Sons of Light, that great FRATERNITY OF THE BUILDERS, known today as Masons, descendants of the Spirit of Fire. Alchemists, Hermetic philosophers and Rosicrucians were all Masons.

Fires of the altars burned upon cubes. The foundation of everything seemed to be a cube or pedestal upon which the altar-fires burned. A

---
(1) - THE CANON, Page 165
(2) - THE CANON, Page 167

cubicle stone was symbolical of man; the spiritual flame, the fire within him. The cube is a six-fold symbol that interchanges with the double triangle or the Seal of Solomon; it is also a symbol of the four quarters of the zodiac, including the zenith and the nadir; and, as a cubicle stone, is identified with the pedestal upon which heaven is supported. The lamp of the alchemist which burned for thousands of years is a symbol of that fire within. Initiates tell us that at the top of the spine there is a little red and blue flame, which through a perfected life creates a transmutation of the lower self into the higher self, the life essence providing all that is necessary to keep the tiny flame burning. The offering of this life-essence becomes the rising vapor from the "Altars of Divinity."

In Christian churches there was always a choir around the altar. In early days the worshippers hoped to invoke Deity through chorus and dance given in rhythmic measured steps around the altar, upon which fire frequently burned. This was in imitation of the measured harmonies of the stars, or the music of the spheres. Among the Greeks, when youths and maidens danced in circular and graceful movements around their primitive altars of sacred fire, this was thought to produce the music marking the Sun's course through the twelve signs of the zodiac in his early revolutions. The chorus, or choir, in our Christian churches mystically represents the Cherubim who sang in imitation of this celestial music.

"The seven planetary circulations are represented by the circumnambulations in the Masonic Lodges. Similarly the Jewish Priests marched seven times around the walls of Jericho, just as the Mahommedan Priests march seven times around the Kaaba, at Mecca," all representing the rhythm or harmony of heaven.

Nearly all old philosophers devised a theory of harmony regarding the universe, which continued until the great changes took place and philosophizing ceased. The sacred animals of the zodiac (heaven's belt) were as much Sons of God as were the spirits of the earth; in fact, they were known and came before them. Astrology, through which all this came, was the most ancient of all sciences, though it is comparatively little known today. But rumor whispers that it will gradually go back and back to its first germ that grew into a tree of Wisdom and Beauty.

The most sacred of all the objects in the Tabernacle was the Ark. The Ark was made of Shittim wood and gold, plated within and without. It contained the Tablets of the Law given to Moses when upon Sinai. On the lid of the golden plate, the Mercy Seat, knelt two Cherubim facing each other, their wings stretched above their heads. This Ark of the Covenant was finally placed in the Holy of Holies in King Solomon's Temple.

The Tablets of the Law had also their cosmic significance and the hand work graven upon them was of the creation of the world as the Word of God. Clement Alexander considers that these would exhibit physical creation: "For by the finger of God is understood the power of God, by which creation of heaven and earth is accomplished ..... for the writing and hand work put on the table is the creation of the world," and the Ark which contained them must have held the knowledge of Divine and human things.

These Cherubim were the Cosmic Angels that had such exquisite knowledge. Moses said that he had seen such figures near the Throne of God, for they were symbolized as the Two Bears -- the constellations near the Pole of Heaven. Clement also considers them symbolical of the Two Bears, and that they held the two-fold principles of life.

The Ark, the two Tablets of the Law, and the Shekinah above were their sacred symbols. As Origen states, in part, in one of his discourses: "But since they are mentioned in a very mysterious manner, on account of the unworthy and the indecent who are unable to enter into the great thoughts and venerable nature of theology, I have not deemed it becoming to discourse of them in this treatise." The starry firmament from whence germinating powers of God were thought to flow has a great symbolical meaning, for the Ark, the Tablets of Stone, and the Shekinah above belong to the knowledge of those great souls who understood and knew.

The Ark of the Covenant, or the Box, was said to contain relics which had been the birthright of every country since time immemorial and was known as "The Fountain-Head of Wisdom." Over this Ark hovered the "Shekinah Glory" as a "column of flame at night and a pillar of smoke by day." The flame is the Spirit of Holy Fire that is within man, enthroned in its holy place. When this flame is lowered its spiritual impulse fades. So it is with a nation; for if it allows its flame to lessen, it is carried away by a few faithful ones to another nation and another people. It is understood that this flame or fire is being carried into our Western world, with its great wisdom of the past knocking at our door. Light hovers over the world today midst rapid changes. Many, seeking allegiance with their higher natures, will be the Builders of mysterious temples and find many sacred relics of the past.

The cosmic symbolism of the Tabernacle has been ably written of, thoroughly proving that it was a mystical image intended as a shrine for the entire universe. Moses, having gone up onto the loftiest and most sacred mountain, difficult of ascent, was instructed in the sacred Will of God and received the drawings from which the Tabernacle was built.

The construction of Solomon's Temple cannot be correctly understood without the key to the Egyptian Mysteries which enables one not to be misled by any historical perversion. From this key the Hebrews were enabled to write their version of Solomon's Temple and all connected with it; and they obtained what they had through astronomical myths, not without their value when understood, but quite useless without the key, proving their universality.

The Egyptian Solomon is the Coming Son of the Apocrypha: "He who comes with peace or fulfillment is the Solomon by name." He was the designer and builder of the celestial temple, and became known as the typical healer and architect of Israel. Sol-om-on, as the Prince of Peace, was a Sun-and-Moon manifestation; and the Sun and Moon were the greatest architects (the god Ptah and the goddess Ma) who built this wonderful celestial temple patterned after the Sun, Moon and Stars. They were said to have a son whose Egyptian name represented the Prince, or Bringer of Peace.

It is stated that the perfection with which the Tabernacle was built intrigued Solomon to use it as a pattern for his Temple, knowing that he could not improve upon it. King Hiram of Tyre persuaded Solomon to invite Hiram Abiff to help in the building. It was to be erected for the Lord as the Everlasting House. Hiram was a Master in the noble Order of the Dionysians.

The internal measures of the Temple were twice those of the Tabernacle. The three divisions, the Porch, the Holy Place, and the Holy of Holies are similar to the three divisions of the churches. They also represent the three degrees of the Masonic Blue Lodge and the three Priests are now accepted as the Entered Apprentice, the Fellow Craftsman and the Master Mason. The court with its open vault looking to the heavens was surrounded by other enclosures.

The table of Shewbread, [1] the altar of incense, and the golden candlestick were assigned to the Holy Place before the veil, as in the Tabernacle, with only slight changes in the arrangement of the Brazen Sea. The plan of the Porch, the Holy Place and the Holy of Holies, together with the chambers, were copied after Egyptian temples. The two Pillars in front of the Porch were named Jachin and Boaz. They took the place of the twin obelisks which stood in front of every Egyptian temple. The Porch was overlaid with pure gold. Gold was everywhere; even the Cherubs were covered with gold; all had the magnificence of fairyland.

The door of the middle chamber was at the right side of the house. There were winding stairs leading into the middle chamber, and out from this middle chamber into a third. The steps of the winding stairs were said to lead to truth.

The symbolic ornaments, forming the chief decorations and the dress of the High Priests, referred to the laws or orders of the world. Two of the three parts in the Temple, as in the Tabernacle, represented the material world -- the earth -- and was open to all; but the third was set apart as God's dwelling-place. The seven-branched candlestick represented the seven planets -- so arranged and regulated as to "preserve the musical proportions and system of harmony of which the Sun was the center and connection." All within was mystical and symbolical.

The court, open to the heavens, was supported by twelve columns, the border around them signifying the zodiac, a sign of the zodiac upon each. The Brazen Sea was supported by twelve oxen, three looking toward each point of the cardinal cross. Temples within were usually filled with sacred numbers, astrological symbols, hieroglyphical signs, which are often emblazoned on floors of lodges. The Holy of Holies in the West was in the form of a cube divided by the outstretched wings of the Cherubim, creating a meeting-place or covenant. The two Tables of the Law with the Ark of the Covenant signified the two sexes.

---

[1] - According to Lightfoot, in the Temple of Solomon "the Shewbread is described as being laid, cake by cake, between canes or REEDS of gold. These canes or reeds were not whole, like the reed itself, but represented it as cloven in two or split up the middle, so that, when the cakes were placed between the halves of the divided reeds, they were the symbol of the food contained in the reed. Fourteen of these halves were used in each pile; twenty-eight for the total of twelve cakes, placed in two piles with three half-reeds placed between two cakes up to the fifth, and only two between the fifth and sixth, the lowest cake being laid on the plain table. The number twenty-eight is lunar in the mystical sense. Every seventh day the old cakes were replaced by a fresh offering." From Gerald Massey, A BOOK OF THE BEGINNINGS, Volume II, page 64.

The Ark was the house of Jehovah, and the name Jehovah is both male and female, shown in the meeting of the cubes between the Cherubim with their outstretched wings "so that the wings of the one touched the one wall and the wings of the other Cherub touched the other wall; and their wings touched one another in the midst of the house." Astronomically the stretching over or embracing of the two cubes signified the quadrant of the year between Cancer and Scorpio, just as the "Cherubim stretched over and embraced the covenant of the meeting of the two halves of the Ark."

The Holy of Holies was deeply concerned with colors, as five were involved, and according to Josephus, it was "built in white, or the color of ether. Inside, it was lined with red cedar. This, again, was lined with orange-gold. The interior was closed against light and was in the blackness of darkness, as the proper place for the Ark of the Covenant (or the meeting together of two opposite principles)." All the colors seemed to have been typical: Silver, the color of the Moon; red, the earth; gold for the Sun, white for the ether, and black for the night or the nadir.

Moses based his religious mysteries on the formula derived from the Sidereal Cycle which is symbolized in the Tabernacle, and upon this the Jewish High Priests built the allegorical Temple of Solomon, which was really non-existent. The astronomical features of the Temple were very plain. It was of heavenly beauty. The entrance faced the East, the rising Sun, representing the Vernal Equinox; the Holy of Holies was West, towards the setting Sun, representing the Autumnal Equinox; the quadrangle found in the winds was oriented North, East, South and West, facing the four winds; the Brazen Sea had on its ledges the Ox, the Cherub or Man, and the Lion, representing three of the four fixed signs of the zodiac and forming the angle upon which it began, Scorpio being omitted. The Lion represented Summer; the Man, or Cherub, Winter; and the Ox, Spring. Dan's sign of Autumn, Scorpio, was omitted, as it represented the setting Sun going down into the darkness and therefore was left out for mystical reasons.

All is conveyed in the description of the building of the Temple. The two squares or the two quadrants of the zodiac are lorded over by Leo, the Lion, or Solomon; and the Summer Solstice, going downwards to the second quadrant, was lorded over by Scorpio, or Dan. The religious culture of the Israelites was located in Dan, or Scorpio, who holds the gate of evening -- darkness. Under another form it was the gate of the woman, or the gate of the evening -- darkness -- the place of the New Conception. The upper square or cube was gold, the fructifying powers of the Sun; the lower square or cube was black (brazen) -- feminine -- the generative powers of the Moon. It was a temple of the Sun, (gold), masculine; and a temple of the Moon, (brass), feminine.

Solomon was of the tribe of Judah, the Lion, and he made all the gold work within the temple; but Hiram made the Brazen Sea and all the works of brass. Hiram was a widow's son of the tribe of Naphtali and was filled with wisdom; and through the generations of Naphtali and Dan all future generations must pass. Hiram completed all the furnishings for this House of the Ever-Living, of prescribed brass. The altar and the table were of gold. Brass was the symbol of the nether world, the darkness of the year, or the Winter Sun. The brass work of the Temple had connection with Dan who held the gate to the depths of the darkness.

The Throne of Solomon was of ivory plated with gold, adorned by bulls and supported by lions. It had six steps and at the arm of each step was a lion -- seven on each side. "The lion that guarded the Ark and held in his mouth the key wherewith to open it, figuratively represents Solomon -- the Lion of the Tribe of Judah, who preserved and communicated the key to the true knowledge of God, of His Laws, and of the profound mysteries of the moral and physical Universe." (1) And he still holds the key to the enigma of the Sphinx.

There is no knowledge of value to prove that Solomon's Temple ever existed, and legends connected with it in no way show it to be of an earthly pattern. Freemasons, whose ritual revolves around this mysterious temple, look upon it as a fabric both mystical and spiritual. The description in Ist Kings is purely allegorical and suggests a spiritual building in the form of an earthly one, as a manifestation of the power and the splendor of raising the Spirit above the material world "through the wisdom and the genius of the Builders" -- building from within outward, creating Light in the subjective self to shine in the darkness of the objective world and draw within its light, Brotherhood. This is the temple to be raised without sound.

When a Mason today becomes a true Builder, he has been taught through his Initiations how to use the rules and principles of architecture, to which has been added the cross, by the horizontal and perpendicular lines supposed to form the foundation of the spiritual temple. It is said in Ist Corinthians, Chapter III, Verse 9-10: "For we are laborers together with God. ..... According to the grace of God which is given unto me, as a wise masterbuilder, I have laid the foundation, and another buildeth thereon." And that other understood that he, too, could build his temple of Wisdom upon a sure foundation, according to the plan of his Creator, who planned the great work by his Infinite Wisdom, performed it by Strength and adorned it in Beauty for man's benefit. There is no greater temple in the universe than Man.

Wherever the Wisdom Religion is studied, its adepts are known as "Builders," building temples of exquisite knowledge and beauty. Active or operative ones build from celestial patterns, whereas speculative ones become the theoretical builders. "The former exemplify in works their control over the forces of inanimate as well as of animate nature; the latter are only perfecting themselves in the rudiments of the sacred science" according to the grace of God. "But let every man take heed how he buildeth thereon, for other foundation can no man lay than that is laid, which is Jesus Christ." - Ist Corinthians III, 10-11.

The building of King Solomon's Temple is less minute than that of the Tabernacle, though the internal measures are twice as great. A work on the oldest plan, which seems to the greatest in serious pretensions, is by Villapanda, the Jesuit. It is practical and workmanlike and has the appearance of being a copy from some traditional drawings preserved by old Masons. Theoretically it gives a canonical pattern for a guide to builders of sacred edifices. It has its place among canonical books, the same as the Ark of Noah, the Tower of Babel, and the Tabernacle.

The Temple of Ezekiel was far more magnificent than that of Solomon, and it has justly been considered a visionary building. Its court, like that

---
(1) - PIKE, Albert, - Morals and Dogma, Page 210

of the Camp, forms a diagram illustrating the squaring of the circle. There is very much to prove the mystical nature of Biblical temples and their allegorical symbolism. It is assumed that the figures and numerals corresponding to Ezekiel's Temple were known and invented by the Pyramid-builders. "The astronomical science of the Hebrews seems to be mystically concealed under the figures of Noah's ark, the Tabernacle, the Temple of Solomon, and the Holy Oblation of Ezekiel, while the Christians added to those their mystical city of the New Jerusalem, described in the last two chapters of Revelation. Each of these mystical structures appears to exhibit a particular aspect of the heavens and constitutes a scientific record of certain known facts of astronomy, which formed the true basis of the ancient theology." (1)

Astronomy, as a science, was a part of the Hidden Mysteries. It is well known that the Christians, at the beginning of their existence, destroyed the early works on astronomy. It is readily cognizable that the Ark, the Tent and the Temple embody astronomical and mathematical calculations.

Temples were places of initiation, and Solomon's was known as "The House of Everlasting Light;" its natural symbol being on the brow of Mount Moriah. It is macrocosmic in character and a symbol of the universe. All great Temples, Arks and Tabernacles were built over or upon water, symbolical of the heavens and founded upon Celestial Waters. A Temple of Humanity is slowly being rebuilt for Man, as his spirit yields to his inner spiritual influence. Slowly behind the clouds it is rising; and "when the Aquarian age is well advanced the Sun will have come into Leo, and it is not alone prophesied but is known that the Secret Religions of the world include once more the raising to initiation by the Grip of the Lion's Paw."

> "And hath he not a Temple, building throughout all time?
> Before historic ages, back in the world's young prime?
> Its walls were based on Service of Gods and men to man,
> And love to all beneath him in Love's embracing plan."

Occultists and writers of the highest authority have given the "Key of Solomon the King" as the fountain-head of all Kabalistic magic of Medieval times. It seems to be well understood that Solomon was an alchemist and a necromancer; and it is said by Josephus that God had endowed him with such transcendent powers that he had understood and was equal to all the great Wisdom of Egypt and that he was assisted by the Wosdom of Hiram, or CHiram, the Universal Spirit.

There was a firm belief among the Eastern nations, before and after the introduction of Christianity into the world, that letters by strange arrangements were made powerful through mystic law. Magical powers and incantations were in vogue at this time and the mystery of the Omnific Word was ascribed to the success of Solomon in building his Temple at Jerusalem. The name Shemhamporesch, or Jehovah, was one which brought forth wonders that were even ascribed to Moses, who, with the Shamir, cut the precious stones of the ephod. Rabbinical writers assert that Solomon secured this mighty Shamir through the power of this Word.

The Shamir was said to be an animal, a magic jewel, and was sometimes called a Worm, spoken of as an insect having power to cut through the

---
(1) - THE CANON, Pages 27-8.

hardest stone. It was said that rocks would split by the slightest pressure from it; and to secure it, Solomon invoked the aid of Elementals to discover where it might be found, as he was required to build his Temple without the sound or aid of builders' tools. So he sought the talismanic potency of the word Shemhamphoresch, and with it trued the rough stones into great beauty. Shemhamphoresch was the blessed and eternal Name, the Divine, Omnific and Ineffable Tetragrammaton.

Shamir, in the Targum, is rendered "Mountain Splitter," and the legend connected with this insect or jewel and its discovery by Solomon is most curious. When Solomon asks the Rabbins how he is to do his great work, they remember this insect that had existed since the time of creation, with powers so great that the hardest substance could not resist it. Thus, by the magic of the Holy Name it was made possible for Solomon to build his Temple without the sound of tool. The hidden meaning in the legend is not far for the Masonic student to seek. There is always a hidden meaning in myth, allegory or tradition.

Solomon was a symbol of Wisdom and Science. His Wisdom was as the sands of the seashore. It was said to be greater than all the science of Mitzraim. He knew the origin of light, of the planets, and of the revolving spheres; he was a great astrologer; and his House was founded on Rest and Peace forever.

Masons who ally themselves with the powers of Light become not only Sons of Light but true Sons of God. The Lodges today are constructed upon the same principles as those of the Ancients; but free and accepted Masons are not subjected to the sacrifices of those ancient brothers. They are not Operative Masons today but follow in the Light of THE FRATERNITY OF THE BUILDERS -- Brethern whose origin belongs in the mysteries of the night and the stars.

Freemasons connect the building of the Tower of Babel with the origin of architecture; and after the so-called confusion of tongues, a new alphabet was said to have been invented. Through legends we are told that the Tower reached up to the Moon, which was the lowest heaven; but we are not told how this work was accomplished; so, how define the legend? "The myth-writers have made the attempt to span the distance from the earth to the Moon, coincident with the commencement of the earthly languages," with the idea of metaphorically intimating that this was a first bestowal of Cosmic Wisdom upon names by joining them to an astronomical invention. It was through this legend that the Freemasons found a "consequent beginning of a practice in building which would make a temple like a name in imitation of the universe." With the collapse of this Elemental Tower came the speech of the gods, which went over the four corners of the world.

The Tower of Babel with its seven tiers was symbolical of the "Great World's Altar Stairs," by which men climbed heavenward. This Tower was one of the most ancient of astronomical temples and was called "The Temple of the Seven Lights." It embodied the astronomical knowledge of antiquity. "The Jews have coupled with this wonderful monument the history of one they called Nimrod. The root of this name means 'the Beautiful Father of Heaven,' a history pertaining to the birthplace of mythological astronomy in the North." The shepherds and princes, or angels, who were said to appear on earth during the downfall of the Tower, had a common origin in celestial allegory or the phenomenon of the heavens. When dealing with things celestial, care should be taken in realizing that all beginnings were heaven-born and that all became veiled in allegory and illustrated in symbols -- a truth which all true Masons understand.

"Throughout antiquity the plans of allegorical temples can be discovered in the multiplication of the cube and the cross surrounded by a circle and the cubic cross moving in a globe." This in Masonry becomes "the root principle of architecture and the science of building."

"The cubic stone and its multiplication explains all secrets of sacred numbers, including the mystery of perpetual motion." The hexagram for many years has been used in the churches as a sacred symbol of Christ and the Trinity. It is the common symbol of the Masonic cube or cubical stone. A cube was a symbol of the mystery of creation, and also of the planet Saturn, as unyielding, solitary, representing the laws of Nature and Thought. A solid having twelve plane faces lies concealed in the perfect cube, indicating, if understood, that the structure of the universe is that of a Dodechahedron. The Master Builders or Initiates became acquainted with this form, which is the geometrical figure upon which the universe is built. Plato was the first to mention this in his writings, though it did not originate with him, when he said that "God fashioned the Elements, Fire, Earth, Air and Water, by form and number," and that "Geometry rightly treated is knowledge of the Eternal." His conception of the Elements was from the original substance, or Spirit over substance, and was purely mathematical. All things come from one substance, and are actuated by one Spirit.

In the completion of any great structure one stone is laid upon or joined to another, just as abstractly one attribute of Nature must be blended to another, so that an inner manifestation, or intuition, may be awakened, making the heart the repository of the great secrets of Nature. Each stone in the truing must bear its Masonic, altruistic mark -- must be hewn and polished out of the rough ashlar before the corner stone is laid in the building of the Temple of Divine Light or Life. The soul of man then becomes most beautiful. Being exalted in its Light and through its beauty, man becomes stilled, for God is never very far from that which is beautiful.

Ancients have left us imperishable records of knowledge; and Masonic philosophy shows conclusively that _it_ was the first science and religion and it will be the last. The Gnosis still lingers in our midst and has its votaries, though they be unknown. "Simplicity is the sesame to the gates of the coming mystery, the great simplicity of attainment encircled in the folds of love;" and there is something charming in the idea of greatness returning to simplicity.

From the ashes of the past a transcendent science is arising, changing human thought, and certainly destroying much irrational and false teaching.

Chapter IX

BUILDERS OF THE MIDDLE AGES

> These Guilds of the Builders deserved their Initiations by making themselves worthy to receive the Wages of the Master Mason, thus setting an example to each worker today.
>
> For by accepting their abstract knowledge "veiled in allegory and illustrated in symbols" the Mason will become conscious of the Great Work for the age of the Incoming Light.
>
> — E. V. S.

ORIGIN of the Builders (Masons) is celestial, its pedigree divine. Cobwebs have appeared at times, hiding many of its spiritual teachings, yet so vast is its inheritance, so sublime, so magnificent, it should always have been true to its Old Self.

My endeavors along the line of research for this origin have been to arrive at ancient truths, by consulting authorities who have given many years of their lives for this knowledge. Their testimonies should not be doubted, belonging as they do to the broad open-minded student. The prejudiced seeker is too content with present changes to delve into that great past where THE FRATERNITY OF THE BUILDERS show their ancient landmarks -- foundations that still exist but are not extant to the unbeliever, the unmaker of today.

Fallen columns of the ancient Builders need to be rebuilded, and through THE FRATERNITY OF THE BUILDERS with their vast inheritance the way has been paved for bringing back the old Masonic Wisdom into its ancient supremacy.

The time for remodelling has come. Masons are now teaching the spiritual messages of that profound Age Old Wisdom which will restore many ancient landmarks, bringing them into the old path of Light. For those who lean toward the Spirit of Truth, all that lies in the mists will be clarified in the sunlight.

Conditions during the Middle Ages were chaotic. Glimpses of architecture and of the Medieval Guilds may not be in a sequential order of events, nor so intended, nor have they been exclusively for Masons of today. Builders and Mystic Brotherhoods belong to the world and to all ages. Legend and truth were closely interwoven during those past ages, oftentimes difficult to unravel; truths have been hidden in nearly all old legends, but were not for the prejudiced seeker to uncover. "Modern Masons, who do not understand the symbolic mode of communication regard these traditions as worthless fiction, deserving no serious consideration. We venture another view of the case -- the statements of the old Masons, like those of priests, were published in the form of grotesque historical allegory, for the sole purpose, apparently, of deceiving those who were considered to be unfit to appreciate the simple truth." (1)

When Constantine the Great became the sole head of the Eastern and Western Empire, in 325, his first care was to establish peace. He had an ardent zeal for the Christian religion which he eventually established in his vast domains. He published an edict in favor of the Christians in the early part of the Fourth Century, when he transferred his capital at Rome to the Empire of Byzantium, which was subsequently named Constantinople. Here many skilled laborers could be found.

At this time Christians under Constantine were allowed to use a number of reconstructed Pagan temples which had been altered to suit their worship; but in the reconstruction many fragments of the earlier temples were substituted and the result was singularly uncouth and tasteless.

One of the first public concessions that Constantine made was in favor of the architects who were under the patronage of the Empire. Each master builder was given a competent salary. In the year 337, three years later, a rescript was enacted by Constantine releasing any master of the mechanical arts that he might thereafter become immune from civil exactions. "Succeeding decrees maintained the integrity of associations of architects, geometricians, stone-cutters and carpenters;" and in 364 corporative privileges that had been earlier conceded by Rome remained intact in the Byzantine Empire.

"Therefore these Guilds of Builders, by imperial recognition, as early as the reign of Constantine, were established on a solid basis in Byzantium." (2)

In 438 these decrees were affirmed by Theodosius. In the Western Empire his laws were more frequently used by the invading Northmen in Italy. Theoderic, the Goth, almost a contemporary with the Byzantine lawgiver, by an edict ordered that the Roman laws should be equally binding upon the Goth and conquered Italian.

During these changes, legends and traditions that had come through the ages became altered in order to harmonize with an ecclesiastical policy; and though the restrictions upon the Pagan Rites and their temple sacrifices were altered, many Pagan Rites were adopted in the early Christian Rites. Their symbols and rituals were appropriated, as well as certain divinities. Byzantine builders, through neccessity in building Christian churches, embodied their conceptions as substitutes for the old heathen legends. This was destructive to the glory of the old Roman arts, for without any scruples whatever these architects changed the head of the mythological Jupiter into that of God the father, and the beautiful goddess Venus into that of the Virgin. Many irrelevant changes, not alone in art, have brought to the world and to the present age a great confusion of unhealthy misinterpretations by turning mythical conceptions into human beings.

---
(1) - THE CANON, Page 241.
(2) - FORT, George F.; THE EARLY HISTORY & ANTIQUITIES OF FREEMASONRY, P. 366

Christian symbolism was introduced into the Rites of a new religion at the period when the imperial residence was transferred from Rome to Byzantium, when works of art became but slavish imitations by imcompetent artists of that which remained of celestial antiquity. Naturally, the beauty of the old architecture and the fine arts of ancient times became demoralized. Embellishment in ornamentation, seemingly in a spirit of rivalry, brought about a tasteless art in which many graceful forms were lost. At this time it was said "the element of art had ceased to exist."

However, Constantine made a supreme effort to bring back some traditions of ancient architecture. He had temples built after the fashion of old Rome. But the symbols adopted at this time were used by Pagan converts who borrowed them profusely from their early ancestors. Constantine, through his apparent love for Christianity, built in his newly-formed Forum a metal statue of the Good Shepherd, and a brazen image of the Thirsty Hart. These two were the most ancient of the earliest Christian symbols -- the Good Shepherd being symbolical of the Christ and the Hart, "athirst for the Divine Presence." But the attempted artistic forms of the older architecture waned, possibly due to the influences back of Constantine's endeavors, thereby hindering any expansion of his artistic knowledge.

When Theoderic, King of the Goths, who was educated in Constantinople, ascended the throne in the Fifth Century, he appointed a superintendent to watch over public buildings, as his tendency was to preserve the artistic form of the older edifices; but the work lacked finish and detail, although the leading characteristics of architectural art were those contributed by the Eastern artists. It was in the Orient alone, especially at Constantinople, that a total loss of art was stayed.

Notwithstanding the earliest sentiments of the Christian church, especially in the East, they objected to images being introduced in religious services, but they could and be tolerated until iconoclasm directed against statues and art suddenly arose in the Eighth Century, particularly where ancient Rites had been celebrated. Byzantine and plastic arts were retained up to the Eighth Century, and then radiated out to distant countries. However, a decided tendenty toward symbolic representations of sacred subjects began to manifest, and various symbols were used, even the Cock, which had always been of importance as the symbol of watchfulness; but the most noteworthy of all was that of the Fish. This symbol was subsequently and frequently used by Operative Masons as a proprietary sign. As a symbol it comes out of a very remote period. Oriental builders used it as a distinctive and personal token. It is found in the Tenth Century on a column of St. Mark's Cathedral in Venice, which was Byzantine architecture. Its secret significance then was disguised except to the "unvelieving" Pagan. It is found on sacred edifices in Greece.

The Cock was a favorite symbol. "French Freemasons, at the close of the last Century, had this as an emblem of vigilance, among other symbols, delineated upon the side walls of the Chamber of Reflection for the Entered Apprentice degree." (1)

Traced to a beginning, before planting-time men were wont to say: "Let us first consult the birds." Birds signified the winds and their

---
(1) - LA REGULATEUR DU MAÇON, Page 13.

direction. The weather-cock is very ancient. At times it was used as a monitor to foretell the future. The Owl, as an enemy of light, is also of ancient usage. If its hoot was heard when it passed a house, or especially a window, its call was thought to hold sinister forebodings. We quickly realize that many superstitions of olden times were no more ridiculous and no more credible than are those of today. There are many practices and superstitions that might be mentioned, lest we forget.

Early incorporation of sacred symbols into church architecture, so frequently found in the cathedrals of Europe, serves to trace the origin and gradual development from early ages into the hands of Freemasons. Sacred symbols were found at the entrance to Byzantine churches which were scattered over Europe. Sides of the main entrance to a church were treated with mystical importance -- even as Christ had become the Portal or door of the Sheepfold; and the columns at the portals symbolized the Apostles, remembering the old message: "Him that overcometh will I make a Pillar in the temple of my God and he shall go no more out." At times these columns were used as substitutes for those at the entrance to King Solomon's Temple. Columns within the church held the same mystical importance as those found in the Masonic Lodge today. On the outer walls, jealously guarding these portals, were depicted or carved various kinds of animals, both real and legendary, grotesque, weird or ferocious, symbolizing conflicts belonging to the outer world; for within, all must be tranquil, calm and harmonious, in the realization that there was the sheepfold whose Shepherd was enshrined in the hearts of those who yearned and were comforted.

In the year 572, at Ravenna, a guild of Greeks was organized. In the Seventh Century, in Ravenna, as well as in other cities, were guilds with regular corporate governments; and as late as the year 1200 an official oath, still preserved, was made necessary on their admission. Stieglitz gives a tradition in his valuable treatise on Architecture that "at the time the Lombards were in possession of Northern Italy, from the Sixth to the Seventh Centuries, the Byzantine builders formed themselves into guilds and associations, and that on account of having received from the popes the privilege of living according to their own laws and ordinances, they were called Freemasons." As early as the Fifth Century, under the patronage of Theoderic, they had oaths of secrecy, usages and customs that had descended from the old heathen temple worship.

Much architectural skill and knowledge of the crafts and plastic arts were brought into Europe at the beginning of the Ninth Century by monk artificers from the Byzantine Empire, also from the Sixth to the Ninth Centuries British monks traveled to Germany in order to propagate the Christian religion.

That builders' guilds or corporations were brought into close contact with Western monks in building religious houses is incontestible. Skilled artists became more or less intimate with Masonic institutions as early as the Middle Ages, and the monks at an early age were initiated into the sublime details of science and became really a component part of it. A monk wears the sign of a woman on his head, and the frock of a woman down to his feet, understanding very well that through the added power of the positive and negative principles acting upon each other, a point of equilibrium is reached. This is found in Masonry today.

During the early centuries the Christian faith took root in the Pagan Mysteries, concealing her symbols within its philosophy. Naturally the Church grew up and around the old Mysteries, whose secret doctrine may have faded but did not entirely disappear, though apparently it was lost at the time.

The cult of Rome is founded upon symbols which were pre-existent and pre-Christian. The Trinity, hexad, and hepdomad or ogdoad, without the original keys, are literally preposterous. Jesus, son of Mary; Buddha, son of Maya; Hermes, son of Maia -- these are the same in Divine Sonship, which is mystically represented at Rome. The Great Father, strangely, when considering the immensity of the known past, is almost wholly absent from early monuments claimed to be Christian.

Religions are but paths or steps to the unfoldment of universal truths. Religion is operative and speculative. It is the latter that has often proved the shifting sands of theological opinions. Gates of Wisdom need special keys with which to open them. Beneath the sublime allegories of the Builders of the Temples is secreted the Wisdom of the Ages.

At Northern banquets, toasts to Odin, Thor and Frey were substituted to the honor of our Savior and the saints. Ancient Pagan festivals were held three times a year, when courts under the direction of the Priesthood were opened for legal business. These fetes were entirely religious in character. "After the politic substitution of our Savior, the Virgin Mary and the saints for heathen dieties," ecclesiastical authorities ordained that these festival days should be made sacred to Christianity but under new restrictions and that the health of Christ and the Virgin should be toasted as a thanksgiving for peace and plenty. Christmas, All Saints' and Saint John's Day were given for this purpose.

"In the Eighth Century there still existed guilds whose express object was the celebration of the mystical, and perhaps repulsive, rites of Thor, Odin and Frey." (1) These guilds and ceremonies were not molested by ecclesiastical authorities. The ancient symbolic ritualism, adapted to the worship of these divinities, was preserved in altered form by succeeding Teutonic associations, among them the Medieval guild of Masons. Medieval guilds were under the direct patronage of the church and arbitrarily controlled by the clergy. "Priestcraft and sacerdotal influence may be found in every guildic document which has escapted interpolation and the zeal of enthusiastic theorists." (2)

A sworn and secret organization of a later epoch was then instituted, but in a limited degree, and banquets under a Christian regime remained as an integral part of civil society. Women were admitted to these associations to make up the sacred number needed for a perfect organization; and in a later history of them, wives and sisters became members.

In 838, monks of the Gallic monasteries formed a guild combining charity with religion. The statute of Saint John's Guild was chiefly composed of goldsmiths, and began with the 133rd Psalm: "How good and pleasant it is for brethren to dwell together in Unity!" This is an integral part of the Masonic Ritualism today.

---
(1) - FORT, GEORGE F.; THE EARLY HISTORY & ANTIQUITIES OF FREEMASONRY, P. 395.
(2) - FORT, George F.; THE EARLY HISTORY & ANTIQUITIES OF FREEMASONRY, P. 399

Oath-bound societies at the close of the Eighth Century had become so numerous and the vice of inebriety so great that Charlemagne and his successors enacted a series of imperial edicts to reduce them to a less objectionable limitation. Penalties were instigated against those who persisted in membership in sworn corporations. Degeneracy through the oath-bound societies had been rampant. These edicts were enacted in an endeavor to cut out Pagan tendencies which persisted, those involving the recognition of Odin, Thor and Frey being among the lists of forbidden usages.

During the Tenth and Twelfth Centuries control of associations passed from the church, and from this followed the struggle for supremacy between the civil and ecclesiastical authorities. The "spirit had gone forth and could no longer be restrained." Oath-bound societies never disappeared from the Teutonic governments and associations. They were preserved through the Middle Ages and initiated members into the Mysteries of secret ritualism, teaching the significance of a mystic language. They had lucky and unlucky numbers, symbolic colors, and certain signs were used by the Initiates for recognition.

There is a striking identity between the appointment of Masonic Lodges and the symbolic appliances of ancient courts. In these ancient courts the same formularies were used by legal bodies in the administration of justice as were used by the Pagans; the procedure was the same. Rites and ceremonies used in Gothic courts furnish Freemasonry with a skeleton of Norse customs upon which Judiastic Ritualism was hung. Evangelists introducing Christianity among Germanic races and their guilds could not blot out Paganistic customs, though intrigued to do so by both evangelists and missionaries. Their history led too far back into the twilight of time, which was in accord with the earliest records of the Gothic races.

Secret arts obtained by the Teutonic races were perpetuated in guilds descending from the oldest form of Germanic government. It does not seem to be known whether sacerdotal sanction was given in the form of charters, but under the Pope they were absolved from territorial restrictions. A charter has not come with the traditions of the craft. Symbolic references, still in use in lodges of Freemasonry, proved they had united with Germanic guilds under ecclesiastical patronage at that period.

In the Eighth Century, a regularly subordinated organization of masters and pupils with lofty ideals was established in the cloisters of Germany, under the patronage of Charlemagne. It is to his credit that he organized these schools of science over which proficient monks and abbots presided. After the extinction of the Lombard Kingdom in the year 774, he recognized the Christian Church for the purpose of having all heathen religion exterminated. In this he was rigorously opposed by the Saxons.

About the end of the Seventh Century, or the beginning of the Eighth, two important events occurred. The first of these, and its relative effect upon the translation of a style in art, was a decree current in Western Europe, made known by an ecclesiastical council in Constantinople in the year 692, prohibiting the use of allegorical or symbolical representations, such as the Crucifixion of Christ or other sacred objects. This was never rigidly adhered to in Western Europe but was modified to an excess that was absurd. At the time of this degree, plastic art compositions were treated hieroglyphically, and to interpret them, it was necessary to know the inner secret.

The second and more important event was the proscription of religious images pronounced by Leo, the Iconoclast, in the year 726. This represented a persecution of the Greek artists which lasted 120 years, banishing from the Eastern churches all statuary and paintings without reserve. Any artist who even dared to prepare an image of Christ, of Saints, or of Apostles, was punished with the greatest severity.

The Greeks were thoroughly imbued with a Judaistic element which had surrounded them in Constantinople and merged into the Gothic guilds of Northern Italy, as early as the Fifth Century. Italy had many Greeks who had fled from iconoclastic wars and who were gradually taken into the Fraternities. Greek corporations possessed exclusive details in church building under ecclesiastical sanction and gave their art to the Northern Italians.

"The profound knowledge of mathematics and astronomy embodied in ancient architecture, and the equally profound knowledge of anatomy revealed in Greek statuary, prove how the fashioners of both were master-minds." Philosophy and logic also permeated the air of Greece.

In Greece the most perfect expression of symmetry was found. Her people cultivated the aesthetic arts as they had the power of rhythmic thinking and harmonious living. Their architecture, therefore, was of beauty and of great importance.

German architectural art was developed and awakened to its highest attainment through the great rapidity with which Germany unfolded, principally due to the incoming Greek and Gothic artists, with the infusion of the cloistered schools and the thorough organization effected through them and their culture. These became divided into the seven liberal arts as we have them today. Grammar, rhetoric, logic, arithmetic, geometry, music and astronomy represented the basis of a finished art in the Middle Ages, and still survive today in modern Masonry.

The maintenance of the arts and sciences by Charlemagne among many of his subjects during a reign of barbarism regenerated architectural arts, sciences, painting and music, and "the Canon of the Council of Nice, urging the worship of images, was submitted by him to a council of bishops at Frankfort, and by his authority re-enacted," in order that the characteristics of the religious culture should be upheld. Then Leo, the Iconoclast, issued another edict that all the churches in his kingdom should be dignified with suitable sacred statuary and imagery.

About the Tenth Century, Teutonic symbolism was incorporated in Medieval Lodges. During the Eleventh Century, ecclesiastical wrath exploded, which led to constructors being united by mutual oaths, thus strengthening their associations. In the monastic orders during the Eleventh Century, workers were received as brothers without having to make the formal vows or assuming the costume of the monk. Neophytes attended to their duties while looking forward to their increase in wages, and in token of their submission, a bell-rope was bound about their throat -- suggestive of the Cable-tow today. A thorough knowledge of all the arts, also given to those not connected with the cloisters, was thus attained. Painting on glass was assigned to the Tenth Century under ecclesiastical instruction.

Endeavors were made to wrest from the cloisters and monasteries the ecclesiastical possessions of architectural and plastic art, through which enormous wealth had been attained. With the decline of religious fervor, deterioration through luxury, dissipation and dissolute habits had crept in, sapping the nervous energy of the clergy. Nearly all spiritual knowledge was ignored, although the building of beautiful churches and chapels continued to attract the popular mind and deceive the people as to the true conditions.

Also, neophytes were allowed in these cloisters without monkish attire or pledge, and many outsiders came there to work. The greatness of the arts was thus taken out into the world. Out of the constant confusion which existed, the citizens were compelled to join more intimate associations at the point of self-preservation, in order to maintain their property as well as their own personal security; yet many monks worked with zealous assiduity. The new social conditions caused the laymen to lose their exclusive possessions.

Very much that happened during these times can be followed further by students interested in those periods of trial, when convents and monasteries became almost like fortresses -- when civilization, under some sainted martyr, was allowed to pursue its way quietly in happiness, in absorbing and creative work through knowledge of "astronomy, arithmetic, geometry, civil law, physics, and medicine. Studies of profane authors were all sheltered within these walls as within a sanctuary."

From the old Dionysian architects "doubtless sprang the guilds of the Traveling Masons known in the Middle Ages." Their works are still found in old-world buildings. The square, compasses, rule, mallet and other tools -- magic tools -- were all incorporated in their decorations. The tools of the Dionysians were used to conceal the Mysteries of the soul and the regeneration of man -- secrets that were revealed only to the Initiated.

The checkerboard floor, under speculative reasoning, was an old Tracing-Board of theirs. The Operative and Speculative Masons went together when the world was in its human forming, realizing that Humanity as a whole was the unpolished ashlar just out of its elemental nature; and by truing, polishing, and squaring the ashlar they hoped to bring the Soul of Humanity into a "Miracle of Beauty."

Even the swing of the hammer was in rhythm with the forces of the Cosmos. Their sacred temples were built on geometrical proportions which they had divinized from the constellations of heaven, knowing that the celestial gave both the spiritual and mystical, which they embodded in their work.

Dionysian architects belonged to a very ancient secret society; they were well known 1,000 B.C. They were closely bound as an organization because of their deep knowledge and understanding of both early and divine calculations. They had a secret language or system in making their stones. It is unknown just what the nature of their secret doctrine was. Their organization was composed entirely of Initiates, their ceremonies were secret, and with the rise of the Roman Empire they found their way into Europe and England. Vitruvious, the mystic architect, was one of the most illustrious of their number.

To illustrate the studies of the old architects and their intensely human and spiritual conceptions, the following is quoted from one of the works of Vitruvious:

"The design of a temple depends upon symmetry, the principles of which must be carefully observed by the architect. They are due to proportion. Proportion is a correspondence among the members of an entire work, and of the whole to a certain part selected as a standard. From this results the principle of symmetry.

"Without symmetry and proportion there can be no principle in the design of any temple; that is, there is no precise relation between its members, as in the case of those of a well-shaped man. For the human body is so designed by Nature that the face, from the chin to the top of the forehead, and the lowest roots of the hair, is a tenth-part of the whole height; the open hand, from the wrist to the tip of the middle finger, is just the same; the head, from the chin to the crown, is an eighth, and with the neck and shoulders, from the top of the breast to the lowest roots of the hair, is a sixth; from the middle of the breast to the summit of the crown is a fourth. If we take the height of the face itself, the distance from the bottom of the chin to the under side of the nostrils, and from that point to a line between the eyebrows is the same; from there to the lowest roots of the hair is also a third, comprising the forehead.

"The length of the foot is one-sixth of the height of the body; of the forearm, one-fourth; and the breadth of the breast is also one-fourth. The other members, too, have their own symmetrical proportions, and it was by employing them that the famous painters and sculptors of antiquity attained to great and endless renown."

Buildings constructed by these great architects were "sermons in stone." Ancient people erected temples to one god or an assemblage of gods, each god representing an attribute of Deity. All had their analogies in the human body. "Initiates of old warned their disciples that an image is not a reality but merely the objectification of a subjective idea." Images of gods were not designed to be objects of worship but reminders only of invisible powers. The body of man is not the individual, but the house of the individual.

When the Guild of Builders became established they concealed their sacred doctrine in their work -- marvelous work, filled with the rhythm of perfect accomplishment. These early workers deserved their Initiations by making themselves worthy to receive the Wages of the Master Mason, setting an example to all workers of today by accepting that abstract knowledge, "veiled in allegory and illustrated in symbols," making an Apprentice conscious of the great work that lies ahead for the age of the Incoming Light.

Guilds spread very rapidly, as well as associations; and the intimacy between Apprentice and Master made for a relationship as close as that of a family. Owing to the rapidity with which the guilds were instituted, having been carried to too great an extreme, they came to an untimely end in the Twelfth Century.

During the Eleventh Century, guilds of Freemasons attained a definite position, and architectural art passed from the property of the cloisters. Certain writers claim that this change took place in the Twelfth Century.

These guilds of Builders -- Freemasons -- were composed of men who were bound by religious vows, and many noble cathedrals were erected during the Eleventh Century, due to the great skill of the workmen. The origin of these guilds was traced to the first Germanic societies. Many fragments of heathen rites and observances passed into them and into succeeding Medieval Fraternities. Teutonic mythology, from its earliest contact with the Eastern builders, as far back as the Fifth Century and through the centuries following, contributed very largely to Masonic symbolism.

"The guilds of constructors or Freemasons appropriated the several degrees which, as we have already seen, existed in the monasteries at a very early age; viz., Apprentice, Fellow and Master. As these fraternities were reorganized under church patronage, they imbibed at their inception a strong religious sentiment -- a characteristic which has come down with Masonic Lodges from past ages." (1)

During the Eleventh and Twelfth Centuries these societies of constructors became established and spread their influence upon architecture in Europe. Many prodigious works were executed towards the end of the Eleventh Century. It was at this time that the arts passed into secret organizations controlled by laymasters and were incorporated into Masonic Fraternities.

The conquest of England by William, Duke of Normandy, occurred in 1066, when artists from France emigrated into England and were initiated into the Masonic order, thereby greatly raising the fame that was contributed by them to the Operative Masonic institution. King William was the builder of the square towers of London, and forts surrounding the country. There was great advancement in the art of building at this time, both in beauty and design.

But it was the Twelfth Century that was called the Age of Architecture, then more advanced in England than at any other time. In 1176, Great Britain depended upon foreign artists for the construction of her principal architecture. It is well known that William, the Conqueror, deluged the whole of England with French artificers, almost to the extinction of the Anglo-Saxon element. Also, Masonic arts or rules of architecture were produced on French soil by Greek or Byzantine operatives.

Under Henry I, third son of William, who ascended the throne in 1100, the Masonic order was greatly fostered and protected. Craftsmen at this time knew nothing of the secrets of their masters, whose symbols were unintelligible to them. Not until they had proved themselves worthy were they raised to the Holy Arch degree. Afterwards they were known as Companions, and if intelligent

---

(1) - FORT, George F., THE EARLY HISTORY & ANTIQUITIES OF FREEMASONRY, P. 73

enough, they were further advanced in knowledge and skill on the way towards discovering that hidden scheme upon which Masonry was founded. It seems to have been through prudence, simplicity, and respectability in their Order that the Masons flourished in Great Britain, when Masonry was almost abolished in other parts of the world. Long after Masonry was extinguished in the Continental kingdoms, it still flourished in England, probably due to English super-prudence, thus eluding the suspicions of its enemies. By some writers it is said that the principles of the order were imported into Scotland, and continued there in primitive simplicity. There is no conclusive evidence that the secrets of English Masonry were given to the Scotch. They were at this time too thoroughly imbued with popery to embrace the Masonic religious point of view; but whenever the spiritual jurisdiction of the Pope was acknowledged during the Twelfth Century, the demands for religious structures prevailed, and in no kingdom in Europe was the church more richly endowed than in Scotland. It is also conclusive that the ruins found in Scotland today were erected by foreign Masons.

The Fraternities of England maintained that at about the end of the Third Century St. Alban brought Masonry into England. Masonry was unknown in England until the time of St. Alban. He instructed the King -- a Pagan -- in Masonry as well as in Divinity. At this time English kings still practised ancient Rites, the ruling monarch disliking intensely the principles of the Christian Creed. The King induced St. Alban to wall the town which subsequently bore the name of St. Alban. He became high in favor with the King and received the honors of knighthood, was a trusted steward of the royal household, and the realm was governed by him under this King.

St. Alban cherished the Masons with much zeal, and truly paid them weekly with higher wages, and enacted a schedule of pay thenceforth to be observed throughout the realm, namely, 11s. and 6d a week; or other than a Mason, 11 d. a week. (It has also been stated that a Mason received 3s. 6d. a week). Up to the time of St. Alban an English Mason received only a penny with his meat for each day of labor.

The King and Council granted the Masons a Charter for better government and further empowered them to assemble in general convention. To this convocation the name Assembly was given. St. Alban attended the Assembly and helped personally in making many Masons. The most valuable contribution from this great prelate to the Craft thus convened was a set of Charges. ("Many of the records containing the history of St. Alban and the Craft were said to have been purposely destroyed in the year 1720, through misguided zeal." (1)

After the death of St. Alban, England was torn with internal troubles from foreign invasions to such an extent that Masonry was practically suspended until King Athelstane reigned and brought the land finally to peace and quietude. Athelstane began building many monasteries, abbeys and other religious structures, besides divers castles and fortresses for the defense of his realm. His half-brother, Edwin, was a genius in geometry, which he sedulously practised, and from pure affection was initiated into the secret Mysteries of Masonry. He gathered about him numerous peoples from other lands. He

---

(1) - PRESTON, - ILLUSTRATIONS OF MASONRY.

procured a charter and commission for the Masons to hold a yearly assembly in whatever locality they might choose to convene within the realm; and among other concessions enumerated in this warrant was the power to correct defaults and trespasses which might hinder the progress of Masonry. Prince Edwin enacted a system of Charges and established certain usages which the Craft must always obey. He himself retained the charter, demanding that it should be renewed under succeeding reigns.

When the famous assemblage of Masons was held at York, with Edwin as Grand Commander, a proclamation was made by him that everything belonging to a Mason, old or young, having any connection with Masonic Charges or usages, whether in writing or given orally, and belonging to this or any other country, must be produced. Many of the writings brought forth were in French, English and Greek, and some were in Hebrew and other languages, the spirit of all being identical. (1) (Halliwell and Cooke, in their manuscripts, say nothing of Hebrew and Greek.) They were gathered together and Edwin caused them all to be drawn up in book form, declaring in his preface how the Masonic science was first invented. He commanded that in the future, at the making of a Mason, these Charges should be read or recited to the candidate; and from that time to this, Masonic usages have rapidly conformed to this order as far as possible.

Since the time of Edwin many new articles have been added to the Charges which seemed essential to the interests of the Fraternities, by the advice and consent of the Masters and Fellows under the sanction of God, and the holy-dome, and upon the Book. This Book was to be held in the hands of a Warden, that he or they who were accepted Masons should place their hands in position upon it while the Charges were being read. If anyone was guilty of violating them, he "must make humble amends to God," for a Mason must ever be true to his God.

The above record of Athelstane and Prince Edwin is generally understood and accepted, as truths always underlie legends; and the tradition concerning the Masonic convocation rests upon Anderson, though but a mere assertion. "A history of this event was written in 1475 by Edward IV, and upon a copy of Gothic articles alleged to have been made by Richard II, between the years 1367 and 1399, nearly five hundred years subsequent to the time alleged for this legendary assembly." The manuscript merely states that Masonry was introduced at the time of Athelstane. This is numbered and lettered in the Library of the British Museum: Royal MSS., 17, A1, folio 5. Positive authority for this definite time is only presumed. It had been copied from an older and more ancient parchment, or transcribed from bits of fragmentary traditions, but it is in tradition that truths are to be found.

Edwin of York lived about the year 926. His half-brother Athelstane was an illegitimate son of Edward, the Elder. Athelstane was really a great king; and it is very likely that an organization of the Craft did eventuate in Edwin's time. In support of this it is stated that no other Lodge laid greater claim to an older antiquity than that of York; and perhaps it may be better to claim that York was the birthplace of Freemasonry in

---

(1) - In Cooke's Manuscript, No. 23,198, it is claimed that "the copyist had before him an older parchment, which contained the following remarkable phraseology: 'And it is said, in old books of Masonry, that Solomon confirmed the charges,' etc."

England, though no additional evidence is given to support the stories of St. Alban, Athelstane and Edwin.

Some old writers look upon this document with suspicion and denial, but ."In Germany this document occupied a very prominent place, even down to our times, and had much influence. Krause, Schneider, Fessler and many more, considered it as genuine, indeed as the most ancient extant." (1)

The destruction of many manuscripts rendered investigation of Masonic history intricate but by no means impossible. Any mystery concerning its development may be solved, as it is written that, by "turning back the leaves of ages may be found many epochs that have arisen from their obscurity."

It is well to seek and learn what may have been hidden in legends of ancient times. Due to their disfigurement and unhealthy translations, truths and many ancient secrets have been hidden and denied the world today.

"A guild of Masons was undoubtedly in existence in London in 1375, 49th Edward III." Some authors claim that Masonry was established in England at the Apple Tree Inn, in 1717, and from there radiated over the world.

During the time of Elias Ashmole, the last of the Alchemists (a Rosicrucian who was born in 1646 and died in 1692), Masonry was a true secret society. About thirty years afterwards, that which is termed Freemasonry became established -- should we not say, re-established? --- on the 24th day of June, 1717, in the Apple Tree Inn. A contributor to the Archaeologia, states that "Master Masons were not organized into a corporation under law as a society of Freemasons until the Thirteenth Century."

Also it is claimed that Freemasonry was first established in England after the death of Canute, at the beginning of the Eleventh Century, when he prohibited in toto the Druidical order. Much seems conjectural, but behind the traditions truth will be found.

---

(1) - FINDEL, J. G., - HISTORY OF FREEMASONRY, Page 96.

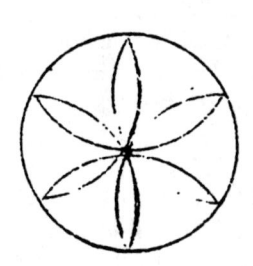

Chapter X

ARCHITECTURE

"Chisel, Man, out of the living block
of the ether, your fate --
Hammer it early; hammer it late;
Out of pulsating Earth, Air, Water
and Fire
Carve the tall Temple of your desire."
-- Mary Siegrist.

WHEN the seat of the Roman Empire was changed to Constantinople, in the year 328, Rome lost her greatness, and from that time philosophy and architecture gradually deteriorated. Those who endeavored to nurture the old arts and sciences resided in Constantinople, and thus it came about that in the Capital of the Eastern Empire everything pertaining to the arts and sciences was preserved; and this light of the East was destined to be carried to distant lands.

Constantinople became the emporium of Masons, architects, artists and skilled artificers. The Ancient Builders for a time were lost sight of, but they were only hidden in the shadows of chaos and confusion so pronounced in the changing of all great world Cycles. (One was being ushered in at about that time.) But old symbolisms representing basic truths never die and are found in all pre-historic legends, myths, and allegories concerning that Ancient Wisdom which is eternal. As the veil lifts, the power and creativeness of the Supreme Knowledge of the Ancient Builder will assert itself in the modern world. Gradually the old and reverenced beauty of architecture will be reborn. The Ancient Builder becomes the Operative Mason, entering the age of unfoldment, uncovering the knowledge of old symbols that always lie in silence at the base of ancient architecture.

At this time efforts were made by Marcus Aurelius to stimulate architecture. He used his power to bring about a return of the true in art, but his efforts failed. Under the Diocletian architects, the perpendicular form of architecture, opposed to the horizontal form of the Greeks, determined a transition period, bringing in gradually a well-defined style that prevailed through the Middle Ages. With its beautiful columns and graceful arches it finally reached the Gothic, and so on to a full development of the perpendicular lines.

"Inhabitants of Northern France, who had a large portion of German blood in their veins, are thought to have originated the Gothic style of architecture; for there in the period between 1160 and 1170 it made its appearance. Thence quickly transplanted to England, afterwards to Germany." (1) "The future improvement of the Gothic style, as well as its perfection was reserved nevertheless for the Germans" who were the creators of the pointed or lancet style, recognizing the vital force connected with it. This pointed style and arch became the prevailing style and was brought to its highest perfection,

---

(1) - FINDEL, J. G., - HISTORY OF FREEMASONRY, Page 53.

developing an infinite variety of pictorial work elaborated on geometrical lines. Its great glory was perfect unity and endless variety of exquisite lace-like detail.

"The mathematical rules of proportion appropriate to this style were brought in the Lodges of German Stone-cutters and communicated to each other as secrets appertaining especially to their art." (1) "These were the Stonemasons, from the midst of whom arose the Fraternity of Freemasons." (2)

Strassburg Cathedral is the finest specimen of Gothic or German architecture. No cathedral or sacred structure has received greater eulogistic praise than this one received when it was finally completed. Its original foundation was constructed of timber and was laid in the year 504. In the year 798 Charlemagne had a choir of stone laid, which was subsequently destroyed. Afterwards Bishop Werner had plans drawn for a new foundation which was laid in the year 1015 by Grecian architects brought to Germany by Bishop Meinwerk. The nave of the Cathedral was finished in 1275. In 1277 Erwin of Steinbach, together with other Master Builders, laid the foundation for further completion. It was through his skill that great beauty was added to the building, especially in the symmetrical exquisiteness of the portals on the south side.

Sabina von Steinbach gave her father most valuable assistance in preparing with her own hands several columns which constituted the chief ornaments of the south portal. She received instruction in the secret arts. At that time, in Germany, such knowledge as she possessed was almost the exclusive property of men. She was obligated to profound secrecy, with the penalty of severe punishment in case of violation. Thus a woman, as early as the Thirteenth Century, had been a Freemason. Some Medieval guilds freely admitted women to share the privilege of membership. Stieglitz makes the statement that "in the case of admission of a member's wife, the fee of entrance was reduced; but an unmarried woman paid the same price as man."

The York Lodge has a manuscript of 1693 giving regulations of the Craft, in which the following appears:

"Thee one of the elders takeing the Booke
And that <u>hee</u> or <u>shee</u> that is to be made Mason," etc. (3)

Saint Stephen's, of Vienna, is a masterpiece of the Gothic or Teutonic art -- the work of Medieval Freemasons.

Among the churches at the beginning of the Thirteenth Century the minster of Magdeberg remains to attest the purity and beauty of the Gothic in its variety of sectional and profusely elaborated style on geometrical lines. This Cathedral was begun under the auspices of Bishop Adalbert, in the year 1208. Bausak was the Master Builder.

---

(1) - FINDEL, J. G.; HISTORY OF FREEMASONRY, Page 49.
(2) - Ibid   Page 53
(3) - HUGUAN'S OLD MASONIC CHARGES, Page 15.

One of the most notable structures of this period, also, was the Cologne Cathedral. This city had possessed a minster as early as the time of Charlemagne. "In the year 1162, Frederick I ...... presented to this church a costly sarcophagus containing the relics of three holy canonized kings of the East. This sacred object attracted many noblemen and rich princes who, together with others equally pious, greatly enriched the cathedral with large sums of money. In order that these gifts might be suitably appropriated, it was decided to erect a minster which should correspond to the dignity and importance of such a monument." [1]

Engelbrecht, archbishop of Cologne, desired to undertake the construction, but he died in 1225. In 1228 a fire destroyed the old cathedral, but in the same year the archbishop, Count Hochsteben, began a new building, which progressed slowly until the year 1322, when the choir was consecrated. At various periods the work was resumed, until it ceased in the Sixteenth Century. The architect who drew the plans for this structure seems to be unknown. The name of Gebhard, however -- a Master Workman -- has come down to us when, in 1872, the work of finishing the cathedral was begun.

Portugal also had a notable specimen of Gothic art in her church at Batalha, founded at the close of the Fourteenth Century by King John I, who brought together many Master Builders. Among them, in the year 1378, is found the name Hacket, a native of Ireland and a member of the Traveling Fraternity of Freemasons; but he had certainly not derived his art from his native country.

Many churches in Holland, the Netherlands, and Belgium showed the work of Master Masons -- also noticed in the city halls of Antwerp, Brussels, Leuven and Vlissingen. Other cities of the Low Countries also possessed the Gothic type. The Antwerp Cathedral was founded in 1422 by Johannes Aurelius, and was completed in 1518.

Through the Scandinavian provinces of Northern Europe, German Master Builders journeyed, creating their mystical art from diagrams obtained in the close-tiled Lodges of their craft -- the airy, beautiful, delicate traceries of Gothic art. At an earlier age the Byzantine workmen reared more sober structures and temples, the finest being that at Upsala, Sweden, commenced in the year 1258 and finished in the year 1453. The Master Architect of this one was Erich, of Pomerania.

Spain also received her impetus from German artists. The cathedrals at Segovia, Toledo and Burgos were masterpieces of style. The foundation of the cathedral at Burgos was laid in the Thirteenth Century; it was finished by German Masons. Many details and plans of this cathedral are identical with those of the one at Strassburg.

In the year 1290 the foundation of the cathedral at Orviete was laid and a Builder's Lodge was held there while work was in progress. A Lodge of Masons existed at this place while at labor on the minster under the jurisdiction of a German Master.

"The word _Lodge_ is, perhaps, immediately derived from the Norman-French, apparently imported into England by French artists shortly after the

---

(1) - FORT, George F.; THE EARLY HISTORY & ANTIQUITIES OF MASONRY, Page 79

conquest." <u>Loggia</u>, Italian, is closely allied to the French, <u>Loge</u>. <u>Logeum</u> was used by Vitruvious to denote a small enclosed space for actors. Houses of ancient Gauls were called Logia. In the Medieval metrical romance of King Alisander, the word occurs to describe a tent or temporary resting-place, which was, no doubt, its signification among nomadic Freemasons.

"Alisander doth crye wyde,
His Logges set on the water syde."

Many other authorities, including Hughan, use the early English word "Loge," meaning resting-place, or lodge.

German or Gothic architecture, during the Thirteenth Century, radiated over nearly all the countries of Europe, with the exception of Italy; but even there a mixture of Gothic and Byzantine was clearly noticed, especially in the Church of San Francisco, at Assisi, and others. "The most striking example of this strange intermingling of the lofty and the sublime with the humble and diminutive is to be seen in the cathedral at Milan."(1) Though the Gothic generally prevailed, Italy perhaps servilely imitated the delicate elaboration of detail of the Germanic architects, but failed to catch the spirit of inspiration that produced it.

Towards the close of the Fourteenth Century, the foundations of the Milan Cathedral were laid. The original plans are still preserved in the Cathedral, and are uniformly inscribed to a German artist. In Rome, the Cathedral of St. Paul, in Gothic style, is the most distinguished for its artistic work. The Master Builder who superintended the work was a German and a very distinguished Mason among the craft in Germany.

In 976, St. Marc's Cathedral in Venice was rebuilt. Grecian artists were imported to build the foundations. St. Marc's was laid on the foundation of a church previously destroyed. No sooner was this work finished than construction of the Cathedral of Pisa was begun under Buschetto -- 1016-1063. He had come with a cargo of statuettes, columns, bas-reliefs, and many fragments of Oriental art. This artist formed an institution or lodge which lived for 150 years, and produced the famous Nicholas Pisano.

The collection of moneys with which to defray their expenses in the building of great cathedrals, together with the wages given Masons in Medieval days, are matters of great interest. The building of the Cathedral of Pisa by Operative Masons was contributed to by the people. Each family was expected to give until the amount necessary had been subscribed, and the sum paid by each family was said to be about twenty shillings, in English reckoning. The city numbered 34,000 families; therefore the yearly income was about 34,000 pounds sterling. In some ways they had difficulty in procuring this amount, but public funds were donated and princely gifts were made by kings, from Sicily, as well as from the Byzantine emperors. In the year 1165, proceeds from important festivals were donated. For the building of the church of St. Antonius, at Padua, in 1265, 4,000 lira were donated, and as a general thing, paid yearly until the church was finished. During the year 1267, Nicholas Pisano worked as a Master Stonecutter in the Sienna Cathedral, receiving for his wage eight pison solidi.

---

(1) - The first clock for public use in Italy was placed in the bell-tower of Saint Eustorgis, in the City of Milan, in the year 1306.

Nicholas Pisano reached a very high attainment in art, and towards the close of the Twelfth Century raised Italy into a far finer and nobler condition of art. His son, Giovanni, was also a Master Builder, and gave to his ideas an expression of all that was ideal. He had been influenced by the German stonecutters and showed a path towards the sublime in his conception of art. Giotto worked under his instruction. He was a marvelous architect, as well as sculptor, and has been immortalized through Dante.

Borghese, a Florentine, received his instruction in the Mysteries of Masonry or Masonic art, and in 1284 was competent, together with another Master Mason, to assume direction of the workmen in the building of the Vatican.

Nicholas Pisano was not only renowned as an architect and stonecutter, but became an exalted celebrity through his most exquisite workmanship on the arch of San Dominico, at Bologna. He it was who added to his "Masonic excellence" and distinguished himself by stealing one of the ribs of St. Dominic which, through Medieval superstition, was claimed to be invested with supernal powers. As a petty crime, this was dignified as a "pious fraud." (Marchese.)

Florence was a city of great art and architecture. Guilds of Masons were thoroughly established in Italy during the Thirteenth Century. In the year 1233, Master Masons there were under the control of particular church organizations; and numerous guilds of Masons were assembled in Florence towards the close of the Thirteenth Century. Over the portal of the Cathedral of Santa Croce, in Florence, is a figure of Christ holding a perfect square in his hand, and in one of the niches of the façade are life-size figures in Masonic attitudes.

For the building of these beautiful cathedrals, people were sent out into the world like radiations, with plenary powers, to accumulate sufficient money for the great structures. So intense, so reverential was the sentiment of the people that even noblemen and their families took part in a financial way, giving many valuable gifts, noteworthy and sacrificial, showing the high standard of help so fervently given because the structures were dedicated to God.

"The mysterious emblem known as the Vesica Piscis is still in the form ⬬ of a fish's mouth, 'or outrance into life'" from which it originated. The first child born was not a human being, as all beginnings were celestial. The Vesica Piscis has since become a co-type, but not in its origin, of the human birthplace, and "this has been continued as a symbol of the birthplace when that which was pre-human was reapplied to the human organ. In the course of doctrinal development, geometrical and astronomical figures are blended in the Vesica." [1]

The true foundation of all Gothic churches is based upon the humanized Vesica Piscis, which ushered in the change from the Norman style of architecture based upon the square, - and endless have been its wonders.

---
(1) - MASSEY, Gerald, ANCIENT EGYPT: THE LIGHT OF THE WORLD, Page 283.

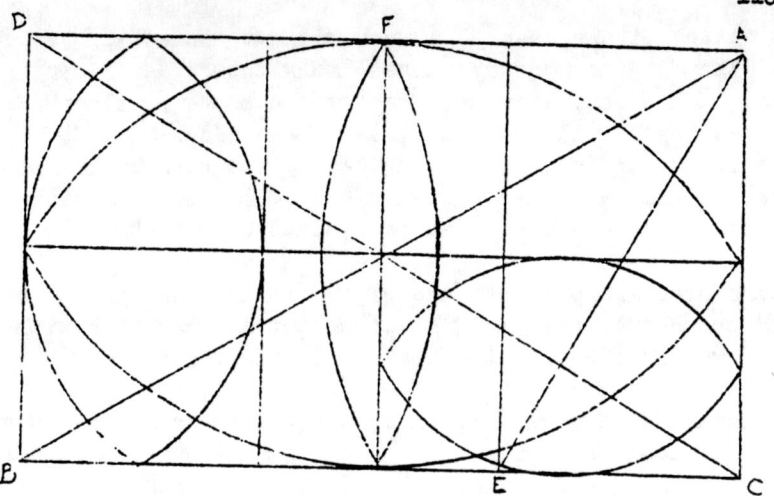

The Vesica Piscis,
Foundation of Gothic Architecture, creating the equilateral triangle. "The diagonal AB of this figure, and the diagonal AE of the subsidiary figure, which is also a plumb line, actually trisect the angle DAC."
-- Frater Achad.

"The rectangle formed by the length and breadth of this mysterious figure, in its simplest form, has several extraordinary qualities; it may be cut into three equal parts, by straight lines parallel to its shorter sides; and these parts will all be precisely and geometrically similar to each other and to the whole figure, (strangely applicable to the symbolism attached at that time to the Trinity in Unity), and this sub-division may be proceeded with indefinitely without making any change in form; however often the operation is performed, the parts remain identical with the original figure, having all its extraordinary properties, and no other rectangle can have this curious property. ....

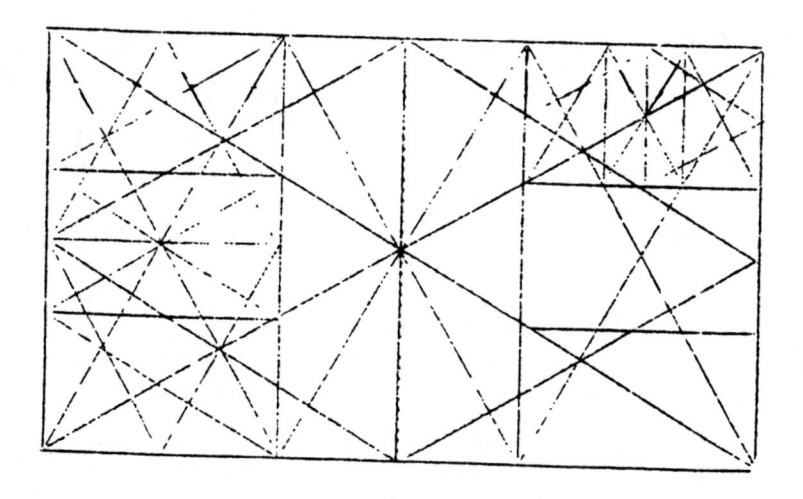

Foundation of Gothic Architecture.
- Frater Achad.

"It may also be cut into four equal parts by straight lines parallel to the two sides, and again each of these parts will be exactly similar to each other and to the whole, and the process may be continued indefinitely, the equilateral triangle appearing everywhere. Once more, if two of the tri-sub-divisions be taken, the form of these together is exactly similar geometrically to half of the original figure, and the equilateral triangle again appears everywhere in both. . . . (See second figure on Page 118.) . . .

"To those who studied geometry and to whom the figure was a symbol of the Divinity in Unity, it was a fact that it actually put into their hands the means of trisecting the right angle. Now the three great problems of antiquity which engaged the attention of geometricians throughout the Middle Ages were the 'duplication of the cube,' 'the squaring of the circle,' and lastly, 'the trisection of the angle,' even Euclid being unable to show how to do it." (1)

Architecture of the Gothic period with its deep religious significance and the beauty of the most important cathedrals and churches cannot be denied. It had been produced from this original figure, which was not only looked upon as a symbol of the Trinity but was that part which was bounded by the area of the two circles and took to itself one-third of each of the two generating circles in which the triangle was formed. This was held in very early times as a most sacred Christian emblem, symbolizing generation and a new birth. The Door of Life, the feminine or Western end of a Christian Church, is figured in the shape of the Vesica.

Early Fathers spoke of Christians as Pisciculi. "When subjects such as these were treated, Maimonides commanded his hearers: 'When you have discovered the meaning thereof, do not divulge it, because the people cannot philosophize or understand that to the Infinite there is no such thing as sex.'" (2)

The unspeakable mystery attached to the Vesica Piscis, save in rare instances, has prevented it from being generally spoken of. "It possessed unbounded influence on the details of sacred architecture; and it constituted the great and enduring secret of our ancient brethren. The places of religious buildings were determined by its use; and the proportions of length and height were dependent on it alone." (3)

It was known to Plato and to his Egyptian Masters in the Egyptian colleges. To the old builders it was "an archetype of ideal beauty." It had also been stated that "the elementary letters of the primitive language were derived from this same mystical symbol."

It is well known to Freemasons, architects and old Masonic writers that the mysterious and mystical figure, the Vesica Piscis, so popular in the Middle Ages and generally placed as a first proposition, and of geometrical

---

(1) - FRATER ACHAD - THE ANATOMY OF THE BODY OF GOD, Pages 9, 10, 11; and Trans. Quatuor Coronati Lodge, Vol. XXIII, 1910, Sidney T. Klein.
(2) - FRATER ACHAD - THE ANATOMY OF THE BODY OF GOD, Page 8.
(3) - OLIVER, George, D. D.

proportions, is found in the 47th problem of Euclid. It was the symbol Masons used in planning their temples. In this 47th problem we find that in every right-angle triangle the sum of the square of the base and perpendicular is equal to the square of the hypotenuse, symbolically giving the great Masonic triad: Wisdom, Strength and Beauty.

To the old Masonic writers the foundation of all geometrical systems, as well as the true system of the universe, was found in this 47th problem of Euclid, as given by Pythagoras; by Plato also, in writing. "The names of the Oriental Hipparchi and Euclid, who solved the first problems of anatomy and geometry, are unknown."

In the East, the Vesica Piscis was used as a symbol of the female productive organs, and when joined to the cross formed the handle of the Crux Ansata. This cross was the symbol of procreation, of life and reproduction. The Great Mother was a type of this cross of Life. As the Vesica Piscis is constructed upon two circles, a double significance has been given to it. "It means astronomically at the present day a starry conjunction; and by a very intelligent transfer of typical ideas"(1) on the higher planes leads to a Divine Marriage.

The two-fold essence of life all ancients gave as masculine and feminine -- the positive and the negative. In early art the Vesica was always symbolically portrayed in its feminine aspect as an attribute of the Virgin, "and the feminine aspect of the Savior as symbolized by the wound in his side, but it commonly surrounds the figure of Christ, as His Throne, when seated in glory. As a hieroglyph, the combination of Christ with the Vesica is analogous to the Crux Ansata of the Egyptians." (2)

In heraldry the Vesica was used as the feminine shield. The Vesica was an ordinary symbol of the church, mystically honored as the Spouse of Christ. In the study of Masonry one is told that geometry is the noblest of all the sciences, and one of its simplest figures has been the intersection of two circles, and the rectangle formed on its length and breadth produced the Vesica Piscis.

Due to the marvelous proportions of the Vesica Piscis, as well as to its Trinity in Unity, beautiful Gothic cathedrals were planned, every detail of which was lovingly watched, for the whole symbolized the highest religious truths capable of the thinking mind of man. The spirit which was back of these is not found in modern architecture; there is not the same urge towards such perfect work.

The name "cathedral" was generally applied to all great churches in the West. In Greek, this word means a chair, or a seat; -- it becomes the Chair of God. Architecture has been called "frozen music," especially applicable to Gothic architecture, for "its beauty is its external promise, its endless upward flight," (3) as pinnacle rises above pinnacle. It has been compared to the Kabalistic Tree of Life as it grows towards Infinity,

---

(1) - THE CANON, Page 13, Edward Clarkson.
(2) - THE CANON, Pages 13-14.
(3) - FRATER ACHAD; THE ANATOMY OF THE BODY OF GOD, Page 43.

ever upward and onward. Geometrical principles of design found in Gothic cathedrals formed the secrets of the Freemasons. An irregular hexagon or the double cube which would enclose a Vesica gives the proportions of 26 to 15, and it has been suggested that the Vesica with these proportions was the symbol of the hidden rule or canon upon which the Tree of Life was built, possibly making it indicative of the hidden knowledge and the truth that had constituted the Sacred Wisdom of antiquity. It is "capable of forming a Symbolical Basis for every idea in the Universe, Natural, Human and Divine." (1)

Architecture is really a great stone alphabet. The first monument was a simple square of rock, or an upright stone -- just a letter -- but the hieroglyphs later carved upon it were fertile with ideas.

In the appointment of Lodges today there are three symbolic columns: the Ionic, which is placed east; the Doric, west; and the Corinthian, south. These are of intrinsic value in the constitution of fraternities. Mystically or ideally they allude to the Pillars of the Universe. From ancient times they have been designated Wisdom, Strength and Beauty.

These three important columns -- Doric, Ionic and Corinthian -- all have names of mystical significance, numerically readily proved. The Doric, the oldest column, was first made in the proportion of six to one, in imitation of man, whose foot was said to be the sixth part of his height. The second to be made was the Ionic, corresponding to the proportions of a woman. At first its height was made eight times its thickness, but usually it is nine times. Lastly, the slender graceful Corinthian was created in the proportion of the slight figure of the virgin, its height about ten times its thickness. These three are the distinguishing types applied to all classical temples and are of the greatest architectural importance. The Doric represents virile strength, the Corinthian, delicacy; the Ionic combines the severity of the Doric with the beauty of the Corinthian.

The Doric became an emblem of the original cause of all things and a "symbol of the generative power of the universe expressed by the sun, which, of all the celestial bodies, most conspicuously appears to measure the whole extent of the Cosmic system." (2)

When the Ionians desired new proportions for the building of a temple to dedicate to their Deity, they used the female figure as the standard, whose symbol was the Vesica. Its design is primarily marked by the double spiral volute of its capital and includes the first two principles of life, just as the universe was built by a two-fold agency. Creations were usually symbolized in double form and architecturally are "identical with the two intersecting circles of the Ionic Vesica, reproduced in the two volutes of the Ionic capital." (3)

"The first measures are said to have been derived from the body of a man 'according to the similitude whereof God formed the world ..... in such sort, that the one is called the greater world, and the other the lesser.'" (4)

---

(1) - FRATER ACHAD, THE ANATOMY OF THE BODY OF GOD, Page 107.
(2) - THE CANON, Page 249
(3) - THE CANON, Page 252
(4) - LOMAZZO, on "Painting," Page 109.

Therefore, man having been made in the image of God and the world, God, the world, and man are synonymous terms, and the human body becomes the standard measure of the world." (1)   And, according to Vitruvius, the temples were to conform to the measures of the human body.

It is also stated in THE CANON that the Corinthian pillar might appropriately be called Aeolic. Aeolus, in The Odyssey, god of the winds, "seems to correspond with Pneuma, breath, or spirit of the Christian Trinity." By the circle of the year, by the winds, and by the sun's orbit, this third column, the Corinthian, was associated with the "center of the universe, and its flowering capital is a beautiful emblem of the fertile earth;" and among other emblems of nature's bounty, the pomegranate was often carved upon it. The pomegranate was a Divine symbol of the Kabiri, who called it "The Forbidden Secret." It was carved on one of the pillars on the porch of King Solomon's Temple.

There is a charming legend of the Corinthian column written by John Shute, architect of the Sixteenth Century: "After that, in the citie of Corinthe, was buried a certaine maiden, after whose burial her nourishe (who lamented much her death), knowing her delightes to have bene in prettye cuppes, and such like conceytes, in her lifetime, with many other thinges appertayninge only to the pleasure of the eye, toke them and broke them, and put them in littell praetie baskette, and did sette the baskette on her grave, and covered the baskette with a square pavinge stone. That done, with weping teares she sayde, 'Let pleasure go wyth pleasure,' and so the nourishe departed. It chanced that the basket was set upon a certain roote of an herbe called acanthus, in French, Brankursine, or Beare Fote with us. Now in the spring time of the yeare, when every roote spreadeth forth its leaves in the increasing, they did ronne up by the side of the baskette, until they could rise no higher for the stone that covered the basket, which, being square, and casting his foure corners over the sydes of the ronde baskette, constrained the branches of the herbe to draw downwards againe with a certain compasse, and so drew to the fashion that Vitruvius calleth Volita. ..... In this citie one Callimanchus, an excellent architectur, passinge or going thereby, regarding the beautifull works of nature," devised a column and set a capital upon it in imitation of the tomb which he had seen; and although this may be called a fancy, it is probably one explanation of the classical architects' connection with the third order of columns.

It is uncertain just when Freemasonry in Germany founded a Grand Lodge or acknowledged the authority of a Grand Master, but a master of masons, in the year 1452, "succeeded in uniting the existing Lodges of Germany in a general or great body, and in the year 1459 the statutes and general regulations of the stonecutters or masons were reduced to writing." "Among all the Grand Lodges of this age, that of Strassburg was preeminent, and was recognized as having supreme authority, and taking precedence over all Masonic bodies in the empire. Moreover, the master builder then at work on the cathedral at Strassburg was declared the Grand Master of the Fraternity in Germany." In 1563 an assembly of Masons reduced the preceding ordinance to convenient form by compilation which received the name of "'stonecutters' law,' otherwise known as 'Brothers' Book.'"

---
(1) - THE CANON, Page 27.

It was when the ancient ritual, usages and lodge discipline began to disappear, during the most flourishing period of its existence, that Masons, fearing to lose a total distinction of these, as Findel states, "began by re-establishing the ancient landmarks by excluding all that was foreign to the crafts and demanding that all Stone Masons belong to the guild or fraternity." They assembled together in the year 1459 for the purpose of renewing, as well as revising their ancient constitutions. Statutes undoubtedly based on ancient law were agreed upon "at the assemblies of Masters and Fellows." Findel also claims that the Statute of the year 1459 "bears the most ancient date of any authentic document extant, and only a little later than the Halliwell document. The revised Statute of the year 1563 contains a repitition of the former laws of 1459" (1) that had seemed necessary at the time.

There is another Stonecutters' ordinance drawn up in 1462, of great importance, and when examined critically and from an archeological standpoint, discloses some details of inestimable value, establishing "the absolute existence of the Gothic or Teutonic derivation of many medieval Masonic symbols" that have come to us today, "facts which the constitutions of 1459 and 1563 utterly ignore and which exist alone in this invaluable Torgau ordinance of 1462."(2)

This constitution adds many links to the "subtle claim which carries Masonic symbolism far back to the dawn of Germanic civilization, long anterior to the introduction of Judaic ritualism, far back beyond the annals of Christianity or before it was born." It was publicly read at each annual communication of the Masonic brethren. Due to the date of this very curious document, we can trace the outline of symbolic references uninterruptedly from the remotest antiquity.

In the year 1707 an imperial Diet published a decree preventing the Lodges in the empire receiving further recognition, and authority hitherto acknowledged was denied them. This was a severe blow to the German Freemasons, and an added decree in 1731 forbade, under severe penalties, all Lodges in Germany from obligating any initiate to silence regarding craft secrets given him; and due to this crushing edict, Freemasonry as an operative body ceased to exist in the empire.

"In order to preserve that striking similitude existing between the productions of Operative Masonry constructed at remote distances from each other, constant communication was kept up with all members of the numerous widely-extended bodies of Masonic craftsmen; and when we consider the unvarying uniformity of style displayed in the construction of churches and cathedrals and the immense number erected in every country, till the overthrow of the ancient religion, we shall perceive how complete the intercourse among Masons of necessity must have been." (3)   With the extinction of Medieval Masonry many of those recondite and esoteric principles of the art were totally lost.

During the Sixteenth Century were seen marks of decadence of those old ideas in architecture which reached back thousands of years, bringing

---
(1) - FINDEL, J. G.; HISTORY OF MASONRY, Page 72
(2) - FORT, George F., THE EARLY HISTORY & ANTIQUITIES OF FREEMASONRY, Page 148
(3) - Ibid. -- Pages 155-6

about a cruder and newer doctrine, which replaced the great achievements in the art of generations of men who had brought it to perfection. It was at this time also that changes brought about the gradual disappearance of the old order of Masons who had builded according to ancient rules. Religious opinions changed, and with them the secret methods of those old Masons, or stonecutters, as they were called.

The secret doctrine of architecture that had been the inspiration of the old artisans had grown fainter and fainter until it had almost passed away, though it will ever be found in the superb monuments which the old Masons have left everywhere, and in the Ritual of the ancient mystical initiations which have survived and through which a Mason was made. This Ritual was a simple one, as is the beginning of all religion. The chief concern of the artisan was to learn the intricacies of architecture and, piece by piece, build a temple, just as an anatomist would build the human body. The esoteric architectural doctrine taught by the Master was symbolically woven into a moral and altruistic nature, always leading towards the awakening of the mind and its creative ability which might build the spiritual within to become outwardly expressed in the great cathedrals. "The utility of those mystic Rites could not be estimated after the religion which gave them birth was no longer known."

A mixed style of architecture prevailed in France, during the Twelfth and Thirteenth Centuries, but the Gothic predominated. "The churches of Saint Remy, at Rheims, the Abbey of Saint Denis, Saint Nicholas at Blois, the Abbey of Jumieges, and the Cathedral of Chalons-sur-Marne are the principal models of this style. It is noteworthy that for a long period the ogive triumphed over the circular arch in Northern France, while in the meridional, Roman traditional types allied to the Byzantine still continued to inspire the construction of sacred edifices." (1)

Among Gallic structures which show their Gothic origin, the most noticeable are: the Cathedral at Reims, dedicated about the year 1215; the Cathedrals of Bourges and of Amiens; while Notre Dame, at Rouen, a specimen cathedral, showing fuller details of the German style, is perhaps the finest example. The churches of Saint Owens and Rouen were completed in the year 1318, erected upon a model of art that had permeated Europe. The foundation of Amiens Cathedral was laid in the Seventh Century; but the Cathedral met the fate of many other old churches -- it was frequently destroyed by fire. However, it was commenced anew in 1220, and was finally completed in 1288. Notre Dame, of Paris, finished in 1275 by Jean de Chelles, a Master Mason, and Sainte Chapelle, built in 1248 (under Louis IX) by Pierre de Montereau -- Master of the Masons -- are connected historically with the Parisian Freemasons and stonecutters whose associations were recognized by law in 1254.

"Lacroix asserts, on a chronical of the time of Dagobert, that Saint Eloi organized the jewelers, whom he selected from different monasteries, into a society comprising three degrees of laborers -- masters, fellows and apprentices." (2) This bishop was prime minister to the king. France is said to possess the earliest authentic record touching the fraternity of Masons and

---
(1) - FORT, George F.; - THE EARLY HISTORY & ANTIQUITIES OF FREEMASONRY, P. 100
(2) - Ibid.; Page 46. This system of dividing pupils into three degrees, alluded to above, brought about a great acquisition of a proficiency in architecture.

upon the authority of Lacroix, that Saint Eloi, whose efforts in behalf of the mechanical trades procured for him the honor of patronage to the guilds of smiths in the Fifteenth Century, had, in the Eighth Century, organized the monks of his abbey into a society of tradesmen. He established two distinct corporations, one for the clerical workmen, the other in which laymen were admitted for membership." (1)

When the laws under Louis IX were revised, the Statutes decreed by Saint Eloi during his lifetime were transcribed, and so far as these rules affected the admittance to the guilds of jewellers and goldsmiths, an apprentice could not be advanced to the degree of Master until he had served and qualified himself by an apprenticeship of ten years, though the time was often lessened. In order that they might attend authorized works of charity, a seal was possessed by the Fraternity at that time.

Etienne Boileau (Provost of Paris) in the year 1254, under the direction of Louis IX, King of France, collected rules and regulations regarding various trades by placing them in manuscript form, and "by royal authority ordained to be the law to which all guilds or ecclesiastical occupations in Paris should be henceforth subjected." (Pardessus).

The 48th chapter of a manuscript of Boileau contained laws of very great importance relating to Masons, stonecutters, plasterers and mortar-mixers. "As the oldest unquestioned and earliest written records touching Medieval Operative Masons and stonecutters, all these were governed by identical regulations."

Anyone could exercise his occupation as an Operative Mason in the French capital, provided he was skilled in the trade and qualified to conform to the ancient usages and customs of the Fraternity. One of the laws stipulated that no Mason could have more than one Apprentice in his employ at the same time, and that such apprenticeship could last only six years, an exception being made with regard to the Master's legitimate children, who could all be admitted as Apprentices. At the expiration of the fifth year's service of his apprenticeship, a Master could engage another, so that he might have the benefit of a more or less skilled worker.

For any inharmony or violation of the rules enforced by the usages and customs of the Fraternity, "the Master of Masons was obliged to compensate by an amend of twenty Parisian solidi." Apparently the earliest account of wages is given in the regulations of Boileau, where he states that the Master Builder received two sous for each one of a party with whom he conferred. A sou in those days was equivalent to twenty francs.

In 1254 a practice prevailed whereby a Grand Master was appointed over the guilds of Masons in Paris. Boileau asserts that it was in strict accordance with the established rules for French Kings to confer Mastership of Parisian guilds upon the nobility, and that Louis IX gave over the Mastership of the Masons, so long as such would please the royal grantor, to Master William de Saint Petre. This mastership over Masons and stonecutters was to be in a Lodge within the palace enclosure, where all matters under Masonic jurisdiction should be enacted and determined by this nobleman. He was obliged to make oath before the city Provost "That well and truly, to the best

(1) - FORT, George F.; THE EARLY HISTORY & ANTIQUITIES OF FREEMASONRY; p. 125

of his ability, both as regarded the rich and the poor, the weak and the strong, he would preserve the ordinances thus promulged as long as the king should be satisfied to retain him in the above-mentioned general mastership." (1)   Thus an obligation by William de Saint Petre was taken before the Provost of Paris within the enclosure of the palace.

It is quite noticeable that the ancient documents of 1254, as well as those of Masonry during the middle of the Fifteenth Century, are drawn from older traditions; also the most ancient records of German Masonry are drawn from much older traditions and do not in any way indicate that the fraternities of Masons were put upon any substantial basis at the building of King Solomon's Temple, or prior to the age of Diocletian, in the Third Century. Operative Masons of France, during the Middle Ages, knew nothing of the Jewish origin of the craft. Initiatory Rites and emblems were not the entire contribution from the Jewish temple builders. Halliwell's Codex makes no mention of Masons during Solomon's time, neither does it pretend to trace Masonic history beyond the time of Athelstane and Edwin, but merely wishes to prove that Geometric Science was the invention of Euclid and was brought to England through Egypt. Manuscripts proceed to define the descent of Masonry or geometry from times of greatest antiquity.

"It was permitted, by the ordinance of 1254, that each Mason, stone-cutter, et cetera, should have as many assistants and aids in his work as suited him, but it was rigidly forbidden to communicate to such laborers or others any of the secret arts of the trade, however slight the disclosure might be."

Boileau states that "Each Master of Masons was obliged to swear that he would, with loyalty and in good faith, guard his trade from breaches and innovations, and would faithfully perform all its requirements so far as he might be concerned as an individual Mason; and also, if he should at any time become cognizant of an infringement upon a rule, or learn that the usages and customs of the fraternity were violated, he would reveal such infraction to the Master whenever it occurred, by the binding force of his obligation."(2)

No Mason of a lower degree in the craft was permitted to ask questions on Masonry belonging to a higher degree than that to which he belonged. This feature is still recognized today. Craftsmen at that time were compelled and sworn to acquaint the Master with the "goodness or the badness" of the materials, that Masonry might not be dishonored. Contemptuous conduct upon the part of any workmen sent the offender to the Provost of Paris who compelled him to foreswear the trade forever.

When an Apprentice completed his term, he was taken before the Grand Master of the Lodge to testify as to his work and that he had lawfully served his term. He was then made to swear that he would always give obedience to the established rules. Unless for some very special reason, a Mason who worked during religious observances or after his hours of work had passed, was obliged to pay a penalty to the Grand Master, who was even authorized to seize his tools until satisfaction was rendered.

---

(1) - FORT, George F.; THE EARLY HISTORY & ANTIQUITIES OF FREEMASONRY, P. 105.
(2) - Ibid,; page 107

The obligation of the French Mason compelled him to inspect the work of plasterers and the accuracy of their measure in materials, and if any suspicion was aroused, the plasterer had to measure out the quantity in his presence. The requirement for precision among all the workmen was most severe, even regarding the beginning or ending of their time of labor; and prior to this period of 1254, earlier records of guilds state that the workmen were compelled to pay strict attention to the opening and the closing of the Lodge.

In Paris, the Grand Master of the Masons was empowered to compel compensation to be paid for every quarrel which arose among the members of the guilds; and if a Mason refused to speak, he was forbidden future exercise of his trade. If he persisted, his tools were seized and complaint was made to the Provost who compelled submission through legal authority.

Plasterers were obliged to perform watch-duty and to pay taxes, but stonecutters were exempt from guard mount. This exemption had descended from the time of Charles Martel. The Grand Master in control of tradesmen was also exempt, by authority of the King. A Craftsman over the age of fifty was not liable for municipal duty.

From the above statements, though scantily given, it would seem that the Fraternity of Freemasons was established firmly in Paris by law in the year 1254; and the Charter from which these facts are given becomes of great value to the Masonic student of research. The Boileau Charter is the oldest record of the Craft yet discovered and is entitled to unbounded confidence.

"The most ancient roll which has yet appeared in other countries does not claim a higher authority than the close of the Fourteenth Century; consequently this charter of Boileau ..... presents claims to consideration superior to the manuscript of Halliwell, which he has assigned to the year 1390 -- a difference of 136 years."[1]

The Halliwell manuscript is numbered in the manuscript list of the British Museum as "Royal 17-AI." It is thought that this manuscript "may have been copied from the return by some guild of Masons, made, as other guilds in England were required to make, to the king's council, in pursuance of an order of Parliament in the twelfth year of Richard II, A.D. 1389." [2]

The Boileau Charter of 1254 states that certain privileges had existed from the time of Charles Martel, who had conceded the same privileges to the Stone Masons' Guild. Then why not apply a similar reason for establishing "the original foundation of European Masonry about the year 774?" The Halliwell manuscript of 1390 alleges that the Masons were first chartered by King Athelstane in 926. Earlier Masonic manuscripts also say that Emperor Charles Martel was noted for his patronage of the Masons.

External knowledge of Freemasonry became beclouded during the Eleventh and Twelfth Centuries, but the marks of the master architects are still to be seen on walls that have defied time. Forty-nine years after

---

(1) - FORT, George F.; THE EARLY HISTORY & ANTIQUITIES OF FREEMASONRY, P. 111
(2) - Ibid.

the death of William, the Norman King, John Moreau, a French Mason, laid the walls of Melrose Abbey. The earliest authentic mural inscription still exists in this Abbey, which was begun in the year 1136 and finished in 1146. The name of John Muruo (or Morow) is engraved on the west side of the transept, and another record, in raised letters, is hewn on a block of stone on the south side of the doorway, which proves that he was architect or Master Mason. A few of these letters, now almost effaced by time, are interesting and may still be deciphered. Mr. Fort states: "From an accurate copy in my possession I quote a portion of the record:

> "John: Morow: sum: tyme: callyt:
> Was: I: and: born: in: Parysse:
> Certainly:"

Tablets similar to this are almost invaluable, showing that as far back as the year 1136 the Craft had been organized by laymasters. Other proofs tend to show that John Morow, or Muruo, was the General or Grand Master. His name was once engraved Muruo, and according to the tablet, he was sometimes called Morow. From this same almost obliterated tablet we see that he must have been the Master, perhaps General or Grand Master, of all Masonic works or Lodges. In Scotland, John Moreau was a Master of Scottish Masons in the Twelfth Century.

The completion of Melrose Abbey in 1146 was thirty years prior to the arrival of William of Sens, in 1176. England is indebted to William of Sens for many of her fine arts. He it was who first introduced the chisel at the rebuilding of Canterbury Cathedral. Previously an adze had been used in the preparation of freestone. He was also the inventor of the turning machine.

"According to the _Archaeologia,_ until the close of the Twelfth Century stones were hewn out with an adze. About this time the chisel was introduced and superseded the hewing of stone. Thus we see that the words 'hew a stone' had descended from the Twelfth Century, at least, to the period when the manuscript first quoted was copied, and, being found in the roll before the copyist, were also transcribed. Moreover, the occurrence of Charles Martel's name in the manuscript as early as that of Cooke, indicates that the tradition of his connection with the Masons or stonecutters had long obtained among the fraternity in England. It is highly probable that this legend was carried there by foreign workmen from the Continent, where, as we have seen, this tradition was extant as early as the year 1254." (1)

From whatever source Anderson obtained knowledge for his ancient Constitution, it also furnished the tradition of Charles Martel. In the French ordinance of Louis IX, no mention is made of Maymus Graecus, but in Cooke's manuscript and in Hughan's Old Masonic Charges he is mentioned as a curious old man who had been at the building of King Solomon's Temple. "From thence he passed, in bold defiance of all chronology, after a mighty slumber, into France." Having amassed a great fund of geometric knowledge or of Masonry, he was royally received by Charles Martel and taught him the science of Masonry. This renowned nobleman of high degree, wishing to learn

---
(1) - FORT, George F.; THE EARLY HISTORY AND ANTIQUITIES OF FREEMASONRY, Pages 117-8

the arts and points in Masonry, selected Maymus Graecus for his teacher and, voluntarily, Charles Martel took upon himself the Charges and customs of the Masons and thereupon began great works. He paid the workmen liberally and was yearly present at their assemblies -- which was a great honor and gave them encouragement. According to the legend, thus was Masonry introduced into France. Subsequently Charles Martel ascended the throne of France.

The name Maymus Graecus signifies Maymus, the Grecian, thus furnishing additional evidence that Masonic guilds recognized the Grecian origin of many things perpetuated in their lodges. "The same Byzantine traditions which had prevailed among the lay-corporations and monastic workmen of an early age passed into Medieval Freemasonry." The age in which Maymus was originally connected with the Craft has passed beyond all recovery. He was a Byzantine artist, or belonged to the Greek builders who were in Europe from the Fifth to the Eleventh Century; and through this old man, Maymus, much can be discerned of Oriental influence incorporated into the Middle Age Fraternities forming an important part of the Ritual.

The Lansdown and Cooke manuscripts assert that Maymus, the Grecian, brought Masonry or the art of building from the East. His name is not discovered among the worldly or profane writers but is the only name found in the old and venerable Masonic records, thereby solving some problems and proving that art was brought from the Orient through Greek artificers, and that through them the secrets of architectural construction had reached their time; also, that the "mystical convocations at York" show that some of the records were in Greek, telling how the English Masons acknowledged themselves indebted to Greek or Byzantine artificers.

Whatever traditions and usages the French Masons possessed at this time passed over with them into England, and a translation of the legend of Charles Martel and a knowledge of Maymus Graecus seem to have been taken into Great Britain also at that time, together with the same usages and customs that were practiced by the Freemasons of France.

German Freemasons added to the construction of English churches, abbeys, and other buildings. A German Master Mason, by name, Kloos, built King's College Chapel, at Cambridge, the finest of Gothic buildings in England. "German Masonic fraternities exercised a decided influence upon architecture in Great Britain at an early age." Many of their magnificent cathedrals are erected in the Gothic style, similar to King's College Chapel, which brought into England a thorough knowledge of the secret details of their art.

There are two full-sized figures or images over the main entrance to the York Cathedral, one holding a rough ashler, the other a polished one; and over them are two others, in a kneeling posture. In the right hand of one is a stone object; in his left arm, the angle of a square pointing above. It is probable that many things still practised within the tiled recesses of a Masonic Lodge had their source in German and Teutonic art, from which came some of the legends that were taught in England.

Trouble had been brewing among the English artisans who refused to accept wages prescribed by law, and a statute had been enacted compelling them to resume labor under the heavy penalty of being branded if they refused. This statute forbade the Masons to assemble as a body of operative workmen in order to regulate wages or to arrange upon what terms an Apprentice should be received into the lodges. As a result of this, the famous statute styled "3 Henry VI; i" was enacted in 1424. It declared Masonic chapters, organizations of Craftsmen, and convocations void and illegal; and though they openly ceased to exist, artificers still met in their Lodges and used the original Rites and ceremonies of initiation.

These guilds continued more as clubs and men devoted much time to benevolent as well as to mysterious works. Through this crushing power everything regarding their laws had been taken from them; the blow had been relentless, and the struggle between the guilds and the law-making power became intense.

A universal language of the Masons originated at this time, consisting of a few words, signs and grips, by which one could communicate with another, according to the degree of initiation. A cipher was then used which could be learned by the Brothers of the Royal Arch Chapter. But today it is of little use to them, as they are forbidden to communicate the secrets of the craft "either in writing, printing, engraving, or otherwise them delineate."

"It is in the highest degree probable that the year 1424 is the proper date to assign for the cessation of English Freemasonry as a strictly operative association, and the epoch of its decided tendency towards a speculative science, such as we now find it." (1)

Men of social prominence became Masons of the Speculative Order, and much of the great beauty of the mystic craft was lost though Rites, Ceremonies and moral instruction were undoubtedly continued. With the current of everchanging civilization and the entry of men of greater social position into Lodges, there came a tendency toward conviviality. This finally extinguished the operative character and a lamentable fact remains; much of the detail of the wonderful architectural art was abandoned, as Freemasons were forbidden to convene at this time as bodies of artificers. They performed their work as best they could in the secret recesses of closely-tiled Lodges, trying to preserve the original Rites of Masonry as a "Moralistic Organization."

In 1495 a statute was enacted by Parliament forbidding artisans of every description the right to use "Signs and Tokens." About the middle of the ensuing century this was rescinded. The license was speedily revoked, except as it related to London.

Some writers consider that Henry VI was an ardent Mason, that he had been initiated into Masonry and had conceded to the Fraternities royal favors. A curious Manuscript was said to have been written by him, which is claimed as spurious. It is well known that his intellect was rather weak and that he had a habit of prowling and prying into Masonic secrets. Through alchemy and its mysteries he hoped to find the Philosopher's Stone.

"This Manuscript in the King's handwriting is said to have remained concealed in the Archives of some convent till the year 1536. About this

---

(1) - FORT, GEORGE F.; THE EARLY HISTORY & ANTIQUITIES OF FREEMASONRY; P. 131

period, Henry VIII appointed the Monasteries to be searched, and commissioned John Leyland, a learned man, to examine and save such books and records as were valuable among them. Leyland is said to have found the Manuscript in a bad state of preservation, to have copied it, and then given it to the Bodleian Library at Oxford. Here, however, it again lay hidden, till it was discovered by the celebrated Locke, in 1696, and a copy of the same sent by him to the Earl of Pembroke, with notes of Locke's own attached to it. The letter supposed to have been written by Locke, precedes the Manuscript; this letter is thus headed: "Certayne Questions, with Answers to the same, concerning the Mystery of Masonry; written by the hande of Kinge Henrye, the sixthe of the name, and faythfullye copied by me, Johan Leylande, Antiquarius, by the commande of his Highnesse." (1)

J. G. Findel, from whom I have copied the above, has searched the Bodlein Library in vain for the discovery of this Document. Some writers have believed this Manuscript to have been written in spite of controversy concerning it. At that time, very much was of a secretive order, and all legendary tales hold foundations of truths to be discovered.

"In the Lansdown manuscript a statement is made that Saint Alban gave the fraternity three shillings and sixpence a week." In 1560, at the time this manuscript was drawn up, this sum was accepted as regular pay, yet it had been shown that wages received fixed amounts prior to this. The Halliwell and Cooke manuscripts, still more ancient, do not mention a specified sum ordered by Saint Alban, though a pay-account probably existed between the Master and his Lodge members, independent of local legislation.

When such a rate was agreed upon, neither the Master nor the workman was allowed to change it. In the Ordinance of 1462, "the Master is expressly forbidden to vary or diminish the daily stipend," due to the assumption of the English Freemasons who, in 1424, refused to accept wages prescribed by law and caused the above Statute to be passed. This modified to a considerable degree the nature of the fraternities and their future standing.

"In the year 1610 the following wages were apportioned by the justices, and were made binding upon the Freemasons: (36 Charles II):

	With meat	Without meat
A freemason who can draw his own plans -	8d.	12d.
A rough mason who can take charge of others -	5d.	10d.
A bricklayer -	4d.	8d.
A bricklayer's apprentice -	3d.	7d.

Subsequently it was enacted that they should be paid in accordance with the subjoined schedule (Archaeologia, Vol. XI, page 203).

	With meat & drink	Without
A freemason	6d.	1s - 4d
A master brickman -	8d.	1s.- 0d.
Servants and apprentices over 18 years -	4d.	0s.- 8d.(2)

---
(1) - FINDEL, J. G.; HISTORY OF FREEMASONRY, pages 109 - 110.
(2) - FORT, George F.; THE EARLY HISTORY & ANTIQUITIES OF FREEMASONRY; P. 200

In 1689 Masons were compelled to take one shilling and four pence a day. Should they accept any more, the fine was imprisonment for 21 days. Wages in the Lodge were paid by the warden at sunset, showing the antiquity of many old Masonic forms. Under Justinian, during the building of St. Sophia, workmen were paid each evening -- a custom coming from Byzantine days and so transmitted to the Medieval Mason.

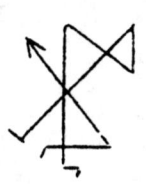

Chapter XI

MEDIEVAL MASONS

> Geometrical forms, in their emblematic relations, taught the Brothers a more profound wisdom, which was to "the Master an immutable clue; and to the Fellows and Apprentices, a fingerboard in the ever-lengthening route to knowledge."
> — E. V. S.

DURING the following centuries many were initiated into the guilds and were received into the mystic Rites of Masonry who had no apparent connection with mechanical trades. It is not quite certain at what period initiations were given to men in high position and wealth who were not in trade, but in the Thirteenth Century Louis IX appointed a nobleman as Grand Master of the Craft. Guilds at that time were so endowed that a Master could be elected from men of high rank.

In the Memoirs of Elias Ashmole, he writes "On the 16th of October, 1646: '4 hor, 30 minutes past meridem, I was made a Freemason at Warrington, in Lancashire, with Colonel Henry Mainwaring, of Kerticham, in Cheshire." Under the date of 1682, an additional entry was put in his diary; "March 10. Received a summons to appear before a Lodge at Masons' Hall, London. 11th. Went, and was admitted into the fellowship of Freemasons by Sir William Wilson, Knt. Was senior Fellow, being thirty-five years since making. Dined at dinner, at expense of the new accepted Mason. This took place at the Half-Moon Tavern."

The earliest use of the words "new accepted" seems to have been found in Ashmole's Memoirs, given in the year 1682, on the 10th of March. "In the year 1670, according to the Harleian manuscript, the words 'accepted a Freemason' were used to distinguish a Mason so received and taken by the Fraternity without professional apprenticeship, from one who was initiated because of his vocation." Gentlemen, professionals, and noblemen began freely to join the Freemasons -- which organization had gradually ceased to exist as a tradesmen's guild by legal interdiction in 1424.

During the Seventeenth Century Freemasonry had practically ceased to be a society composed of Operative Masons, and guarded doors were then opened to the more professional people. The earliest authentic record of professional men being admitted into Masonry is found in the rolls of Saint Mary's Lodge at Edinburgh, the oldest Lodge in Scotland, where the name of Thomas Bosswell, of Auchinlick, appears. He was present at an assembly of the Lodge in 1600 and chosen Warden of the Lodge. Also Robert Moray, a Quartermaster-General of the Scottish Army, was admitted and made a Master Mason in the year 1641.

The earliest record of Lodge meetings was in 1599, but there are copies of Old Charges that date from the Fourteenth Century. When the Old Charges ceased to be influential, those who did not follow the trades became Speculative and preserved the old Order which was near to passing out entirely.

Speculative Masonry taught as a spiritualizing art is "exalted to a Brotherhood of symbolic builders who, in place of visible, perishable temples, are engaged in the erection of that one invisible, eternal temple of the heart and mind." It is intensely human and spiritual and opens the way for Masons to become the advance guard in the New Era of civilization which is to bring with it the opening of a new consciousness.

The entrance of Elias Ashmole had paved the way for what has been termed the Masonic Revolution of 1717, which forms an important epoch in the history of Masonry. "Dermot mentions eight persons, among them the Rev. Dr. Desaguliers, who was elected Grand Master in 1719, as the author of this remarkable Revolution."

Drs. Anderson and Desaguliers became the two moving spirits of the time and brought together the four old Lodges of England which met in London, and on June 24, 1717, formed the first Grand Lodge of Free and Accepted Masons. In other countries Lodges were introduced under the authority of this Grand Lodge of England. Writers upon this subject claim that this was the parent stem of the common mother of all Speculative Lodges in the world.

This did not include a Masonic body at York, which remained independent and formed a Grand Lodge of its own. It continued until the year 1790, but had evidently chartered no other Lodges.

The term "Freemason" applied to all "Craftsmen who had obtained their freedom as Masons to work within the Lodges with the Fraternity." From the time of the earliest Charges, the word "Accepted" was used to distinguish them from the working Masons.

Drs. Anderson and Desaguliers, with others under authority, formed a later and better method and history of Charges and regulations. It is said that as a result of it "we have the Free and Accepted Masonry, founded upon the apochryphal legend of Hiram and the symbolism of King Solomon's Temple,"(1) which came into use about 1723.

The constitutions of 1723 and 1738 were written by Anderson for the first Grand Lodge of Free and Accepted Masons of England, and though many manuscripts were said to have been destroyed by fanatical reformers, many famous ones, giving sufficient knowledge concerning the old Operative Masons, are in the British Museum and the Bodlein Library and other well known places.

Dr. Mackey, a great authority, claims that the divisions of the Masonic system had been the work of the Revivalists and that they had been taken chiefly from Ancient Mysteries. He further claims, through the opinion of the best scholars, that the divisions into Entered Apprentices, Fellows and Masters "were simply divisions of rank, there being but one initiation for all."

---
(1) - VAIL, Rev. C. H., ANCIENT MYSTERIES AND MODERN MASONRY, Page 154

Allegories of the Egyptian Mysteries had to be disguised in order that the real purport of Masonry might not be defeated; but those Mysteries were ages old before Operative or European Masonry arrived. The Egyptian Mysteries, originally Masonic, came through from Atlantis.

The Ancient and Accepted Scottish Rite was derived from a body in France, "which organized in 1758, in Paris, a Rite called 'The Rite of Perfection,' consisting of 25 degrees, to which eight or more were subsequently added. The immediate source from which French Masonry derived these Rites is unknown." (1)

Albert Pike, a great authority on the Ancient and Accepted Scottish Rite, accepts the view that the direct source from which this Rite came was, very likely, one of the Metropolitan Lodges in Paris, instituted by Jacques de Molay while in prison. The Rite was said to have been brought to England in 1736-38, in the cause of the Catholic Stuarts.

"Every Degree in the Ancient and Accepted Scottish Rite, from the first to the thirty-second, teaches by its ceremonial as well as by its instruction, that the noblest purpose of life and the highest duty of a man are to strive incessantly and vigorously to win the mastery of everything of that which in him is spiritual and divine, over that which is material and sensual; so that in him also, as in the Universe which God governs, Harmony and Beauty may be the result of a just equilibrium." (2)

The Scottish Rite has become a teacher of great truths, and the "true Mason is he who labors strenuously to help his Order effect its great purpose."

"A Grand Lodge was formed at Charlestown, South Carolina, in 1783; a Supreme Council, 33rd Degree, in 1801; and the Rite has been called by its present name, Ancient and Accepted Scottish Rite, since that time."(3)

The Grand Lodge of Ireland was probably formed in 1725; the Grand Lodge of Scotland in 1736. The Royal Arch, probably of English origin, appeared in 1740; its founder is unknown. It was worked into chapters in 1762. "When a Chapter of the Royal Arch was formed at York, it became the fourth degree in the Ancient Grand Lodge System. The 'Moderns' did not recognize this degree or adopt it officially until 1767; upon the union it became a part of the English Rite."(4) It separated from the Blue Lodge Masonry and began an independent existence.

According to the copy of an old constitution, Anderson states that a general feast was held on St. John the Evangelist's Day, December 27, 1663, when the Earl of St. Alban was elected Grand Master. Regulations were made at this time "that no person of what degree soever be made or accepted a free mason unless in a regular lodge, whereof one to be a Master or Warden in that limit or division where such lodge is kept, and another to be craftsman in the

---
(1) - VAIL, Rev. C. H.; ANCIENT MYSTERIES AND MODERN MASONRY, Page 175
(2) - PIKE, Albert; MORALS AND DOGMA, Page 855.
(3) - VAIL, Rev. C. H.; ANCIENT MYSTERIES AND MODERN MASONRY, Page 176.
(4) - Ibid., Page 158.

trade of freemasonry. That for the future the fraternity of freemasons shall be regulated and governed by one grand master and as many wardens as the society shall think fit to appoint at the annual general assembly. That no person shall be accepted unless he is twenty-one years old or more."

During the revolution of 1688 only seven lodges could be gathered together for the roll of London. Sir Christopher Wren had become a Grand Master of Masons in 1685, when he distinguished himself in the construction of St. Paul's Cathedral and presided over a Lodge of the same name. Halliwell, in his EARLY HISTORY OF FREEMASONRY, quoting Aubrey, states that Sir Christopher was chosen Grand Master in 1698 and gives an account of the revolution which took place at this period.

Under Queen Ann, Masonry languished and a proclamation was forthcoming which provided that privileges of Freemasonry and the right of initiation should be given to all men of whatsoever profession, and if regularly approved and elected, should be entitled to the degree and thereby become a member of the Order. Evidently before the time of this announcement, Freemasonry was recognized as resting from its Operative labors and had cultivated the social and speculative side.

In the Common Hall of the London guild of Freemasons, meetings were held, with Christopher Wren as President. The real object was political; the restoration of the Monarchy. Exclusion of the public and the oath of secrecy were then necessary. The pretense of promoting architecture and the place of meetings were blinds to deceive the existent government. Although the society convoked in London and established branches throughout the country, furnishing the members with means of secret recognition for political ends, this was not the commencement of its real existence.

Anderson states that "in 1716, the few Lodges in London, finding themselves neglected by Sir Christopher Wren, thought fit to cement under a grand Master as the center of union and harmony." "These were the four Lodges that had united and met, first at the Goose and Gridiron Ale-house, in St. Paul's churchyard; second, at the Crown Ale-house, in Parker's Lane; third, at the Apple Tree Tavern, in Charles Street, Covent-Garden; fourth, at the Rummer and Grapes Tavern, in Channel Row, Westminster."

"The members of these lodges and some old brothers met at the said Apple Tree, and having put into the chair the oldest master mason, they constituted themselves a grand lodge, pro tempore in due form, and forthwith revived the Quarterly Communication of the Officers, called the grand lodge, and resolved to hold the annual assembly and feast; and then to choose a grand master among themselves, till they should have the honor of a noble brother at their head."

Accordingly, on St. John the Baptist's Day, the 24th of June (the summer solstice) 1717, "the brethren again met, and by a majority of hands, elected Mr. Anthony Sayer, Grand Master of Masons, who being forthwith invested with the badges of office and power by the oldest Master, and installed, was duly congratulated by the Assembly, who paid him homage."(1)

---

(1) - FINDEL, J. G.; HISTORY OF FREEMASONRY, Page 146

The Grand Lodge was formed with the express purpose of sacredly perpetuating the immemorial usages and landmarks. Thus we find the Operative features became extinct and were consummated in the Speculative details which accepted and clung to past traditions and the old and venerable Rites, with their symbols. These are with us today, though many modifications have crept in.

The foundation-stone of Freemason's Hall was laid in 1775; the dedication took place in 1776.

"The coming to light of all sorts of mystical knowledge that had been carefully concealed in previous times is one of the notable features of the Seventeenth and Eighteenth Centuries." (1)

Legends of English Freemasonry trace their origin to far earlier periods and are more complete than those of the Germans which go no further back than the time of Diocletian, when workmen refused to build heathen temples. The writ or ordinance of 1462 furnishes information not found elsewhere. Legends in Masonry previous to the time of Athelstane seem to be a group of stories connected with a traditional history of geometry, brought into Europe at an early age, possibly by Byzantine artisans. All legends of Freemasonry lead through Grecian corporations back to the Orient, and in lodge appointments, the road leading to the Gothic is very wide.

Traditional history of the Germans and French patron saints can readily be referred to the time of Diocletian, and by a strange consistency, may be followed through the Ancient Masonic corporations of Europe, though much has been lost or has drifted away. "Speculative Masonry has perpetuated intact for centuries that which has come down from the very twilight of time." The rigid adherence to all that guided the old builders in the ancient Lodges, through the hewing out and polishing of the rough stone with the beautiful designs of those old master builders, is still apparent in Speculative Masonry today.

"The earliest approach to the use of the word Freemason is in the statute of 24 Edward II, of the year 1350," published in the French language, in which the laws of England were written at that time. In the third chapter, regulating the price of wages, we find the following:

"ITEM: -- Carpenters, masons and tilers, and some others, shall receive no other pay than fixed by the law of 1346, viz.:

```
"A master carpenter . . . . . . . . 3 den.
 Another (joiner). . . . . . . . . . 2  "
 Master of freestone . . . . . . . . 4  "
 Other masons . . . . . . . . . . . 3  "
 Their servants . . . . . . . . . . 1  "
 A tiler . . . . . . . . . . . . . 3  "
 Their knaves . . . . . . . . . .    ".  " (2)
```

During the Middle Ages, Masons, carpenters and tilers existed as a union, but tile-coverers had their own guilds. The Master of freestone was

---
(1) - THE CANON, Page 239.
(2) - FORT, George F.; THE EARLY HISTORY & ANTIQUITIES OF FREEMASONRY; Ps.147-8

called "mestre de Franche peer," meaning literally a worker in stone, used here to distinquish a Mason adept in preparing freestone from the ordinary rough-stone Mason, the polisher, as it were, of the rough ashlar. The earliest mention of the word, Ashlar, seems to have been about the year 1389. It is probable that the nearest approach to the name Freemason appears in the above date.

Great diversity of opinion exists concerning the origin of the word Freemason. In the Seventh Century the word Caementarius was the earliest form used synonymous with mason. In 1077 it was used for classification, later, in 1212, caementaru was used for cutters of freestone. In 1217, caementarius became the equivalent of massun. In 1396 the word Lathomos, in this connection, corresponds to a hewer of stone, and is identical in signification with German Steinmetz and the French Tailleur de peer, or stonecutter.

During the Twelfth and Thirteenth Centuries the word mason was fixed by law, and had continued without further alteration than a prefix, when a Fraternity of Builders was established by law. The word Freemason is not met with in manuscripts until 1376; and, in this country, in the oldest Lodge records, dating from 1598.

If the word "Masonry," as some writers of distinction claim, is a corruption of the Greek "Mesouraneo," that in itself signifies "I am in the midst of heaven," -- in fact, in the center near the North Pole -- around which sailed those Ancient Companions, THE FRATERNITY OF THE BUILDERS. "Freres Maçons, in the French, adopted by way of secret reference to the Builders of the Second Temple, was corrupted in English into Free-Masons." (1)

Frere Maçons was a term used to distinguish them from other Masons. Between the Eleventh and Fifteenth Centuries the majority of architects in England were French. The Norman conquest brought the French language into England. From the French name macon we have Mas -- an old Norman noun meaning a house; and from this has come the English name, Mason, a house-builder.

In its earliest application, the word Mason seems to have represented one of a body of artificers and is found in an almost obliterated condition on one of the walls of Melrose Abbey, hewn there not later than the Twelfth Century.

The word Fremaceons, also used in 1396, indicates that these two French words -- frere and maçon -- being merged, readily meant an artificer, one regularly initiated into a fraternity recognized by law, thus becoming a "Brother Mason." It is well known that at the end of the Fourteenth Century, in England, builders of this class were called Freemasons; and at an early date, as Freemasons, they called themselves Brothers. "That ye one another call brother or fellow, and by no other foul name" is quaintly given in the Manuscript Charges. When the craftsmen entered a Lodge they would immediately speak to their fellowmen in words of affection and fraternal regard as Brothers. This practice, as well as other observances, has been transmitted to Speculative Masonry, and remains today.

---

(1) - PIKE, Albert, MORALS AND DOGMA, Page 816.

An interesting article in "Maconnerie Occulte" states that "rightly or wrongly, Ragon, a learned Belgian Mason, reproaches the English Masons with having materialized and dishonored Masonry, once based upon the Ancient Mysteries, by adopting, owing to a mistaken notion of the origin of the craft, the name Free Masonry (and Free Masons). The mistake is due, he says, to those who connect Masonry with the building of Solomon's Temple, deriving its origin from it. He derides the idea, and says: 'The Franc-Maçon (which is not maçon-libre, or free masonry) knew well when adopting the title, that it was no question of building a wall, but that of being initiated into the ancient Mysteries veiled under the name of Francmaçonnerie (Freemasonry); that his work was only to be the continuation or the renovation of the ancient mysteries, and that he was to become a mason after the manner of Apollo, or Amphion. And do we not know that the ancient initiated poets, when speaking of the foundation of a city, meant thereby the establishment of a doctrine? Thus Neptune, the god of reasoning, and Apollo, the god of the hidden things, presented themselves as masons before Laomedon, Priam's father, to help him to build the city of Troy -- that is to say, to establish the Trojan religion.'"(1)

The author of THE MASTER KEY TO THE DOOR OF FREEMASONRY states that the word "Free" was added to Masonry by the society because none but the free-born were admitted. This was in conformity to the established rule in the Egyptian Mysteries.

Lodges in early days met at sunrise, the Master Mason taking his place in the East, while the Brethren formed themselves about him into a semi-circle or oblong square. Prayer was essential and harmony was demanded before the invocation was given.

It was also the custom in those early days to dedicate the Lodges to some martyr or saint. The Fraternities in Paris placed themselves under the patronage of Saint Blasé. In Masonic legendary history, French Masons of the Middle Ages and earlier, claim a very high antiquity for their corporations, with Saint Blasé as their patron saint; (he had suffered martyrdom through Diocletian in the year 289). Legendary tradition has it that this Saint gave great relief to all those who suffered from physical or mental distress. Fires were kindled in high places in his honor, -- on the second of February, purposely, because of its being an extremely cold day. Masonic Fraternities in France during the Thirteenth Century donated all fines arising from any violations of their rules, to the Chapel of Saint Blasé.

In these early days St John was invoked by the British Masons. On the walls of Melrose Abbey, carved by a Master Mason or Master Builder, are these words:

"I: Pray: to: God: and: Mary: baith:
And: sweet: St: John: keep: this: Holy: kirk:
fra: skaith:"

Fraternities in Italy invoked St. Luke's protection, and when incorporated into their lodges, no work was allowed to commence without an appeal to God for aid. From these early days has come the goodly office of invoking aid and inspiration from the Deity. We have evidence that the celebrated artist, Fra Angelico, never started any one of his important works without being under the inspiration of God, whose aid he invoked.

(1) - BLAVATSKY, H. P.; THE SECRET DOCTRINE, VOL. II, pages 795-6.

During the Middle Ages, English Freemasons convened in the crypt of the old Cathedral of York, whose gloomy sombre vaults became sacred places, their massive columns folding in, as it were, a mystic glory among the aisles and arches. To them, high hills and lowly valleys were not sufficient to guard against the unitiated. In Northern countries, meetings were held on high hills and in lowly valleys. These places were greatly venerated. Legends of all great peoples do not center around the lowly parts of the earth. Ancient teachers sought the mountains for inspiration and attainment. The beauty of song, the sublimity of wisdom, color and sound, all originated on the mountains, where they seemed nearer the heart of the Supreme; for high mountains stand as witnesses of the "Great Reality." As far back into the ages as we can go, we find primitive man going to or lifting his eyes toward the mountains, in recognition of the greatness symbolically given there.

A Masonic dress for Medieval Masons was thoughtfully worked out; every detail was given attention. They wore short woolen tunics in winter and linen ones in summer, fashioned with a girdle about the waist to which a small hanging satchel or sword was attached. Their heads were covered with a tight-fitting skull cap; and their trousers were close-cut, making a distinctive dress, easily recognized by other brethren. Uniformity of dress was by no means compulsory.

"All Masons, whether Masters of Fellows, were obliged to be present at every assembly, upon due notice, if convenient, and within ten or fifty miles of any place where the same convened." Every Mason was obliged to revere his elder and "put him to worship." The Harleian manuscript very distinctly states that the Master must be addressed as "Worshipful."

A candidate for admission must be free-born and of a certain age. When found worthy, he was entitled to the degree of Apprentice; greater privileges were given when he advanced to that of Fellow; and when he became Master, he has given the geometrical secrets. But just how far the Apprentice was initiated in the Mysteries of the order is not known. Essential knowledge was given with the grip, password and sign. It was necessary for a Mason to be of sound mind and legitimate birth. In the Thirteenth Century this was insisted upon, under the penalty of a heavy fine. The time between the three degrees -- Apprentice, Fellow and Master -- varied according to the degree given.

French Masters were allowed one Apprentice whose time was six years; but at the end of the fifth, a Master was allowed to have another. The Master of the Royal Masons, in Paris, was allowed two. His sons could serve as his Apprentices, provided they were legitimate. Any infringement on this order would immediately bring a fine, which was paid to the Chapel of Saint Blasé.

In Germany, no Apprentice could be accepted for less than five years. In England, seven years of service were demanded. When the Apprentice advanced to the degree of Fellow, he had to take oath with his hand upon the Scriptures and the Holy-Dome,[1] held by the Warden. Just how long he remained

---

(1) - An Oath was sworn under the sanction of God, the Holy-Dome, and the Book. The Holy-Dome was usually a chest, -- containing the bones of some martyred saint -- in imitation of a small house. Holy was symbolical of the sanctity of the relics; and Domus -- Latin for house -- became holidomus -- later, holy-dome.

a Fellow is not known; but when sufficiently proficient to be advanced to Master, he was initiated into the mystic Rites and given fullest details of architectural art and the geometrical mystical secrets of Freemasonry. Thus he became capable of directing a lodge. He had no further instructions than his initiation into the Emblems incident to a Master's power and the legend of the Builder, Hiram Abiff.

In most of the guilds, when a Fellow desired to become a Master, it was customary for him to prepare a piece of his own workmanship of an exceptional order, which was placed before a syndicate of tradesmen for them to discuss and pass upon. If his work was favorable, he took an oath of allegiance to the King and became a Master. Today, an Entered Apprentice, before being raised to the degree of Fellow, similarly presents his gift which is symbolic of the work he has mentally accomplished as a Speculative Mason. When the Apprentice had filled his term of service and was recognized as a Fellow or Companion, he had privileges of greater moment than those of the Apprentice. He was given permission to wander as he pleased in search of work -- a privilege which was denied the Apprentice; but if the Master could not supply the Apprentice with necessary labor, he would loan him a Mark -- which would permit him to go in quest of labor.

An Apprentice, when initiated into the Fellow Degree, was given a special Mason's Mark, never to be changed unless by unanimous consent; and it has been of inestimable value. These marks are found in sacred ancient structures, as well as in other marvelous works belonging to olden times, when men had loved and had served the beautiful. It was to God they built those magnificent cathedrals and sacred houses.

At the present time, initiatory Rites are concluded with a banquet. This was a common practice during the Middle Ages; and upon such occasions prayer opened and closed the festivities. After prayer, the Master would drink the health of the newly-made Brother from what was known as a __Welcome Cup__, or __Drinking Horn__. It was answered by the Initiate as he emptied the __Horn__, giving a toast of prosperity to the Craftsmen. In those days, toasting was required to be "performed in three cadences of motion." The hand which held the Horn must be gloved or covered with a handkerchief, and the drinking given in three regularly-timed draughts; after which the Horn was placed upon the table with three regular movements. Very often the festivities were prepared by the Initiate, though frequently the expenses were born by the Lodge and the Craftsmen. The Ordinance of 1462 declared the corporation's share of accounting was definitely fixed, and anything over and above that became the Brother's private expenditure.

Teutonic nations closed their judicial terms with drinking bouts and banquets, early imitated by Freemasons. Wine and beer were the principal drinks. "Judges were allowed the preliminary draught, after which the people indulged ad libitum." These festivities were especially elaborate. Though convivialities at banquets were the object of ecclesiastical censure, this censure was ignored at almost every turn; and due to this, a standing regulation among the numerous associations demanded a fine for drunkenness. A charge brought against a Mason at a comparatively recent date was due to the hilarity of drinking bouts which followed Initiations.

Due to internal discipline, "it was a standing order in the English guilds, that 'Whoso makes any noyse in time of drynking where throw ye breyers and sisteren shul be greyd he shal pay to amendment of the lyzth (light) di pound of wax.'" Also, in another ordinance "was a 'rigid prohibition, under penalty of xii d., (a large sum in those days) for any member to enter the ale chamber without leave' . . . . .'The master or alderman scal have evere nith wilis ye drinken ij galoun of ale.' Two gallons of ale for a master in one drinking bout." (1)

"Oftentimes a burlesque initiation (2) was performed upon the applicant, in order to render the genuine mysteries more solemn and impressive. The brethren divested themselves of their implements and short swords in entering the mystic lodge, for the reason that the highest symbolism of harmony and sanctity was to be impressed upon the suppliant. (3) The lodge being opened in suitable form, the Master presiding directed a brother Mason to prepare the candidate. His weapons, and all substances of like material, were taken from him; a portion of his clothing was removed, so as to bare his breast." (Fallou claims that the left knee and the breast were both bared in initiation during the Middle Ages.)

"With bandaged eyes and left foot unshod he sounded three distinct blows upon the lodge door. (4) Upon his entrance, a Warden received him and conducted him before the Master, who stood in the East. The candidate knelt, and a short prayer was offered, after which he was led thrice around the room and back to the door where, with his feet at a right angle, he was ordered to advance by three upright, measured steps. The candidate was then placed in position to take the prescribed obligation, which involved the contact of his right hand with the Sacred Scriptures -- holy-dome -- and the square and compasses."(5)

"He swore to be true and loyal, to faithfully adhere to all the charges and regulations of a Mason, and to conceal with care and fidelity the secrets of the fraternity. The bandage was then removed and the three great lights explained. An apron was presented to him, and having received the password, 'Wortzeichen,' and grip, 'Handschenck,' he took his seat as a member of the Lodge." (6)

White gloves were presented to the Initiate at the termination of his degree -- a usage which seems to have had its beginning in the year 1688; yet in 1686 it was obligatory to present gloves before an initiation. "White

---

(1) - FORT, George F.; THE EARLY HISTORY & ANTIQUITIES OF FREEMASONRY, P. 212; (In footncte, he quotes from Toulman Smith's "English Guilds.") pages 61, 90 - 92, 95.
(2) - FALLOU; MYSTERIEN DER FREIMAURER, page 60: In this ludicrous ceremony the initiate was obliged to carry a staff; for what purpose does not appear.
(3) - IBID., Page 58. ..... The sanctity of a medieval lodge mounts up to the opening of Teutonic judicial organizations. . . .
(4) - IBID., page 243; This custom seems to have come from the Benedictines....
(5) - FINDEL, GESCHICHTE DER FREIMAUREREI, page 71; and FALLOU, IBID., - The wardens ..... were sworn upon the square and compass. .... ORDNUNG DER STEINMETZEN, 1462, Art. 18: This explicitly declares that the patron saints of the order were invoked during the obligation.
A curious regulation in one guild - St. Edmund's, states that "No man ne come in time of drinke beforn ye alderman and ye gild brethren in tabbard, in cloke, ne barlege, ne barefoote, under penalty of 7d." (Smith Toulman, ENGLISH GUILDS. Page 95)
(6) - FORT, George F. - (This note is continued on Page 143)

gloves were used in the mystic ceremonies in French lodges at the opening of the present Century to symbolize purity, and after the degree was conferred, were donated to the aspirant's wife."(1)

"When operative Masonry flourished, the 'prentyss' entering a guild had to present each member with a pair of gloves. In modern Speculative Masonry he receives two pairs of white gloves, one pair to fit a man's hand, the other for ladies; and he is told that a Mason has to keep his hands always spotlessly clean, and that he may present the other pair to the lady most esteemed by him. ..... Many and important are the mysteries covered by the symbolism of these two pairs of gloves." (2)

A great deal of esoteric wisdom has been conceived from the symbolism concerning these white gloves and the relation of the sexes. It has deep esoteric meaning concerning the dual nature of the soul, and though veiled, is connected with inner development.

A mystic branch of Masonry was practised secretly during the Eighteenth Century in Germany, France, Italy and in Scandinavian countries, consisting of three degrees which were only accessible to Masons who had passed the Rose Croix degree. "In the first degree, the newly accepted 'Seraph' received a pair of lady's gloves to remind him constantly that from now on he became a 'true daughter of Jehovah,' and as such he was not called 'brother,' but sister.'"(3)

"The custom of calling a man 'Sister' originated also in the Fourteenth Century."(4) It may also be found in the Zohar of the Hebrews.

An Apprentice, having received the degree of Fellow, was permitted to travel as he pleased; and when he went to a Lodge in search of work, as he approached, he gave three distinct knocks on the door. The Brothers within immediately disposed of their tools and formed themselves into geometrical positions awaiting the entrance of the seeker.

When the Fellow entered, he advanced by three upright and measured steps, gave the salute or hailing-sign to the assembled Brothers, and after this formal greeting, he addressed the Lodge in this manner: "May God greet you; may God direct you, and may God reward you, Master, Wardens, and you, good Fellows." After these words, the Master, or if he were absent, the Pillirer (Warden), as he was then called, responded with thanks. In this way the visitor discovered who was Master of the Lodge.

The Fellow then resumed his fraternal intercourse, saying, "My Master (giving his name) sends you cordial greetings." After the greeting, he went around the Lodge with a friendly salute for all the Brothers, which they returned in the same friendly way. It was the custom for Traveling

---

(6) - (Continued from Page 142.) FORT, George F.; THE EARLY HISTORY AND ANTIQUITIES OF FREEMASONRY; page 213. (In footnote he states that "Unless noted, the above details have been taken mainly from Fallou.)
(1) - REGULATEUR DU MAÇON; page 33; -- Grade d'Apprenti.
(2) - MAYER, Francis; THE GLOVES OF A MASON; from THE WORD; Vol. XXV, page 134.
(3) - Ibid, Page 135
(4) - Ibid, Page 140

Masons to go around the Lodge from one Brother to another, thanking each in turn. If the visiting Mason needed assistance, he was at liberty to demand it of the Master whose obligation compelled him to give it. If this need was financial, he must see that the distressed Brother was cared for, to the extent of his ability; and if perchance no work was at hand, the Master must go with the applicant, together with the other Brothers, and aid him.

When a Traveling Mason requested a piece of stone and a chisel upon which to carve his Mark, it was immediately given him. If his appeal for help was urgent, as a last resort he would say, "Help me, that God may help you;" at which he would take off his hat, and say very humbly, "May God thank you, Worshipful Master, Pillirers, and worthy Fellows." Very naturally his needs were cared for.

By means of signs, grips, and passwords, Masons and their Lodges were recognized everywhere. Great secrets of the Medieval Masons could be found in the rudiments of art and science with which they produced their wonderful and superb structures -- sacred edifices that were so truly "built unto God;" and these are still well preserved in symbolic, geometrical form, each sign having had its origin in the heavens and on a celestial basis which was thoroughly understood by the Masters.

Geometrical forms referred directly to art and architecture, and in their emblematic relations taught the Brothers a more profound wisdom, which was "to the Master an immutable clue; and to the Fellow and Apprentice, a fingerboard in the ever-lengthening route to knowledge." Albert Pike truly writes:- "We wonder and are amazed at the power and wisdom of the Maker; they wondered at the Work, and endowed it with life and force and with mysterious Power and Influence."

We must travel far into the past to realize the language of symbols in which ancient peoples gave their great unspoken thought. It is an old saying, "Mother Earth has shaken many civilizations from her back." Our modern world may be indebted to both Lemurian and Atlantean civilization and culture bridging many thousands of years.

The portals of old and Hidden Mysteries, whose origin lies above, are wide open to those who are seeking. Astrology and its principles were evolved millions of years ago, and it is prophesied through this Ancient Wisdom that psychic energy will come into this, our great changing era, but it will be directed toward life -- not death.

CHAPTER XII

EARLY MASONIC REGULATIONS

SYMBOLS

> Symbolism is a celestial language
> and through its alphabet can be traced
> the workings and patterns that have
> descended from the seats of the Mighty
> Ones above, who are ever watching in
> silence.
> — E. V. S.

AS SOON as a Mason became a member of the Lodge, great attention was given to his moral instruction and spiritual uplift. Any infringement of Lodge rules was severely punished. Dignity, simplicity, refinement and culture were taught and explained. The Master, through his authority, made no distinction between the Fellow and the Apprentice. Any partiality between Warden and Fellow, or any attempt at bribery, was strictly forbidden through Lodge regulations. There must be no slander among the Brethren, showing the tendency of the Master to teach his Brethren the principles of truth and morality. A profound religious sentiment pervaded the Lodges.

The 1459 ordinance of Strassburg states: "Since God, the Almighty, has graciously favored us, masters and workmen, in devoting our talents and labor in a praiseworthy manner, for the erection of His sacred edifices and other artistic works, and by such handicraft are enabled to earn an honest living, therefore, in humble imitation of Christian people, will we for the future, with pure thankfulness, continue, moved by our hearts' impulses, to serve God, and in that way deserve our soul's salvation." Religion was thus made a prominent part of Lodge secrets. It was deemed necessary to elevate the Brothers and have them realize that their Lodges were consecrated places.

Wardens gave scrupulous care and watchfulness to all implements and material used. Fellows and Apprentices at labor were equally compelled to care for their tools. The square must never be left hanging upon a stone, the gauge must be returned to its proper place, and the level hung up where it belonged; and so on, with all tools. Without permission, no laborer was allowed to take additional working tools. Any carelessness on the part of a laborer, or any infraction of these rules, must be paid for with a fine.

The ordinance of 1462 unequivocally enacted "that any fellow craftsman failing to close the shutters of the window at his work-bench after a lodge had ceased to labor, should be punished." Certain implements used in building had their mystical, moral and spiritual usages and taught through their symbols that which was ethical, venerable and constructive. Even the humble artisan became impressed with the beauties of the mystical, represented by the square, compasses, gauge, level and plumb-rule. Each implement had its inner interpretation, its inherent power, which gave the worker ability to grasp and interpret nature in its broadest sense.

Wardens were compelled to show kindness towards Fellows and Apprentices. If a Warden was accused of backbiting, he was made to stand before the Lodge, dishonored. His duty charged him with restricting the craft from excessive indulgence in regard to drinking; and similarly the duty of the Director of Ceremonies today is to watch and superintend his craft during the hours of refreshment, as well as to see that all things are properly taken care of.

Operative Masons labored in Lodges under the direction of a Master, or Warden. Every fragment of material was under critical scrutiny regarding its artistic preparation; hence as an efficient architect, he (the architect) was "deeply skilled in the traditions of Masonic government, and equally accomplished in abstruse geometric problems." He was capable of quickly determining questions, "in conjunction with two others, affecting a Master's prerogative, and was able to adjust properly elegantly-wrought stones according to architectural diagrams."

The Warden had to test the accuracy of the squares and gauges; and as an example in stone-work, he placed a rough ashlar before Apprentices and Fellows for them to draw out suitable designs upon it. If the slightest fraction of a mistake occurred upon the stone, or its position was changed, the one responsible must pay for it in stone. A Mason was severely punished even if he allowed an implement to slip or become loose, especially when needed for some delicate work, lest injury render the work less accurate. Minute regulation in every detail was insisted upon -- a model for Speculative Masons today, by which they might adjust their lives with the same exactness and minute regulation as did the Masons of Medieval days, as well as those of an even earlier age.

The office of Treasurer of a Lodge today is an inheritance from earliest times. Then, he was selected from the Fellows and his place was filled weekly, by appointment of the Master. A true account of every expenditure and receipt was necessary; all fines and dues had to be accurately accounted for; and when his term of office expired, his statement of accounts was handed over to his successor.

During the absence of a Master the Warden assumed his duties; every responsibility became his. He was the first to be present at the opening of the Lodge, at noon, and after refreshment when the Lodge was ready for work -- thus setting the example for all. The Warden was chosen with the greatest care and his competency acknowledged, that he might faithfully perform the duties entrusted to him. To make this a trustworthy position, he took a solemn oath with his hand upon the square and the gauge, in this way obligating himself under invocation of the patron saint, to be faithful to and protective of the Lodge and its Master. His installation exacted of him that which was demanded of the Master when he was placed in office; and according to the Rites of the age, a banquet followed.

During the installation ceremonies of a Master, the Brethren marched around the Lodge room before him, with an appropriate salute, signifying in symbolic manner that the new incumbent had reduced the Lodge to his possession. Great importance was given to the selection of a Master, as he had charge of all that pertained to the work of Masons under him. No detail could be left unnoticed; his authority was absolute.

When contracting for a new building, two to four Master Builders were called in, who were obliged to swear by solemn oath as to the proficiency of the Master they were to select for the new work. If in any way the Master whom they selected should prove inefficient, or damage should result from his work, or if he showed his inability to consummate the work, Lodge justice required a payment of twenty pounds of wax. Wax was a necessity for the burning of tapers. If a strange Master wished to enter the Lodge, he must pay each time for his admission five pounds of wax.

A command was given in a very old and valuable document that no workman was allowed to bring into the Lodge any woman whose character had the slightest taint of immorality; and if any worker spoke to her "he must go as far from the Lodge as a stroke-hammer or mallet could be hurled." This is a custom hoary with age. If a disreputable woman was taken into a Lodge or workshop, the penalty was four pounds of wax.

A master was compelled to regulate the affairs of the Lodge in strict accord with ancient landmarks. In every secular duty he was obliged to be absolutely upright and just, and it was the supreme duty of every Master to keep his Lodge free from discord, and demand that it be kept as sacred as a court of justice. This foundation of a perfect Brotherhood of Masons, reaching far back into the dim past, has been brought down through the ages to the present, when Masonry may become the greatest moral support of the entire world.

If an officer committed theft, defrauded anyone in the Lodge, or in any way injured a Brother, he was expelled from the Fraternity, and was thereafter "Masonically dead." Occasionally there was an opportunity for preferment by the Master, when he might select as Warden an Apprentice (whose time had not expired) because of his thorough knowledge of his art and proficiency during his term of service. Also, occasionally, an Apprentice was granted a privilege, similar to the privilege granted a Fellow, of becoming custodian of a Mark, by reason of a thorough knowledge of his art. He was then at liberty to travel, with the information necessary to gain him admission to strange Lodges -- an honor which, when conferred, was considered very great. It invested him with the Mystic Key which opened the doors to the symbols of construction, thus enabling him to aptly and correctly apply that which he had in part learned as a common workman.

If a Mason borrowed money and failed to refund it upon request, he was held degraded, which effectually severed his connection with the craft. In cases of this kind the creditor could have the matter investigated, and should the Master or Warden neglect to liquidate the debt within a stated time, the Mason was accused of un-Masonic conduct and debarred from further intercourse or assistance. The consequences were very serious. In all cases where a Master was "put to his proofs," it was necessary to have two other Masters present. It was a universal custom that if one Master, by word or act which proved to be unwarranted, slandered or injured another, he was expelled from the Fraternity; but before such penalty ensued it was indispensable that judgment be given by two Masters in conjunction with the district deputy.

During the Middle Ages every cathedral or large structure was surrounded by several Lodges of Masons over which a Master or Warden had exclusive jurisdiction. A Master had unlimited power: he could withhold work from any Mason whose private life was not above reproach, who associated with public women, who belied the character of his Brother, addressed improper language to the "maidens at the tavern" or within his home or in any way deported himself indecently.

The Apprentice was very carefully taught in the matter of preparing the rough stone, using the gauge, the measuring tool and other tools as he evinced aptitude in the rudiments of exact geometric science. A secret meaning attached to many things was withheld from him until he had attained to full knowledge and was able to interpret mystical symbols. He was obliged to learn his work just as an anatomist learns how the bones of the body are put together -- in fact, everything pertaining to the body; for the efficiency demanded of Masonic workmen who were called Apprentice-stonecutters was such that their work was sure to be progressive. His teacher was his Master, and every instructive essential was given him throughout his apprenticeship. His advancement, though gradual, was thorough, until he was ready for the next degree. He then had perfect knowledge of the intricacies of his art, and he had reached perfection of detail in his work as far as he had been taught. He could carve, mark, and delineate intricate designs in architecture with infinite skill; and to work in such beauty must have raised his inner life to a very high plane of sensitive moral ability.

For combinations used in the construction of magnificent cathedrals, their great columns, graceful walls with their wealth of floral beauty, the perfect arches whose traceries were symbolically divine in their beauty, and for the many details put together to form these great earthly temples, the key to all was the secret left untold until the candidate had finished the degree of Fellow. Then, and then only, were the interpretations and symbolic allusions given to him which were filled with the details of the emblematic treasures of his Lodge. When unfolded to him, they could easily be seen, read, and understood in all their mystic import. This was to be his "Finger-board on the highway, with no other significance than the necessary ornamentation applied to a sacred edifice or as an inexplicable appurtenance of the Lodge furniture."

No greater or finer example could ever be given our Speculative Mason today, as he too, slowly and gradually, like the Operative of old, traces his highway on the Tracing Board of his Lodge while building his own temple for Humanity.

In the old days, if the Operative Mason failed to attend prayers or worked on holy days, he was under the ban of ecclesiastical censure and forfeited his right to further Masonic Instruction.

The minute regulations regarding the explicit conduct of the Brothers have become inherently recognized in modern Freemasonry. The Brothers had to be upright and just, so that peace and justice toward all might be maintained in the Lodge. Holy days were held sacred and only those of pure and undefiled reputation could enter the Lodge. A deep religious note was held to be fundamentally necessary. If a Brother Mason knew anything dishonorable and failed to divulge it to his Master within a certain time, he was branded as faithless and unworthy as a Brother. No Brother was tolerated who in any way opposed the Master's or Warden's orders. Harmony was ever one of the great essentials. In the York manuscript it is stated: "Ye shall be true to ye Lord or Master ye serve, and truly see his pfitt and advantage."

Dangerous implements were rigidly excluded from the Lodge, or if admitted, conformed to specific rules: A Brother could not carry with him to his Lodge a knife or other weapon over half an ell in length; nor could he carry the same to banquets; all of which goes to show the strict morality of those Medieval Lodges. A fine was exacted if this law was disobeyed.

No architect was at liberty to use a Craftsman without the consent of a Master. A striking craft regulation had descended to us in its original force: No member was allowed, within the tiled recess of a Lodge, to depart without the Master's consent. Also, in Medieval guilds, if a Brother, through illness or other circumstance, was unable to support himself, he was entitled to relief from the Lodge fund; but when health was restored, or fortune came, he was compelled to return the expenditure.

Operative Masons were always urged to adhere closely to the rules of their Lodge to keep intact harmonious relations; these regulations are sought and understood by all Masons of the present time, for symbolically the Operative Mason of old becomes the Speculative Mason of today. A continuous effort was made to infuse into the life of the Fraternity the principle of honesty, not alone towards themselves but to all men, and to uphold the dignity of the Lodge, thereby maintaining the divinity, grandeur and supremacy of the living God. This law, venerable with age, was the written law of the Ancients.

Two systems of judicature were in vogue during the Middle Ages. They were termed Lesser and Greater, the Lesser having jurisdiction over petty cases arising amongst Masters and Wardens and members at large. "Larger courts possessed a final jurisdiction over matters of greater importance" which came before the yearly convention. Craftsmen were forbidden to constitute themselves judges of personal quarrels. The ordinance expressly states that a Master, and no other, due to the obligation taken previous to his installation, shall be judge.

Extraordinary power was delegated to a Master, to be used at his discretion when great edifices were to be erected, that all might proceed without interruption. Four times yearly, the presiding officer of a Lodge propounded questions to his Craftsmen as to whether envy or hatred existed among them, so that no prejudice might creep into the building of their great cathedrals and churches -- just as today, in the building of our Temples of Humanity, there must be no flaw to mar the perfection of the work. The Torgau text states that the Master, in this as in all cases, was solemnly sworn to fearlessly wield the authority of his office according to the law, that he "should do right and let alone what was not right." No detrimental thought was ever allowed to intervene in their work. This has become the heritage of Masons today. The Masonic Constitution during this cyclic period should be sought, read, studied and digested by each Brother in the Lodge, that he might know how great is the foundation of true Masonry.

The places where ancient Teutonic and Norse nations assembled for their tribunals were vigilantly maintained as sacred. Originally courts were held in the open, under the broad expanse of heaven, amid the beauties of nature. Gothic tribunals assembled on high hills or uplands as such eminences were thought to be of a high degree of holiness, and the sacerdotal fire offerings to the ancient divinities were there given as an invocation to help in judging the perplexities due to law. Though the Christian religion ceased from keeping these sacrificial fires, the sacredness of the courts was maintained.

Under some Norse tribunals, valleys claimed veneration, and the courts of law were held within such enclosures under safeguard of the Norse deities. During the Carlovingian age, these law courts were ordered changed from the open air and were to be held in sheltered places. Though Charlemagne attempted "to crush out, beneath the weight of his imperial power, this venerable and popular judicature in the rural districts, these outdoor tribunals still perpetuated a vigorous existence." At the close of the Middle Ages they were extinguished.

COURTS

The earliest form of a court was circular; subsequently this shape gradually changed to an oval; and finally, to an oblong square. The earliest information regarding these courts claims that the Brothers assembled around the Master in a semi-circle. At the close of the last Century, Lodge banquets were formed in a semi-circle. Since that time, Lodges have been described as oblong squares. Scandinavian antiquities state that this method of making a circular form, subsequently becoming an oblong square, was begun with stout hazel-twigs fastened together with strong cord; and though at times the excitement due to adjudication of disputes was so great that the pressure from behind snapped the cord, the sanctity of the place prevented a forceful entrance.

"In 1283, the posts surrounding the allotted place were called 'Pale,' or 'Palings.'" In its most ancient form or generic name it was pal. Pale or post has been retained. These posts were to guard against outsiders. There were two main entrances into the enclosed courtyard, but from which cardinal points they were arranged is unknown. They were under the charge of two guards who were careful to admit only duly authorized persons. These two guards, due to the duty they performed, were called "Pallirers." The original meaning of this word was "a guardian of the court, pale, or post."

When the Ordinances of 1459 and 1462 were committed to writing, this word "Pallirer" had become defined as "Warden" -- one who guards; "and in this sense it occurs in the Torgau book of Masonic Law." In the ordinance of 1459 the word is given as Palirer or Parlirer; in the Torgau it is Pallirer.

Heathen antiquity gave deep reverence to the changes of the Moon, a new Moon or a full Moon being especially favorable. When the orb was waning, it typified that which was sombre and sinister -- a singular notion which was held by the Germans during the time of Tacitus. "Civil courts were assembled by an almost universal usage on or before the full Moon."

Medieval Lodges began their work at Sunrise and closed at Sunset, due to a superstition sanctifying all diurnal business. Gothic courts or Lodges, during the Medieval Ages, opened before the Rising Sun. Day and sunlight were thought to be essential. They were suspended exactly at Sunset. Time and place were most important. At the first ray of Sunrise the signal was given for silence; and after that Lodge function began, with the Master of the Lodge in full authority, placing the sacred enclosure under the ban of peace and harmony. Uninterrupted silence was demanded; and when stillness ensued, announcements were made or proclamations given.

The opening of all ancient Gothic courts was similar in significance to the inauguration of Masonic Lodge work. "Judicial appointments, or furniture, consisted of benches set up with careful formality, and a sword as an emblem of justice was invariably suspended." (The sword is typical of light and the source of light. The sword, in the Lodges of Germany, was always placed before the Master.)

"A shield hung near the judges' seat and, perhaps, in remote times, may have been affixed to a spear thrust into the ground. Other symbols, such as an iron gauntlet, swords, shears, an axe, and a cord, lay exposed upon the bench at the commencement of the court, and remained there until it concluded the session. Upon the close of the tribunal, benches were upended, the emblems of judicial authority removed, and the justice stood up."[1] This meant silence and peace. In the Middle Ages a judge was required to remain in his seat during business of a regular order. If he arose, it was the signal for all argument to cease. This has become a fixed regulation. When a Master rises, or at the stroke of his gavel, all debate must cease, this being the signal for silence.

Medieval courts were often designated Lodges. Identical operations of Lodges and courts in Medieval times are too frequently known to be accidental. Perfect stillness and silence was at all times insisted upon; no one could leave or enter without permission; nor could he leave his place without permission. Discussion of private affairs was prohibited, without qualification, unless permission was given. All applicants for the Mysteries of the craft were obliged to give undeniable proof of their legitimacy and freedom of birth. No serf or bondsman was allowed to be within nine paces of the Lodge were justice was administered, the idea being that slavery debased or degraded a man. Lodges were jealously guarded against the serf. His presence would have tainted the sacred enclosure.

THE ROSE

Hanging from the ceiling above the banquet-table of Northern peoples was a garland of flowers with a rose placed prominently in the center, to symbolize that everything spoken or accomplished at the banquet must be held secret. From this we have the two words, "Sub Rosa." In the Gothic code the rose was an emblem of secrecy — as it was, also, with the Medieval Masons. This rose is often sculptured on the walls of European churches and elsewhere. From the rose in its emblematic form we have the mystical message of the three roses on the apron of the Master Mason.

---

[1] - FORT, George F.; THE EARLY HISTORY & ANTIQUITIES OF FREEMASONRY, P. 269

THE GAVEL OR MALLET

The antiquity of the Master's Gavel or Mallet is of absorbing interest. It has been the emblem of Power — the governing instrument of the office of the Worshipful Master. It is a symbol of the tenure or right by which a Master holds his office. Without it he is impotent to rule his Lodge or assembled Brothers. The Gavel was invested with Divine and extraordinary power, which has come from the Ancient Past into the Lodges of today. In the hands of a Master, it shows his power and perpetuates the Medieval idea of possession, directly alluding to its ancient usage. When a decision is announced, the sound in <u>that blow</u> is merely the re-echo of a power current many centuries ago in the administration of justice. Used in our courts and in the hands of an auctioneer, its blows have a similar significance. As a symbol of Power, it goes back to remote antiquity. It is the emblematic pledge of a Master's ownership over his Lodge.

In 1462, the Gavel or Mallet was recognized as a Masonic symbol when used to define, as well as to symbolize, the territory surrounding a Lodge. It became a religious symbol establishing proprietary rights over land and water, accomplished by throwing the Hammer (Mallet) as far as possible. The ground thus covered was given into the possession of the person who wielded the Hammer.

The original Gavel was a double axe, belonging to the Neolithic age, representing a double force or symbol of Power and Divinity. It preceded the single one. From the double axe has evolved the Common Gavel and the Master's Gavel — symbols held as sacred then, as they are today. A stick with two others crossing it was originally used by the Pygmies to denote a chief; and as an emblem of Power and Might, is found among the chiefs of Central Africa. African tribes were the offshoots of the Atlanteans; the earlier Paleolithic men of Europe were of pure Atlantean stock.

Weaving began in the Neolithic age and was used by prehistoric man on both hemispheres. He spun fibre on what we call a spindle. It belonged to the same sign as did the Swastica. The Swastica heads the religious symbols of every nation. It was the Worker's Hammer, the magic weapon of Thor; but when he lost his magic Hammer, part of his divine strength — his "Resistless Force" — was taken from him. When the Hammer was brought back by his sons, it was no longer a weapon of war but was used to consecrate a new heaven, a new creation, and a new earth. Then it became known as "the Hammer of Creation" — a potent charm so famous that it has been engraved on churchbells and on cathedral walls; and it is found engraved in the Tower of London. When used with the guildic cup of consecration in an invocation to Thor, its symbolism is most profound, for it is said to have been imbued with magical properties. This Hammer, when used in symbolic reverence, becomes the Mallet or Gavel of the Worshipful Master in Masonry.

Thor, the great Scandinavian god, is always represented with a hammer. He was the God of Thunder. His hammer, when used in the solemnities of marriage, was laid on the knee of the veiled bride and foretold her new destiny. Food and drink among the Norsemen were blessed with it, or the hammer sign; and even the banquetting cup was rendered hopeful and prosperous by it. And when Thor's Hammer or sign restored the dead goat to life, it had an important Masonic allusion.

Prior to the Nineteenth Century, in Masonic Initiations the candidate was consecrated into the Mysteries with the Mallet. During the stone period in Denmark, the flint mallets were cross-shaped, having a hole in the middle for the handle. This design was used in consecrating sacrificial offerings in the mystical ceremonies belonging to Thor's worship. A hammer was placed in the tomb of the ancient Celt. It was also an emblem in the Buddhist religion. Medieval cloisters had a wooden hammer, used when a monk in agony was in a dying condition. As the "Worker's Hammer", it struck sparks from flint, and mystically speaking, the sparks were said to create new worlds.

As of old, when a Master of a Lodge grasps his Mallet, he becomes immediately the symbol of "Resistless force," typical of absolution and authority, when the Mallet is wielded with skill and energy. As the Master now wields his Gavel it constitutes his possession of the sacred environment of the Lodge. No other symbol in Masonry can claim a more remote antiquity. The Gavel, or Hammer, belonging to Thor, was placed in the West; but by an unaccountable translating, the Gavel has gone to the East.

Thor's Hammer, as an emblem of destruction and an instrument of death, was used by the Priesthood to solemnize burial ceremonies and the Rites of cremation. The Mallet, or Setting Maul, as a Masonic symbol, is used for like purposes, with all its tragic attributes -- and there were many of them. It comes from legendary times into modern Masonry and into the Mysteries of Hiram Abiff. Both in Teutonic and present Masonic times, this Hammer, as the Setting Maul, originally of destructive power in both systems, is made an emblem of death and is so used today.

It is known that Charles Martel carried a little hammer in imitation of Thor's, assuming that he had near him a symbol of "Resistless Light," (Martell is a diminutive of the Latin word, Malleus, and signifies a small hammer,) to prove that it was not a weapon of war but a symbol of Power when used in battle. Legends of English Masonry claim that Charles Martel was a patron of the Craft of Masonry and highly skilled in geometry. The Mallet was finally substituted by the Sword, as it was thought to be of equal power. The Setting Maul, like all Masonic symbols and tools, is traced back to a time almost beyond reckoning, appearing in all parts of the world and persisting as we know it today. The Setting Maul, the Gavel, and the Hammer were names differently expressing the same tool. All tools of the ancient workers symbolized the secrets of the soul and of human generation. The Secret of Secrets was known only to a few, others were not thought worthy to receive, or meet with reverence, the profundities of Life, of Creation or of God.

L I G H T S

Light or Fire is the most sacred of all Elements, the most sacred and supreme of all symbols. Light is the vehicle of Life, for where God is, there Light is. He who worships Light worships God and the Mason who serves Light serves God. Hiram resembled the Element of Fire, and a supreme secret taught in the Mysteries was a quick release, called Regeneration, perpetuated in the third degree of the Blue Lodge of Masonry today.

As an emblem of a Triune Deity, the Trinity is represented in the three chief officers presiding in Lodges, and in the three Greater and the three Lesser Lights, the three movable and immovable jewels, the square, the level and the plumb, as well as in the three Pillars that support a Lodge. Kabalistically, the central Pillar symbolizes equilibrium; the one at the right

(Jachin) symbolizes the outpouring of the Wisdom of God, and the left Pillar (Boaz) is understanding, receptive of the coming forth of Wisdom.

The Three symbolic Lights in Lodges had their place back in Pagan and Teutonic superstitions and mythology. In Norse Temples, three symbolic Lights are placed before the columns of Odin, Thor and Frey. In the magnificent Gothic Temple at Upsala, Sweden, they are sacredly revered -- each column symbolizing his or her divinity. Odin holds a sword; Thor, at his left, grasps his mallet; and by his side is Frey, Goddess of Beauty and Plenteousness. The column consecrated to Odin was called the Pillar of Wisdom; the one to Thor, the Pillar of Strength; while the one to Frey was consecrated to Beauty. At the column of Frey, a sheaf of wheat was placed, to typify the maturing prosperity of the Southern Sun, hastening the ripening of the corn and wheat.

The word "Shibboleth," symbol of the reddening corn, according to the Hebrew, comes from "Shabal" - to flow, synonymous with plenty. In a translation from the Vulgate Testament, it was rendered "an ear of corn," -- corn being the type of productive, generative nature. It became Frey's symbol when traditional worship prevailed. In the Brahman temples the sheaf of wheat was placed West.

In arcane reading, this peculiar word "Shibbolithon" "is recorded to have been used as a test for the separation of two peoples." It was due to the pronunciation of this name that the Gileadites distinguished the fleeing Ephraimites, who said "Sibboleth" instead of "Shibboleth." (Judges XII, 6). It has been a disputed, argumentative subject of Masonic writers. Hutchinson claims that, from its root-words, it means "cherished stone," having mystically something to do with the stone of Saturn and Jupiter. "The flinty stone which, in making bargains the swearer held in his hand and of which he said, 'If knowingly I deceive .... cast me away from all that is good, as I cast away this stone,'" refers to a ceremony which by some has been connected with the Abraxas stone. "The word 'Shibboleth,' said to mean 'plenty;' also 'waterfall,' and sometimes 'waterford,' is also translated 'floods.'" (Ps. LXIX, 2) (1)

Cups and bowls of terra cotta found in Babylonian ruins are covered inside with inscriptions as charms against calamities. These inscriptions are composed in the Chaldean language, mingled with Hebrew words. The bowls are thought to belong to descendants of the Jews who were captive in Babylonia. "The word 'Halleluiah' appears upon them; and here is a word with which ancient Syro-Chaldeans conjured -- one which, through the vicissitudes of language, has become the 'Shibboleth' of modern revivalists." (2)

CHAIRS

The Master's Chair in the East typified the rising Sun -- and Light; that through him the warmth and power of the Sun might be transmitted to the Brethren, Seekers of Light, that they might gradually rise into a greater harmony with THE GREAT ARCHITECT OF THE UNIVERSE. In Lodges today this chair of the Master in the East is approached by three steps. It symbolizes the rising Sun, Light, or the Seat of Wisdom. It is unknown just when this Seat of Wisdom was translated to a place in the East. Anciently, Wisdom was represented by the Great Mother, or the Moon -- darkness -- out of which Wisdom

---
(1) - GOULD, S. C. - SOCIETAS ROSICRUCIANA.
(2) - LAURENCE, Richard; THE BOOK OF ENOCH (Footnote in Introduction, Page IV)

was said to come. The primary was assigned to the Moon in celestial making. In Babylonia, their principal god endowed with the male sex was the Moon -- Sin -- which regularly preceded the Sun. Sacred calendars regulated religious life and its ceremonies according to the Moon. The gender of an object was in the language of the country; the divinity who bore the name was masculine or feminine; the Moon was a god, and the Sun a goddess. All created a perpetual variety in Ancient Mythology.

The Senior Warden's Chair is approached by two steps, and the Junior Warden's, by one step above the floor. They represented the three stages of life: youth, manhood and old age. The mists of time have obscured the original meaning, but youth provides all that is fresh and joyous, and typifies beauty, which belongs to the sunny South where the Junior Warden sits; manhood provides all that gives Strength, and all that goes with the setting Sun, in the West; but old age, with its accumulation of Wisdom, is given the East -- the place of the rising Sun, or Light. The Scandinavian legend, coming from ancient Masonry, often portrays Odin as an old man with a long white beard. The Point Within the Circle and the Cube were his emblems.

S Y M B O L S

THE FRATERNITY OF THE BUILDERS, when working under the plans of the Master Architects of heaven, were given celestial signs for Masonry, used today. These were followed by gestures, originating with the "gesture language," the oldest known form or idea of language. Masonry is primarily founded upon Truth -- immutable and eternal. It is found among the Stonecutters, who must use Truth in their work with the square, the compasses, the twenty-four-inch gauge, the rule, the chisel, the mallet, trowel and shoe, and the interlaced triangle -- all alluding esoterically to Speculative Masonry today. The extended hand is a beautiful symbol as it makes its sign of Brotherhood. It was an ideograph of the ancient Mother, as was also the crossing of hands in the mystic chain. The early form of rule and measure was to stretch out the first finger -- a rule of Truth. The twenty-four-inch rule is symbolical of the twenty-four-hours of the day -- representing a double truth on the basis of which all things were made perfect. The eye is also a Masonic symbol -- the "All Seeing Eye" that Masons may see deeply into the world if their services are to be complete and true.

The newly initiated candidate was read to from a book of stones called "The Petroma." The Petroma was a book of Truths, belonging to the Great Mother as her two-fold truths. The two stones cemented together represented an interpretation of the Mysteries. We have this today in the double tablets of the Ten Commandments.

T H E C R O S S

The first Cross was celestial, known as the Ankh or Ansated Cross, an Egyptian symbol of Eternity and Continuity. The earliest shape of the Ankh Cross was a mere loop containing both cross and circle in one image. It was first connected with the earliest of all Mothers and was carried in front of her as a symbol of Life, an Oath, and a Covenant. In early times this cross was made of cords or of grass, -- a symbol of atonement. As the cross of cords, it is used in Masonry today.

156

One of the most primitive forms of a cross was made of two human figures. This dated back to the Neolithic age; it also represented the four quarters of the world and the four Elements -- Fire, Earth, Air and Water. In Masonry the cross enters into the mythology of the Eighteenth Degree and higher ones.

The first primitive form of a cross "was two human figures crossed, and is found depicted on one of the seal cylinders found in a prehistoric grave at Naqada, dating back to the Neolithic age."

These "two figures were blended to form the so-called Swastica, as here seen cut on a sepulchral stone found at Miegle, in Perthshire. From this form was evolved various other forms throughout the world."
-- Albert Churchward.

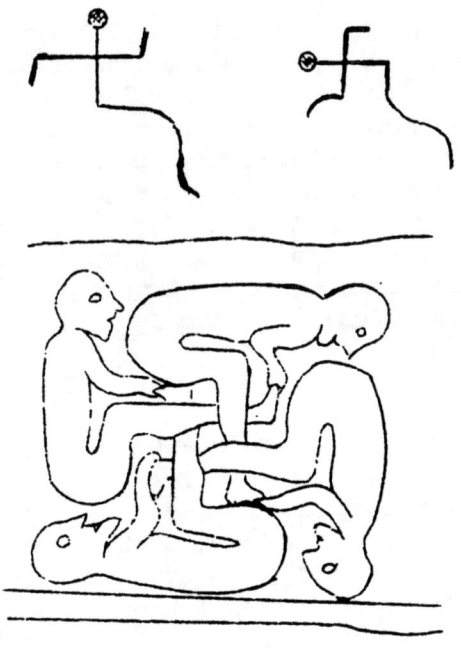

It was on faith "founded upon the Mystery of the Cross over 30,000 years ago" that the dead received their burial. "The gnosis of the Crucifixion, however, was the same in the Stellar Cult, 300,000 years before this, as is witnessed" by a "pictograph taken from the Central American Ruins. It is over 200,000 years old, and represents the Crucifixion during the period of the Stellar Cult. He is crucified on the two Poles -- North and South. He is God of the North and the South. ..... A Crown of Thorns is depicted on his head. His side is pierced with a spear from whence blood and water is falling on his Spiritual Name. ..... He is supported by four brothers ... representing Matthew, Mark, Luke and John, of the Christians, represented by four squares," with other symbols. "He is the Great Lord and God of Heaven situated at the North Pole. He is God of the Pole Stars and God of the North and South, and the Heavens, and Paradise; and his age is given as thirty-three years in the Mexican Codices, - 95 f.; It is written in the hieroglyphics of Egypt as '33 years.'" (1)

This curious Crucifixion of long ago, though varying in name according to time and country, holds the same signs and symbols as are found in all parts of the world.

The Mystic Chain is formed from a circle and a cross -- by crossing both arms from one Mason to another -- deriving all its significance from the circle and cross of heavenly origin. The Masonic square is a form of ninety degrees, or one-fourth of a circle; the circle is a symbol of heaven; and the

─────────────────────
(1) - CHURCHWARD, Albert; SIGNS & SYMBOLS OF PRIMORDIAL MAN, Pages 479-480.

square, of earth. The circle was broken to form the square. The Tau, so important in the Mysteries, is a symbol of nine, as a three-quarter symbol, when it becomes the generator.

The perfect square is the Swastica, which represents vivifying Fire, or Life as a generating Fire; and out of the vastness of antiquity this Firey Cross of Life calls us today. The Cross is of immense antiquity. The Tree of Life and the Cross are identical. "The Tree of Paradise was called the Tree of the Cross, and this Cross was the original four corners of the world, created by the Seven Stars encircling the Pole." These Stars, THE FRATERNITY OF THE BUILDERS, were among the first fundamental symbols of Creative Cause. The time draws near when Masonry will be truly re-identified as a mystic craft with foundations in facts which go beyond any religious mysteries known. The way of the Cross and the way of Life are the same, the Crucifixion being needed before union of the Human and the Divine can take place.

The rising of the river Nile in Egypt was marked by a column having one, two or three lines across it in the form of a cross. Sometimes this was surmounted with a circle or a globe. This pole with one line came to represent the Tau Cross. Later, two points of flame, or two serpents, were annexed. It was the Egyptian Nileometer, known as a symbol of life, health, prosperity and happiness, with power to avert evils resulting from the inundation of the river. It is now one of the most famous symbols in Masonry.

In one of the modern degrees named "The Brazen Serpent," the jewel is a Serpent entwined upon a pole or Tau Cross. This Cross, when emblematically formed of one perpendicular line, is a symbol of matter, or the female ray. It also belongs to the oldest form of letters, glyph of the Third Root Race at the time of its symbolic fall. The Egyptians added the circle above as an attribute of the Great Mother, when it became known as the Ankh Cross, an emblem of Life. It is the same Cross as that used by the Atlanteans. In New Zealand, it was generally known as the Totem Pillar.

The Tau Cross is the Alpha and Omega of secret and Divine Wisdom. The triple Tau, although its origin is too old to trace, came to represent the Trinity, or the attributes of Deity. The headless or Tau Cross is also a figure of the three quarters of a zodiacal circle, or nine signs; the fourth quarter, or last three signs, was, for mystical reasons, not completed. In the Kabala this number Nine is the Broken Wheel, the wheel which cannot be completed until man becomes the perfect number Twelve.

If the three spiritual degrees of Masonry -- those of the Entered Apprentice, the Fellow Craft, and the Master Mason -- are symbolically added to the nine months of embryonic creativeness, this allows the candidate to prepare a way for the completion of the Broken Wheel; for in future, we are told through occultism, man must spend twelve months in embryo before birth, until those mystical gates are opened for completeness.

THE ARCH

The mystical building of an Ark, or Arch, in the Masonic Ritual, is similarly one with the Ark or Arch of heaven. Nine Companions in the Royal Arch Chapter, who hold their hands meeting above their heads, must be present to form this Arch. The candidate passes under this living Arch, and, at the entrance, the Companions give "The Sign of Sorrow." When the candidate rises from an imposed darkness, it is as one of the Builders of the Temple of the Great Arch or Ark of celestial making. It represents that which is known as the Put Circle, in heaven, composed of nine gods who formed a three-quarter circle, with one quarter left out for the Abyss. When the "Sign of Sorrow" was given, it was similar to the mourning of the Egyptian gods for Osiris, who had to pass through the gate, or Ark, to his resurrection.

The Final form of the Ark in heaven was the completion of the zodiac of twelve signs. Hermes describes this final form of the Ark as the "Twelve Signs of Necessity," by which the twelve torments of darkness are overcome and driven away. This was the "conquering of the Twelve Signs of the Zodiac called the 'Wheel of Necessity.' The zodiac represents the material animal existence of physical life on earth, and every sign must be lived in its symbolical rendering and conquered, if the soul is to receive its freedom and awaken to the realities of a spiritual existence, the lower consciousness becoming merged with the Eternal." (1)

---

(1) - E.V.S. - "THE CELESTIAL SHIP OF THE NORTH.

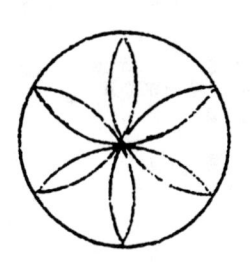

Chapter XIII

S Y M B O L S

> The science of numbers relating
> to the art of will-power has been the
> Key of Magic. It will open the gates
> of the universe.
> — E. V. S.

THE NORTH

NO LODGE of Masons today illuminates the North with a symbolic light. The Frisians called the North the "Fear Corner," in harmony with the Scandinavian superstition. In the details of Norse tribunals a superstitious notion arose that caused the people to regard the North as the deadly night. They made it a place of death, which was ingrafted into craft formularies. Masonic Lodges have either directly or indirectly indicated this superstition. The North was denominated sombre and black, but, going beyond this to its origin, the North was looked upon as the place of birth -- of creation -- not of death. It was the creative point in the heavens.

"Early Christian ecclesiastics assigned seats on the North side to new proselytes, emblematic of the darkness of unbelief from which they had barely escaped;" and "at the close of the 18th Century, the candidate for the degree of Entered Apprentice was stationed directly in the North, for the reason that he was typically able to sustain but a feeble light."[1]

THE HAT

Masons always had their heads covered when convening. This is not always carried out today, meaning that the old sublime significance of the Master's Hat is nearly doomed. In French Lodges it was the privilege of the Master, at the conclusion of the Rites, to hand his hat to the candidate with these words: "For the future, you shall be covered in a Master's Lodge," meaning that a hat contained the secret symbolism of authority, liberty and superiority. In the transference of property the purchaser received a hat from the hands of the judge, the title passing in this way; and when the hat was placed upon a pole, it indicated both subjection and authority. It was also used as a symbol of freedom from servitude.

KNOCKS

As early as 1462, Operative Masons opened and closed their Lodges with knocks, a usage belonging to ancient times -- an exacted law. Three strokes from the Master convened members of the Third Degree; two were given in rapid succession by Wardens to call those of the Fellow Craft Degree; and

---

(1) - From "REGULATEUR DU MAÇON" - Grade d'Ap. - Pages 36 -39

one blow was for any degree of workmen belonging to the Lodge. If one were late or dilatory in beginning his daily work, a penalty was recorded against him on a stone -- generally a rough ashlar; and should the Warden allow the penalty to go unpaid, he himself was obliged to assume it.

In Gothic courts three knocks were of symbolic import. We still find this to be true in Masonic bodies. The numeral 3 became separated, for symbolical reasons, by dividing the strokes, as 1-2 (one to two); and 2-1 (two to one). Masonic strokes are sounded in cadences in Lodges today. The sacred circle of Medieval times had three stakes of entrance. Three drinks were of mystical import, suggesting the origin of an ancient Masonic custom at banquets when a toast was given in three drinks, and with three distinct motions of the horn, when placing it on the table. Three fires in the homes of the Northern races were typical of their three great divinities. Superstitions concerning this number seem almost endless; even crimes came under the three; robbery, arson and theft; and the entertaining of guests was limited to three days. In Teutonic courts, three judges were required to open a lodge; the maximum was seven, but at times only five were required.

N U M B E R S

Numbers play a most important part in Lodge Ritual. The fundamental numbers are 3, 5 and 7. The number 3 constitutes the minimum of the Lodge. The numbers 3, 5 and 7 are representative of the three, five and seven steps in Speculative Masonry, which show the circular or winding walk. They are mystical numbers greatly honored by the Masons.

The number 3 symbolized in the Triangle comes out of ancient times -- hundreds of thousands of years ago. Morality in the art of living, Science of being and Philosophy of life, were thoroughly understood by the early Builders and constituted a trinity of great knowledge, which belongs to the Lodges today as it did to the Operative Builders of long ago.

The 3 is of the most archaic significance, and has come to the Freemasons today in its ancient characteristics. Similarly, the 7, though archaically not so prominent, is filled with sacred symbolism. Pythagoras called 7 the "Vehicle of Life." It is also the symbol of the Seven Steps of the Ladder leading towards complete union with the Divine; and in the oldest of all records, signifies the Seven Great Stars, THE FRATERNITY OF THE BUILDERS.

The seven-fold classification of the universe and man is the teaching of the "Secret Doctrine," and from the zodiac a key is given for a better understanding of the seven-fold system of all the Rounds and Races down to the present time -- which passes on into the endless future.

1, 3, 5, 7 and 9 were said to be perfect numbers. They became thoroughly mystic and have played a part in every cosmogony and evolution of human beings.

"All countries relate to what the Masons affirm to be symbolical of the nine names or attributes by which Deity is known to all Initiates; yet the old heathens seem to have known what the greatest of the Supreme Chapters of Masonry knows." Why its loss? Why the secret vault?

The number 9 represented the great harmony of the universe, ages before history began. Its significance was known and recognized beyond a time of reckoning. If this number 9 is multiplied by any other number, from 2 to 9, the resulting number, when reduced to a digit, will always equal 9. To illustrate:

```
        2 x 9 = 18:   1 + 8 = 9
        3 x 9 = 27:   2 + 7 = 9
        4 x 9 = 36;   3 + 6 = 9
        5 x 9 = 45:   4 + 5 = 9
        6 x 9 = 54:   5 + 4 = 9
        7 x 9 = 63:   6 + 3 = 9
        8 x 9 = 72:   7 + 2 = 9
        9 x 9 = 81:   8 + 1 = 9
              396:    3 + 9 + 6 = 18:  1 + 8 = 9
```

The resultant multiples (i.e., 18 to 81, as above) when added together become 396. Add this to 270 -- representing the period of gestation -- and we have the sacred number 666; which indicates the incarnation of the solar logos in humanity. Nine is the symbol of fire; and the sacred fires in the temples were under the care of nine Brahmans.

The pentagram is a five-pointed star. When the upper point is reversed, it symbolizes the hand of a magician; when the two hands are clasped, they represent the number Ten and belong to the Master's symbols. They are the pairs of opposites, or union of the Divine with the human, teaching the harmonizing of body and Spirit; and by the strong Grip of the Lion, meet in Brotherhood and Peace.

"All events, like all forms, result either from conflict or from a balancing of forces. These can be represented in numbers. The future may thus be determined in advance by calculation."

Pythagoras revealed God to the world as the Great Geometrician and concealed his doctrine in a numerical and geometrical system — the only form in which he gave it to the world. The secret Pythagorian Doctrine of Numbers was preserved by the monks of Thibet, the Hierophants of Egypt and Eleusis, at Jerusalem, in the circular chapters of the Druids, and especially concealed in that mysterious book, the Apocalypse of St. John. Plato also concealed his doctrine of a numerical and geometrical system, as did likewise the Jewish Priests of the Kabala, who elaborated a system of numeration used by the Rabbis in the Talmud. Due to this, the greater part of the Ancient Mysteries have not been understood, as numbers were symbols in all esoteric doctrines. They had constituted a connecting link between the early gesture signs and the spoken language; but the theories of numbers which formed a part of the Ancient Mysteries have ceased to be understood.

The oldest form of numbers is in the esoteric doctrine of the Egyptians from whom the Greeks received it and then transmitted it to the modern world. Pythagoras had his knowledge of numbers from the Egyptians, teaching that God was Number and Harmony. He instructed his disciples to honor numbers, geometrical designs or diagrams, with the names of the gods. Just how the Egyptians demonstrated their use of numbers has not been discovered, but it is known that numbers formed a part of their dogma in the laws referred to by Plato as having been "ten thousand years old and perpetuated as one of the bases of religion and art by all subsequent peoples."

Numbers held an important place in the theological and spiritual systems of the Ancients. "These they fixed, and exhibited patterns of them in their temples; and no painter or artist is allowed to innovate upon them, or to leave the traditional forms, or invent new ones."[1]

As Plato stated, "Their works of art are painted or molded in the forms that had been used ten thousand years ago." Pythagoras and Plato were the two greatest teachers of the Aryan Race; and in the centuries to come they will still be honored for their true greatness of soul. The world is destined to go back gradually and gain a broader mental outlook through the knowledge of those illuminated souls. What the Canon of Art really was, is practically unknown, but traces of it are found in the religious art of the Greeks and Christians today.

The Ancients held that the division of time and numbers was divine and was revealed to mankind through the motion of the stars. The veneration given to numbers had its source in the stars. The progress of mathematics must often have been the result of the progress of astronomy. "Eternal mathematics and equilibrated forces were the sovereign principles in all things." The science of numbers relating to the art of will-power has been called the Key of Magic. It will open all the gates of the Universe.

The guilds of initiated artists which existed throughout the world knew that the Ancient Egyptians held their theology to be the epitome of arts. It was their guide and the law was their sacred arcanum, only communicated in symbols and allegories. Today theology has seemingly lost these symbols, though they may be found in the ornaments, meaningless to the uninitiated, as well as in modernized parables. It becomes a great and divine privilege for Masons today to unveil false imitations -- to once more restore to the world the mystical meaning of religious symbols in art and thus bring back the reverence and beauty that belonged to ancient races.

When all was mystical and metaphysical, it was natural that numbers should be brought into the service of art; and geometry provided a symbolical code whose symbols enabled the mathematicians to use the Secret Mysteries in their works. Traces of the old geometrical system survive in the Masonic Orders today. Architects and Masons insist upon geometry being the foundation of their work. This explains the notice over the door of Plato's sanctuary: "LET NONE IGNORANT OF GEOMETRY ENTER HERE." Plato was initiated into Masonry and acclaimed as an Ancient Brother.

All systems of religious mysticism are based on numerals. Their very sacredness begins with 1 (one) and ends in 0 (zero) -- the boundless infinite circle of the universe. All science is based on geometrical calculation. Pythagoras claimed, of the Point Within the Circle: "The element of all existence is a point;" "extended out in length, it forms a line; expanded in every direction, it is a surface; the line curved round a center becomes a circle; hence, a point in a circle represents the element of all possible mathematics or created figures in the universe and their origins."[2]

---

(1) - THE CANON, Page 9.
(2) - GARRISON, Rev. J. F., M.D.; HISTORY OF THE LOST WORD, Page 467; from FORT, George F.; THE EARLY HISTORY AND ANTIQUITIES OF FREEMASONRY.

TREES

The Ygdrasil, or Ash Tree of the Norse legend, so often quoted, had three widely-spread roots, upon which Northern mythology based its entire physical world. The branch towards the land of the Giants contained the fountain in which Wisdom was concealed. Odin drank daily from its waters to replenish his Wisdom. The Ash is the most sensitive of trees and only unfolds fully and truly under favorable conditions. Her roots spread widely and quickly, a little below the surface of the earth, and like life itself, soon exhaust the soil. "Its inherent strength and profundity lie in movement; and Nordics divined this in mystery." They would not kill an animal before it had propagated its young species, so that it should have knowledge before passing. It is the Ash Tree that cannot die until the last battle of life is fought; but constantly its roots are being gnawed by the mighty serpent Midhoger.

The fruit of the Sycamore, or Fig Tree, gave a divine drink which was used during certain ceremonies in order that one might become wise. The Sycamore was called the Tree of Abnormal Knowledge. This divine drink is used in one of the higher Masonic degrees.

Trees were the first temples under which man worshipped. They were made emblems of spirituality, as their branches stretched always towards the light. A mystic silence penetrates forests, a silence which has neither beginning nor end. Primitive man seemed to feel that the Holy Spirit was there. The Great Mother was imaged in the Tree whose branches spread over the entire world. This was the Tree belonging to all nations, a Tree of the Universe, of Time, and of Life.

In the promise of Esdras, [1] seven mountains are given with the Tree of Life in a twelve-fold form: "They shall have the tree of life for an ointment of sweet savor; they shall neither labor nor be weary. ..... I have sanctified and prepared for thee twelve trees laden with divers fruits, and as many fountains flowing with milk and honey, and seven mighty mountains, whereupon grow roses and lilies, whereby I shall fill my children with joy." This was the zodiacal tree; its leaves, the planets.

The Crown of Thorns placed upon the head of Jesus was a bit of the Acacia Tree — a tree found in every part of the world. It will easily take root anywhere and will bud and branch luxuriously. A sprig of Acacia was placed over the grave of Hiram Abiff. It was like a cross on the altar, a cross which led through the grave into the realms of reality.

The Acacia is held most sacred by all Masons and plays an important part in their symbolic Ritual. It was an ancient and revered emblem of the Mysteries. Candidates entering the tortuous passageways in which ceremonials were given, carried in their hands branches of Acacia, or a small cluster of its leaves -- to them, sanctified flowers. The shittim wood in the Tabernacle and the Ark of the Covenant is said to be of Acacia; it is the thorny tamarisk. In Egypt, the Ark that contained Osiris floated over the waters until it became entangled in the branches of the tamarish (or Acacia) which had grown to the height of a tree. His body was within the trunk, which made it a Tree of Life. To both the Egyptian and the Jew the Acacia became very sacred. Philosophers

---
(1) - ESDRAS II, - 12-19.

and Priests were often referred to as Trees; Initiates belonging to certain Mysteries were called Cedars; and the famous Cedars of Lebanon used in the building of King Solomon's Temple were illuninated Sages or Initiates.

In the Kabala the clustering together of the Seven Great Stars was called Kabbing and the Kabala meant the Doctrine of the Stars. The Sephirotic Tree of the Kabala had its roots in heaven and its branches upon earth. The Great Pyramid of Egypt has been thought of as an inverted tree with the roots at the apex and the branches streaming or diverging in four streams towards the base -- a Great Tree of the World.

It was under an Oak Tree with its mistletoe that the Druids performed their most sacred Rites in honor of the Supreme Deity. They were often called "Men of the Oak Tree."

In the Island of Delos, the inhabitants believed in gigantic Palm Trees. In Samos, Athens, Arcadia and Dodona all the people worshipped in sacred groves. The Oracle in the grove of Zeus at Dodona was an enormous dovecote. The trees were full of doves; and the answers to all questions were given in the cooing of the doves.

India's worship of the tree is of very ancient date. According to an ancient Indian legend their sacred Aswatha Tree was only to be touched on the Seventh Day, for then it would be lucky, as it was the dwelling-place of the beautiful Lakshmi -- the Great Mother.

In Ceylon, in the courtyard of every monastery, a Bo-Tree is planted. Its origin remains unknown.

The Acacia, Sycamore, Pine, Ash, Cyprus, Palm and Olive Trees are all of greatest importance and should be studied by all Masonic Brethren.

The Tree of Life, and the Tree of the Knowledge of Good and Evil, held the mystery of Equilibrium -- the Great Arcanum of antiquity. By partaking of the Tree of Life, immortality was attained; by partaking of the Tree of the Knowledge of Good and Evil, polarity was attained, but not unbalance.

"Spiritual development is the Fruit of the Tree of Life; and all Prophets, Seers and Wise Men have partaken of its Fruit. ... When Eve ate of the apple, it represented a procreative process. ... Her yielding closed for her this Spiritual Wisdom, for the awakening brought about the material universe, or so states this Cosmic myth; but contained within it is that creative mystery which is one of Nature's most profound truths." (1)

The Tree of the Universe, of Time, of Space and of Life is ever fresh and green, as it is daily sprinkled with the Waters of Life by the Norns: the three sisters of Fate -- the Past, the Present and the Future. It is said that it will only disappear on the day when the last battle between good and evil is fought. If won by the good, "Life, time and space pass out of life, and space and time."

---

(1) - E.V.S. - "THE CELESTIAL SHIP OF THE NORTH."

THE WAND

Court messengers in Medieval days were given a staff as a badge of authority with which to stimulate all matters within their province. The Masonic Director of Ceremonies may hear the echo of this far-off signal as he carries the official Wand, with which he should be very alert and oversee everything pertaining to the Lodge and its Ritual. The Director of old saw that the whispered word was properly given, and to the proper officer. In the year 1408 the regulations required the Guild Masters to carry the Wand. The carrying of the Wand by Directors of Ceremonies is traced directly back to ancient stellar mythical time when the dove was a symbol of the soul, and the soul was ever the Mother -- the Soul of the World. This was primary.

The Staff or Wand as the shepherd's crook was the guardian of the emotional body. It became a symbol of the mastering of the mind. Its service now belongs to the Director of Ceremonies in Masonic Lodges.

COLOR (BLUE)

The ceiling of a Masonic Lodge should be symbolical of heaven and night. When ancient courts were compelled to assemble within closed doors in order to continue their ancient symbolism, they adorned their ceilings with stars, in imitation of the heavens. An azure-colored dome strewn with stars belongs to Masonic Lodges.

To the Teutons, Blue always meant Fidelity and Fortitude. In their processions, Blue banners were carried as a sign of Fidelity and Faithfulness. Blue was worn by mourners of the dead. The most solemn oaths taken among ancient Teutons were sworn to on a Blue Stone. Druids gave equal prominence to this color and reveled in it. In all official acts the bard wore his sky-colored robe. Masonic altars are covered with Blue. This symbolic color has survived in modern Masonry. Their places of assemblage are designated Blue Lodges, signifying the sanctity of the ancient emblem.

Many of the earlier languages did not possess a word for "Blue" as a color, yet Blue as a thing was indicated by using the sky, the celestial waters. The early Egyptians used lapis-lazuli to represent Blue, and their heaven was either a Blue stone or a Blue sky. In their Ritual, Blue was called the "Upper Heaven" -- the Blue woof of heaven.

Early men seem to have been deficient in knowledge of color. Max Müller affirms that the Blue heaven does not appear in the Veda-Avesta nor in the Old Testament. In the primitive system of color-making, the name for color itself signified a form, a shape, a likeness or an appearance, through things suggesting ideas, like the bottom of a pond, the ground, an egg, blood, to spring up and shoot forth like verdure, represented by green. It was the same with the rainbow as it sprang up spontaneously. In this way the primitive thinker thought in things; and they suggested ideas which later became words.

Language did not originate in abstract roots, nor with dictionary words, but with things, objects, involuntary sounds, and the living gesture-signs. Every sign was a picture, a symbol of the object suggested. Hieroglyphics, which came later, are far older than letters.

Colors are the effect of vibratory action. Color and Sound are inseparably connected with vibratory activity. Colors do not belong to the world. They are due to this vibratory activity within the individuality, which descends into the personality. Colors are therefore known subjectively, not objectively. Manifesting its color within, color vibration had to be there or there would be no color.

"According to esoteric philosophy, Blue is the true and sacred color of the Sun. The apparent orange-yellow shade of this orb is the result of its rays being immersed in the substance of the illusionary world."

THE SQUARE

Masonically, "Acting on the Square" goes very far back -- back to the ancient Mother whose creations are all according to eternal law -- the Law of Heaven. In Egypt, the Square was an emblem of justice. Truth and justice were in the scales of perfect poise -- so perfect that it could be turned by a feather. Truth to the Egyptian was geometrical. Egyptian hierophants wore square head-dresses; they never went abroad without them.

OATHS

Medieval Masons obligated themselves by placing their hands upon a square and a gauge. This taught the candidate to be upright and obey the laws of moral integrity. The Warden, prior to his installation, placed his hands upon these two Masonic implements which seemed to be conjoined. The right hand touching an object was often used in formal swearing during the early ages; and when the solemn oath was taken, the left hand was placed over the heart or the breast. All implements upon which oaths were taken possessed power, or were symbols of holiness -- so holy, it may have been due to this that the bondsman, or slave, was not admitted to the guilds.

Among Norsemen, the oath was always taken with the face towards the rising Sun, and with hands upraised; but the Saemund Edda states that an oath must be taken with the face towards the Southern Sun. Many of the Ancients swore with the hand grasping a ring which was besmeared with blood. Christians used crosses, relics of saints, sometimes a missal or bell -- the latter having first been consecrated during a religious service. Earliest Christian oaths seem to have been sworn upon the shrines of saints -- sacred Scriptures were not used. The Egyptians swore by their dead.

Many are the legends connected with the taking of oaths at wells, when the Rites were connected with them. "Sevening was an ancient mode of swearing. Abraham, when he took oath at the Well of Seven, Sevened, or did Seven." Sometimes oaths were taken on a sword, on grass, water, rocks, cliffs, and other objects in nature; but among them all, the most binding was made upon a Blue stone -- which at times was found in the middle of a court. Usually a Blue stone was raised, or erected, upon which sacrifices could be offered. To swear upon Thor's Hammer was a very binding oath. Ancient Jews placed their hands above or under the thigh when calling upon the name of the Most High; but the most sacred oath among the Israelites was that in and by the name Jehovah.

To reveal any of the severe oaths of Rome, Egypt, or Greece was punishable by death. These oaths obviously concerned their doctrine of a

Supreme God.   Polytheism was commonly accepted by the profane, due to the many myths and legends of gods and goddesses that had arisen. The true secrets were only given, under oath, to the few. Any disclosure of the secrets of the craft was atoned for, through the Middle Ages, by terrible reparation.

Many oaths were very minute in detail concerning the secrets of religious architecture -- an architecture created in reverence to God. Any profanation of these buildings was dealt with by the acme of cruelty, in some instances with a profligacy which was almost incredible. Terrible and most inhuman were the penalties inflicted during the Middle Ages -- the cruelest of which was exacted from one guilty of robbing a Pagan temple. For such desecration the Frisians had the criminal dragged to the seashore, and his body buried in the sands where the tides ebbed and flowed.

Hipparchus relates that in the days of the so-called Pagans "the shame and disgrace that justly attended the violation of his oath threw the poor wretch into a fit of madness and despair, so that he cut his throat and perished by his own hands; and his memory was so abhorred after his death that his body lay upon the shore of the Island Samos and had no other burial than the sand of the sea."

Also, a creditor could subject his "delinquent debtor to the awful penalty of having the flesh torn from his breast and fed to the birds of prey. Convicts were frequently adjudged by the ancient Norse code to have their hearts torn out." (1)

"The oldest death penalties of the Scandinavians prescribed that the body should be exposed to fowls of the air to feed upon. ... Sometimes it was decreed that the victim be disembowelled, his body burnt to ashes and scattered as dust to the winds;"(2) or, that the body be severed in two, so that "the air might strike together between the two parts." Many other inhuman tortures were inflicted -- even to tearing out the tongue.

The oath of secrecy administered to all candidates for initiation has been religiously kept, according to manuscripts of the Middle Ages. It has always been profound. When administered, the hand of the candidate is placed upon the Book of Sacred Knowledge constituting his particular religion. In Lodges today the candidate is obliged to hele, and conceal, and never wilfully to reveal the secrets of his Order, and to preserve all charges given to him with fidelity.

In the Book of Enoch we are told of the power and strength of the oath. The Most High "established this oath of Akae by the instrumentality of the Holy Michael. There are the secrets of this oath, and by it they were confirmed. Heaven was suspended by it before the world was made, forever. By it has the earth been founded upon the flood. ..... By this oath the sea has been formed, and the foundation of it. .... By this oath the sun and moon complete their progress, never swerving from the command given to them for ever and ever. By this oath the stars complete their progress; and when their names are called, they return an answer, for ever and ever." Such we find to be true with regard to the Ark of the Covenant; and such was the oath of those Watchers in heaven: THE FRATERNITY OF THE BUILDERS. One could go on almost indefinitely with examples of these oaths and their obligations.

---
(1) -- GRIMM: DEUTSCHE RECHTS ALTERTHUMER, Page 690.
(2) -- Ibid.

It is claimed that Freemasonry was established in England soon after the edict of Canute, at the beginning of the Eleventh Century, when the strongest oaths, binding to secrecy, were made necessary. The oath imposed upon the Brothers was revived in 1717. It had its foundation in past ages, when it was too sacred to have been made merely for the sake of swearing. It does not in any way apply to an association of architects today; neither does the science, or art, of building require or warrant such appalling oaths. In the Brotherhood of the Servants of God there are no oaths, no vows of secrecy. Only that which the soul dictates is needed. A true Initiate has never been known to reveal a secret of Divine Knowledge.

W A X

Initiates of the Norse guilds took their obligations under the light of a burning taper. Many penalties among the Medieval Masons, as well as in the secular guilds, were paid in wax, which shows the usefulness and the sacredness of the burning of wax tapers. The Bee which produces the wax was valuable in those ancient times. It has been proven that an occult mystery underlies the wax candle. In the original system of idolatry one realizes with what unanimity nations very remote from each other used wax candles during their sacred Rites — a general practice which proves its primeval source and a very mystical one.

T H E   B E E

The Bee is a very mysterious insect and has a very mystical meaning. The "worker" Bee is sexless and works for the good of all. The Bee Hive manifests the spirit of the hive, and mystically "represents a state of consciousness where everything is being done for the whole — Cosmic in its highest sense." As the Bee Hive manifests the Spirit of the hive, and also of the Bee, so can a Mason build his own hive within and fill it with the honey of a spiritualized life.

Before the advent of Christianity, the ancient Jew commonly spoke of the coming Messiah as Dabar, or the WORD. In Chaldean, Dabar signified a Bee —also a Word. Its primeval meaning was the Enlightener, the Great Revealer, the Sun; and the Bee became a symbol of this Great Revealer, the Sun, which was often used as a substitute for the Word. "The light of the wax candle is the light of Dabar. The Bee was set up as the substitute of the light of Dabar, the Word," the shadow instead of the true light. The Word at first was but a wavering shadow of things, and it became definite only in the ideographical phase -- a truth which has been almost ignored by the Aryanists.

Lighted wax tapers were set up on the altars of Saturn, "because by Saturn men were reduced from darkness of error to the light of Truth." The Persian Sun-god was made the symbol of "The Great Revealer of the Godhead" under the name of "Mithra," the Sun -- the Lion, with the Bee, as the Word, between his lips. The Lion belongs to the zodiacal sign, Leo, the Lion. This Lion has been sculptured with a Bee between its lips to represent the WORD, thus showing how the WORD could be conveyed. (See illustration on next page.)

The Lion sculptured with the Bee between his lips identifies the Sun-God as the Great Revealer of the Godhead. The Bee signifies "The Word."

In ancient maps of the heavens, the Sun Sign -- Leo, the Lion -- was represented with bees passing in and out of the Lion's mouth; Leo represented the summer month of the year, giving the greatest profusion of flowers -- a time when bees become very busy.

Our Bible tells of Samson meeting the young lion in the vineyard and killing it, yet "he had nothing in his hand." When returning from his errand, he turned aside to see the carcass of the lion he had killed and found a swarm of bees within it; and the bees were "booming," which meant, mystically, that the state of his soul -- the Bee principle, or his consciousness -- was the only thing active, the only thing alive.

A great riddle ensued and was thus answered: "What is sweeter than honey; what is stronger than the Lion?" The Sun, the Bee, the Wax, and the Word; and the Word is the great mystery under the Bee, the Wax and the Candle. "Thus should be Bees be extolled, for they gather the honey with their feet, yet the flowers are not injured thereby; they bring forth no young ones, but deliver their swarm through their mouths."

The Bee was sacred to the goddess Venus, and is one of the three forms of life which came from the planet Venus, millions of years ago, and has always been considered a sacred feminine symbol -- so old that its origin cannot be traced.

The Bee was a hieroglyphic expression of great gods as mediators. The Ephesians called their chief Priest a King Bee. There were many Mysteries connected with the Bee. Among the Ancients it was a symbol of chastity. The Bee Hive belongs in Masonic symbols, where it is considered an emblem of industry as well as chastity. The Bee was a symbol of the Hindu Krishna. In a Roman Catholic work, "Pancarpium Marianum," the Lord Jesus is expressly called by the name of the Bee. Referring to Mary, under the title of 'The Paradise of Delight,' the author thus speaks: 'In this Paradise that celestial Bee that is the incarnate Wisdom did feed.'"(1) Wisdom was always the signature of the Great Mother -- the first and greatest of all.

H E L E

"Hele, conceal, and never reveal," forms a triad of importance in all Masonic Ritual. Apparently up to the present, research has not learned the true meaning of this ancient word "Hele," or it may have passed beyond recognition. In the Medieval oath it meant "concealment," as it does today. During the Middle Ages, a judicial obligation was as follows: "Will bewaren, helen and halten." An older form was "Ik will helen and hoden;" and a similar obligation was used about the Ninth Century. A very ancient Frisian oath contained the word "helen." "I swear the secrets to conceal, (helen) hold, and not reveal." Much discussion has arisen as to when it became a part of the obligation.

The word "helen" is archaic, belonging to a past too far away to admit of much controversy, but its antiquity should be of interest to all Entered Apprentices.

C A B L E - T O W

First knowledge of a rope, or cable-tow, belongs to the order of celestial creations found among primordial symbols. There were "seven tow-men of the starry vast, and haulers of the solar boat, the bark of millions of years." In the course of precession, these were the Seven Pole Stars known as the great Cosmic or Polar Gods, who were the presiding Powers of the Sidereal (26,000-year) Cycle -- agents of the upward progress of the race. They were represented by the seven ropes or bonds to be considered, that were to lead "towards the dwelling of Better Things." They were the seven who in turn hauled the ropes, "makers of the ties, bonds, knots, or fastenings of the cable to the Pole when the rope was a primitive link or connection that preceded Newton's law of gravitation."(2) Each maker of the cable towed the boat through the ecliptic, the zodiac. (3) Originally there was but one rope belonging to this cable-tow, when it represented a Power -- an Attribute. Afterwards six ropes were added, making Seven Great Powers originating at the Pole.

Far back in the night of time, a sort of rope was made of grass and worn by primitive peoples as an expiation of sin. A grass rope connected with Horus represented one of the Seven Powers or attributes that led from darkness to light. This grass rope originating in the primitive myth existed ages before it was brought into Egyptian eschatology (eschatology: a doctrine of the final cause, so important in Masonry).

During the Middle Ages a cord was wound about the neck. One of its uses was to hold in check people surrounding the sacred enclosure of a court. Masons today well know its symbolical meaning. (4) The cable-tow, as a chain

---

(1) - HISLOP, Rev. Alexander; "THE TWO BABYLONS," Page 196
(2) - MASSEY, Gerald - ANCIENT EGYPT: THE LIGHT OF THE WORLD, Page 598.
(3) - These Seven were later given as the Horses of the Sun.
(4) - In Masonry the cable-tow holds the candidate against unauthorized advance or fearful retreat.

or a rope, was worn by the Initiate, or one about to be initiated, to signify his belief in God, his dependence on Him, a binding obligation to submit to His Will and Service, thereby leading him from earthly to spiritual life. A chain was likewise used by the Druids and by the Egyptians in their Mysteries.

In India, "the Initiate was seated with a cord of three threads, so entwined as to make three-times-three and called Zennar. Hence came the cable-tow." (One of its origins, as given by Albert Pike.) This triple cord was called the Cord of Creation, and is the string upon which the Lamas hang their Yu-stone.

A beautiful thought concerning the cable-tow has been written: "The spiritual life of man floating on celestial waters above and sending his message through his cable-tow to the lower man on earth."

SHOE

The shoe, or slipper, was a sign of subjection, adoption, lawfully begotten, or legitimization. It was sent to inferior princes as a sign of subjugation. When carried on the left shoulder of a person whose feet were bare, it was a sign of humiliation. The sacred symbolism of the footprints of Buddha without shoes is widely known. In the Middle Ages dispensing with the shoe constituted the surrender of title or claim to property. In the fourth Book of Ruth, seventh verse, it is stated that the owner of the land "plucked off his shoe and gave it to Boaz." That was the ancient way of transferring property or land. The bare foot meant not only the giving up of land or property, but also complete humiliation or subjugation. It belongs to Masonic installations, when the candidate becomes, in a way, an acceptor of certain possessions in his Lodge. Jesus illustrated this idea when he washed the feet of the disciples, showing his humility and his desire to serve.

Uncovered feet also meant reverence. Priests always offered sacrifice in bare feet. In Eastern churches, shoes are left at the door, that reverence may be assumed on entering the sacred enclosure. The twenty-four-inch gauge in Egypt represented two feet; and two feet read "Mati," a pair of foot-soles, -- at that time meaning two truths, the basis upon which they stood. A pair of shoes and a half-opened compass have been found on tombs of Masons in Rome.

SPADE

In the Masonic Brotherhood the spade is known as a symbol of Immortality. For many centuries it had been a symbol of death. The sacral bone at the end of the spine is in the shape of a spade. It is at the beginning of the Great Path. The spade suggests the grave; and in the Masonic Ritual, the grave, with a bit of acacia and a coffin, typifies the death of the lower man and his liberation into the Light of higher consciousness.

The trowel is indispensible for building purposes, as it was with the ancient Brethren, with whom it was based upon a geometrical formation for its proportions in architecture. It is differently formed from our regular tools; it "is a geometrical basis of the combination of square and compass; the point of the trowel represents an angle of sixty degrees, its base ninety degrees, in which the handle is placed."

Esoterically it was used by the Master Masons to smooth over and gather all fragments relative to life. When "breaking the sword of the Templars it was converted into a dagger, and their proscribed trowels henceforth were utilized only in the erection of tombs." (1) The sword and the trowel finally became the insignia of the Templars when they concealed themselves under the name of Masonic Brothers, with the sword in one hand and the trowel in the other. "The trowel of the Templars is four-fold; the triangular blades are disposed in the form of a cross, constituting a Kabalistic pentacle known as the Cross of the East." (2)

The triangle came to be known as the trowel -- symbol of life -- an emblem of very extensive application, containing the most abstruse mysteries. It signified equally Deity, Creation and Fire.

The mallet, shoe, trowel, compass, and the five-pointed star -- all are of esoteric significance and have been used as symbols. They conceal great hidden mysteries wholly unintelligible to the uninitiated. Tools were the working forces at man's disposal, subject to his influence and under his control. Morality is a force, and a very great one. Some forces are of expansion; others, of contraction. They come under the influence of the two powerful planets, Jupiter and Saturn.

S W O R D

The Sephiroth were emanated by means of the __Flaming Sword__ or __Lightning Flash__, descending from the highest Sephriroth, Spirit, to the lowest, Earth.

Whenever a Hungarian monarch was crowned with his royal tiara, he wielded a sword to the north, south, east and west.

The sword is not alone the symbol of Justice and Peace, but is, mystically, the symbol of the Word of God, called the Sword of the Spirit -- effectual in prevailing against the temptations of the flesh. As the Flaming Sword, it was the Word of Power, slaying the illusions of the material world -- the sword that turned every way to keep the way of the Tree of Life. Thus may it become the guardian of the Pillars and the Sacred Jewels of the Lodge. The sword of true discrimination is one that ever separates the false from the true; and Wisdom is a sword of quick detachment.

---

(1) - LEVI, Eliphas; THE HISTORY OF MAGIC, Page 271.
(2) - Ibid; Page 266.

CHAPTER XIV

THE FACULTY OF ABRAC - SYMBOLS

> It becomes a great and divine
> privilege for Masons today to unveil
> false imitations -- to once more re-
> store to the world the mystical mean-
> ing of religious symbols in art, and
> bring back the reverence and beauty
> that belonged to ancient races.
> -- E. V. S.

OF ALL MASONIC SECRETS claimed in ancient records, the "Way of Winning the Faculty of Abrac" is one of greatest consequence. It was the arcanum of transcendental importance in tracing the inner history and emblems of Masonry, when the Mysteries and their inherent powers were found in the natural sciences, interpreted through the exact law of nature, together with the various manifestations of the one Universal Life in nature, and the mysterious powers belonging to the Divine.

Abraxas, or Abrac, is the name which the Alexandrian Gnostic, Basilides, gave to God, who, he said, was the author of three hundred and sixty-five virtues, powers or intelligences. He claimed that he had received the knowledge from the Apostle, Matthew. He was a religious of the Second Century and it is said that he pushed his investigations into the Infinite, asserting that the name Abraxas mystically expressed the Supreme God. He was an Egyptian who had embraced Christianity, and his complete system was a combination of Christian, Jewish, Pagan and Egyptian notions.

The word Abraxas among magicians is said to have the essence of Wisdom and Strength within it; and, according to the ancient numeral system, the word gives the number 365 -- a number which also refers to, or corresponds to angels or aeons, each having a specific power due to its sacred name. Aeons were arranged in pairs -- male and female. This is also found in Hindu mythology, where every god has a female consort through whom he acts.

According to Basilides, Abraxas is depicted with the head of a cock -- a bird sacred to Phoebus -- or the head of a lion, which was the symbol of Mythras. His human body is clad in a cuirass, signifying his guardian power; his legs are serpents, types of the Agathodaemon; his right hand wields a scourge, the Egyptian badge of sovereignty; his left hand holds a shield, usually emblazoned with a mystic word, denoting, as does his cuirass, his perpetual warfare with the powers of darkness belonging to all ancient myths and legends. Based upon darkness and light, the tragedies of the celestial world have been brought into material manifestation as historical.

The Gnostic hierarchies in their speculative philosophy, including Basilides, claimed that God, the uncreated Eternal Father "had first brought forth Nous, or Mind; this the Logos or Word; this again Phronesis, Intelligence; and from Phronesis sprang Sophia, Wisdom, and Dynamis, Strength;" and from these, as many as 365 angels which represented the number of the pretended heavens.

The emblem of Phronesis, or Prudence, is placed in the center of Lodges for pronounced reasons; it is of a most exalted nature and holds various manifestations, especially as "she leads us forth to worthy actions, and as the Blazing Star enlightens us through the dreary and darksome paths of life."

A branch of the Gnostics called the philosophic sect, held the figure of Abraxas in great esteem; and to the statue of Abraxas they directed transcendental and mysterious doctrines, using it as a token or password among the initiated to show their unity. It was also used as a talisman, an amulet, and a seal for their documents. The Gnostics were a secret society of early Christians, having particular tenets of faith. As the word Gnostic implies an enlightened person, they claimed to have extraordinary Light. They forbade the Gnosis to be used by Christians, and so closed it to high initiations.

From ancient records we have evidence that the Pythagorean doctrine and Basilidean principles were the foundation of our religious morals and rules; the chief emblems came from Egypt.

Bellerman's description of this composite image of Abraxas as the Supreme Being is represented by five emanations; "From the human body .... spring the two supporters, Nous and Logos, expressed in the serpents, ... His head -- that of a cock -- represents Phronesis. .... His two arms hold the symbols of Sophia and Dynamis, the shield of Wisdom, and the whip of Power."

Iraneus asserts that God, the uncreated Eternal Father, had brought forth the Nous and Mind; and from these two, the virtues and principalities, as powers and angels; and again, from these, other angels -- to the number of 365 -- who governed the celestial orbs committed to their care.

The numerical or Kabalistic value of the name Abraxas directly refers to the Persian title of the Sun-god Mithra, worshipped from the earliest ages as IAO. IAO of the Mysteries was distinct from Jehovah; but the "IAO and Abrasax" of some Gnostic sects was identical with the God of the Hebrews. The same was applied to Horus, who is seen seated on a lotus inscribed "Abraxas IAO." IAO and Abraxas were indeed Holy Names borrowed from the Ancient East, and were words of great power.

The Jewish synonym for the Ineffable Name of Jehovah is "Shemhamphoresch," -- the "Holy Word" -- turned by the Rabbis into "The Name" or "The Word." In Coptic it has been called "The Blessed Name," the nameless and unutterable Word. Under the word Abraxas, with its various names, it links itself with Hebrew, Egyptian, Christian and Gnostic traditions and theology. It finally enters Freemasonry, representing the Lost Word. The faculty of Abrac has come through the ages, and has been transmitted with other Oriental matter into the guilds. This name, used in connection with the six-sided stone, is a symbolical part of the corner stone of the Masonic Royal Arch degree.

There is a curious legend about this stone. It is said to have been brought by Adam from the lost Paradise of a previous world, and to have gradually come down through endless periods of time and found its way to King Solomon, who used it for the foundation-stone of his Temple — a legend of great significance. A stone which fell from heaven is the opener of many myths. It was an ideograph of the Great Mother.

For the antiquarian, Abraxas was an antique gem upon which the word Abraxas was engraved, and together with other variable symbols, came from the Third Century. It was always worn with great veneration. On this talisman there is always the name IAO with the title Abraxas. "The prayer on the amulets gives IAO, Abraxas, Adonais, Holy Name, Holy Power defend ..... from very evil spirits." These names are united and are followed by the affirmation: "Thou art the Father, Eternal One." The normal invocation ΑΒΛΑΝΑΘΑΝΑΒΛΑ addressed to IAO, through slight corruption became Abracadabra.

The virtue of Abrax was its irresistible charm to avert evil, cure fevers and aid in innumerable ways, especially if written in the shape of a triad, a sacred name, or in the form of a triangle, when it was endowed with great magical potency and was used for invocations.

A Pentagram is a five-fold star; and a Hexagram, a six-fold star. "Unite the Pentagram and Hexagram, and an Eleven-pointed Star gives us the Key to the Aeon with its word ABRAHADABRA as our Magick Formula. Thus we unite with the Word, the Logos, and finally the Divine Breath which produces it."(1)

In Astro-astronomy the number Five, which is so important in Masonry, represented the first planetary heaven that was completed. "The five runs into the six in the 'Five Orders' of what are termed the 'Six Periods, the Grand Architect;' which expression is used to designate the six days of creation." (2)

Primarily, creations are incalculably old, created by the first Great Builder, the Mother. "In 'passing the veils' in the Masonic Mysteries, the candidate proceeds from the figure six, the double triangle; and, at the figure nine, the triple triangle, the Word is communicated by the Companions."(3)

The Great Celestial Architect of the Egyptians was their god Ptah. He was the Father of all the Fathers, founder of the earth and former of men; and was called the Father of the Pygmies (all origins being very small). Ptah was the founder of the sixth creation, upon which a Fraternity was inaugurated, typifying the Abraxas or cubical stone, completing the 365 days found in the Mysteries under the name of Abraxas. Numerically, Abraxas gives: A-1; B-2; R-100; A-1; X-60; A-1; S-200; = 365. This numeral is found in Latin, Greek, Coptic, and earlier still, in Egyptian.

"Acacian" is a title signifying a Mason. The Acacia is the typical Masonic Tree. The Cube was squared in Acacia wood, as it was in stone, because

---

(1) - FRATER ACHAD: - THE EGYPTIAN REVIVAL; Page 22.
(2) - MASSEY, Gerald; - THE NATURAL GENESIS, VOL. II, Pages 81-2.
(3) - IBID, Page 84.

of its hardness, and a figure of the six-fold heaven. If we go a little further in creations, we find the seventh heaven was founded on the six-fold heaven. Abraxas is a word of seven letters signifying the seven creative powers, planetary angels, or spirits; and the letters added as numerals (given above) taught that the powers of the universe were divided into 365 Aeons or Spiritual Cyclos, given as the Supreme Father. His name Abraxas was the symbol of His Hidden Divine Powers.

Mount Meru, the Tower of Babel, the Pyramid of Sakkara, and other similar monuments were forms of the Great World's Altar Stairs with its Seven Steps; and the highest, the seventh, was that of Saturn.

Mosaic art was in use in the early Fifth Century. In many instances the mosaics were composed largely of triangles, spheres, circles, the double triangle and the pentalpha, which was surrounded by curiously-wrought blocks and was typical of Divinity. The original significance of the mosaic pavement and Blazing Star in Lodges has been altered, but historical data still claim that these checkered floors of inlaid work typified a "Primordial state of uncreated nature, and that the triangle or Blazing Star within it symbolized Deity in His work of creation; or, in other words, this star is the glory radiated from the creative Jehovah (י), the letter 'G.'" This letter at the close of the Eighteenth Century became the symbol of THE GREAT ARCHITECT OF THE UNIVERSE.

In the center of a Masonic Lodge, within an irradiation of the Blazing Star, is the letter "G," denoting the glorious science of Geometry as cultivated by our venerable and ancient Masters. The Egyptians found Geometry of such importance that they deified the science; hence the great respect given its Initial in Masonry. The "G" is a substitute letter, meaning mystically "Stone Squarer." It is really meant to represent the Deity.

Sirius is the Blazing Star of Masonry, and is undoubtedly one of the most interesting stars of heaven. It was "the herald star which measured whole ages by its rising light as it dawned for a moment in the Eastern horizon." Its ancient name was Sut, Son of the Great Mother, and it was called the Star of the Celestial Immaculate Conception. It was known later as the planet Saturn, the Great One in the night of Time. Saturn is the planet of Justice, Chastity, Wisdom and Prudence, and as the Blazing Star of Masonry, represents that "Prudence which ought to appear conspicuous in the conduct of every Mason." As the star Sirius, it was called the "Star of the White Spirit." In the myth of stellar reckoning, it was known as the Star of Hathor, and of her son Horus, (the Mother and her Son). Most important and most sacred were the Rites connected with the rising of this star, which is mysteriously connected with Hermes. It has a mystic influence over the whole living heavens and is connected with every religion of antiquity.

MARKS

When a candidate had passed gloriously through the ordeals of initiation, an engraved stone was given to him for his admission into the Brotherhood. This was the Mason's Mark -- a secret Mark that was often stamped into the flesh, indelibly incised or tattooed.

Medieval guilds were corporations composed of actual workmen who served their regular apprenticeships; and after producing trial pieces to prove their competency, they were admitted "free" by the guilds and "accepted" as members. Every Mason had a mark or cipher assigned to him on his admission which he was compelled to put upon every stone that he dressed, so that his work might be distinguished from that of other Masons.

Marks have a history filled with interest and obscurity, many being traditional, going back to antiquity, and found wherever a hewn stone was used. Undoubtedly many of these marks were religious, and by them followers of different gods were distinguished. They have, however, degenerated with time.

Mason's Marks are of infinite variety and are found on monuments of architectural art in various parts of the world. In their earliest and simplest form -- in their pure geometrical design -- they are traced to the Byzantine architects who brought them into the West.

Eminent Oriental builders had distinctive personal marks by which their workmanship could be known. A rigid rule made it necessary for every Mason to choose his mark which was to be based on a geometric figure; but inconsistencies brought deviations from this rigid rule. The Mark, in a mystical sense, is a part of the Lodge Ritual today. A Fellow Craftsman must never change his mark except by unanimous consent. When an Entered Apprentice was given a mark on admission to the Fellow Craft degree, this ceremony was always accompanied by a feast, and his Mark was copied into the Master's book of tokens, to be preserved for its Lodge. The "ordinances of 1459 and 1562 both prescribed certain rules for these marks and their preservation."

Tokens were worn by members of secret societies for superstitious purposes, a custom that had come down from ancient Paganism, at a time when Priest and citizens carried their favorite deities around with them. Architects of Europe can be traced through the Syrian and Jewish builders by their proprietary tokens; and during the Middle Ages these became an important part of Lodge Ritual.

A six-pointed star was often left as a Mason's mark in ancient churches especially in England. It is the double triangle that had been called the Macrocosm, or God. This double triangle or six-pointed star as a Divine Nimbus was anciently used for God the Father. It also represented the mystical marriage of Fire and Water, or the union of Father and Mother. The snowflake also represents this six-fold or six-pointed star which contains the two halves of all nature.

"All things are said to have proceeded from the Primal Water under the action of Spirit, that the Substance should Crystalize in exactly the same way that any drop of water, or any crystal, is found to take form under the direction of the lines of polar force which always form six radiating lines or axes in every rain drop which becomes a snow flake. ... Thus the Pure Essence of the Soul of Man may also crystalize and become a Center of the Great Star." (1)

The five-pointed star, the Pentagram, has always, in a mystical way, been used to represent man; its importance depends upon the direction of its

---

(1) - FRATER ACHAD, - THE ANATOMY OF THE BODY OF GOD. Pages 54-5.

point. When it is used in sorcery or for evil purposes, its point is downward; but when the direction of the point is upward, it represents "the masculine and feminine powers in one human body, or, motion and will uniting, invoking the conscious use of consciousness." Just "as the Microcosm, Man, is symbolized in the Pentagram, or Five-Pointed Star, so is the MACROCOSM, GOD, symbolized in the HEXAGRAM, THE SIX-FOLD STAR. The attainment of 'Union with God' is considered in all religions to be the Great Work which is before us." (1) The Great Work is to unite the Microcosm with the Macrocosm.

Israelitish traditions and legendary lore were acceptable to the Byzantine workmen or were substituted into Byzantine corporations for Pagan traditions, and then emerged into Gothic associations. Jewish Rites and ceremonies in connection with their traditional lore helped in making architectural guilds, which were of Byzantine origin, harmonize with Christian ideas. They were antedated by sacerdotal Rites ages and ages old. The Hellenistic Jewish traditions, such as the Legend of Hiram, the great importance of Jehovah's true name, or Omnific Word, and those of lesser significance were introduced by Byzantine workmen into Teutonic sodalities; but when "the merging of the Jewish legendary element into Germanic guilds occurred" is not definitely known or assumed, but possibly it was near the time of "Theodoric, the Goth, who ordered the Greek builders from the East." It was not fully perfected, however, until centuries later.

When the Gothic and Jewish elements of Freemasonry were united by the merging of the Byzantine art corporations in the Germanic guilds in Italy, "the Norsemen contributed the name and orientation, oaths, dedications of the Lodges, opening and closing of colloquies, Master's mallet and columns, and the lights and installation ceremonies. On the other hand, Judaistic admixture is equally well defined" (and brought a great many Lodge appointments and ritualism which had come from the Gothic courts that had been closely allied to heathen temples). "From this source, Masonry received the Omnific Word, or the Faculty of Abrac, and Ritualism, including the Hiramic legend." (2)

Ancient Rites, worship and symbols caused great confusion in the beginning, during the period when they were being merged with Christian symbology, and from this came the Rite of Baptism belonging to Pagan consecrations. The Pagans sprinkled water to purify the soil, as well as the people, and to endow both with holy properties. Sprinkling of water is used in the church and in Masonic Ritual today. Gallic craftsmen used water for purposes of lustration and purgation. In the Chamber of Reflection in a Lodge, where the candidate remains for meditation, a bowl of water is or should be placed. During initiation, water is given for purification and for symbolic purposes. Pagans lighted torches in their temples. These torches symbolized their deities and were used as sacred fires, borne aloft amid burning candles. The burning of frankincense and sweet odors was done in their honor.

Early Christian Mosaic Rites were held in great veneration; they spread with rapidity. The building of King Solomon's Temple was deeply rooted in the minds of the Jewish exiles. His Temple at Jerusalem was open to both Jew and Gentile. Both the moral and spiritual changes in Rome to Christianity made great strides in the Judaic meetings, interwoven with marvelous old traditions and symbols. Similarity of the Teutonic and Jewish emblems which have

---
(1) - FRATER ACHAD; Q.B.L. or THE BRIDE'S RECEPTION; Page 63
(2) - FORT, George F.; THE EARLY HISTORY AND ANTIQUITIES OF FREEMASONRY, P 406, (foot note) During the 9th and 10th centuries Christianity and Heathenism were strangely mixed.

aided in uniting the two systems is further indicated, and made more interesting through legends, especially those of Hiram, the Good, and Baldur, the beautiful; both having astronomical foundations. The twelve companions of Hiram Abiff are related to the twelve Drotters of the Odinic legend, showing that they came from the same source.

The legend of a Dying God belongs to every secret school of the Mysteries and is its supreme allegory. It has been perpetuated in all colleges teaching the Sacred Wisdom; it is also found in Christianity. In Greece, it was Prometheus; in India, Krishna; in Central America, Quexacoatl; in Scandinavia, Baldur; and in the Masonic legend, Hiram Abiff; and the body of this martyred god became the Holy Sepulcher.

This legend or allegory of a Dying God is not only a key to universal redemption and regeneration, but applies to the individual as well. In all its sublime beauty it belongs, in Freemasonry, to the very dawn of creation, is very spiritual and is deeply revered. A murdered and dying god brought back to life is recovered from remote antiquity. If a Mason winds his thoughts about this legend of Hiram Abiff, he raises himself into the holy aura of Divinity. Hiram Abiff is, mystically, CHiram Abiff, -- "My Father, the universal spirit, one in essence, three in aspect -- type of the Cosmic Martyr, the Crucified Spirit of Good, the Dying God."(1)

Sun-worship is so old it can scarcely be reckoned with. It was prominent in all Pagan Mysteries; it played a most important role in all those of ancient times, and has its part in every religion of today. It is readily traced back to the last Lemurian Race and to the first of the Atlanteans, whose people absorbed Divine knowledge from the Sun, Moon and Stars, especially from the setting of the Sun in the West and its rising in the East. All Mysteries have their source in this Sun-god, who was often represented with golden locks -- symbol of the rays of the Sun, and through all traditions, myths and allegories belonging to ancient nations and coming into our century, we have the youth with the Golden Locks who was slain by wicked robbers, or the murky forces of the universe and of life. Through sublime Rituals and ceremonies symbolical of purification and regeneration, this Sun-god of Good -- the Youth with the Golden Locks -- was brought back to life and became the Savior of Humanity. The secret ways by which he was resurrected symbolized those good influences which enabled man to overcome his lower nature (subdue his passions), master his appetites, and so evolve through his higher nature.

When the Atlantean Priests fully realized the doom awaiting their continent, they carried their Sacred Wisdom into all parts of the world for preservation. It is through them that the original mystic schools branched out everywhere, including in their Wisdom-teaching this, perhaps, greatest and most profound allegory: that of a Dying God, which was the setting of the Sun in the West and its resurrection in the East -- the seal of a spiritual Initiation, with all its symbolic meaning, which has marvelously raised the standard of morality and religion throughout the entire world.

That which so often and so contemptuously has been called Paganism contained the Ancient Wisdom, filled with thoughts of God; and primitive Masonry naturally having been a source of Light, the Pagan or Mason paid honor to the Sun

---
(1) - HALL, Manly P.

as the source of Light when circumambulating his temple or his Lodge, by following the apparent course of the Sun from East to West. "In man the light shines towards the north but never from it, because the body has no light of its own; it shines with the reflected glory of the Divine life particles concealed within the physical substance." (1)

Old Mysteries, and Masonry, are founded on the journeyings of the Sun through the twelve signs of the zodiac, which revealed to the Initiates all arts and sciences and all that was necessary to mold and create a perfect life through the lessons taught in this "Great Wheel of Necessity." No matter how religious in concept, no mystery can be solved today that did not pre-exist in the conception of a Sun-god, though the name of the Sun itself was a hidden one. For instance, in Egypt their Sun-god was at one time called "Ra." His hidden name was identified with that of Osiris; and this name was H U H I, and must of necessity have been the pre-Israelitish name J H V H. Ra, in Sanskrit, properly spelled, is RCH, which means Light. Ra's symbol was the solar disk. Similarly the Sun had hidden names in other nations; and through one of these hidden names, has been given the story of the murder of Hiram Abiff by the three Craftsmen, Ju-Bel-A, Ju-Bel-O, and Ju-Bel-Um, who were determined to procure the secret of the Master's Word -- that Lost Word in Masonry -- or take his life. (The names Jubela, Jubelo, and Jubelum are not found in Hebrew or Arabic.) The middle name of these Craftsmen (Bel) was the Babylonian Sun-god but, for some reason, the Jews turned this Sun-god into a demon. These three names are also variations of the Latin word "Jubeo" -- "I command" -- suggestive of the command for the Master's Word. The faithfulness of Hiram in refusing to reveal the Word caused his murder.

In the search for his body, which followed, the cardinal points of the world were traversed; and when it was finally found, though apparently dead and buried, he was raised by the Grip of the Lion's Paw. This is similar to the raising of Krishna, and of Buddha, venerated as incarnations of Deity; also of the raising of Lazarus in the early Christian Mysteries; and of Osiris by Anubis. An Egyptian monument shows Osiris being raised by the left paw of a lion, the right paw holding aloft the Ansated Cross -- the symbol of immortality and life everlasting; all, except that of Anubis, represent hidden names of the Sun. In this Mystery, Anubis personified a spiritual physician assisting in the passing of the soul, that it might be made perfect for its rebirth into a spiritual life. Similarly in a Tibetan ceremonial, the Lama kneels at the side of the passing Initiate, assisting in the re-awakening of the soul, that it might be perfected -- a ceremony which, in its administration, has become the most sacred office performed by the Worshipful Master in Masonic Lodges today.

The three Craftsmen associated with this age-old Mystery are astrologically symbolical of the three months of the Winter Solstice hidden in the darkened realms of the constellations, cut off from the rest of the zodiac, and made to represent the irresistible powers of darkness -- the murderers, or the three winter planets, Mars, Jupiter and Saturn, rulers of those winter signs. In the darkest hour the Sun, Hiram, was extinguished, and ready for his resurrection. In the York Masonic Rite, twelve Fellow Craftsmen were sent in search of the body of Hiram. When the Temple of King Solomon was nearly completed, fifteen of the Fellow Craftsmen grew impatient about receiving the Master's Word and agreed to extort it from him when opportunity offered. Twelve recanted; the other three persisted.

---

(1) - HALL, Manly P.: MELCHIZEDEK -- AND THE MYSTERY OF FIRE, Page 38.

Many principle festivities throughout the ancient world represented the incarnation of the Sun at the Winter Solstice, which took place on December the 25th -- the darkest period of the year. While the Temple of Solomon was being built, this death and resurrection of the Sun (the Dying God) was performed at the Winter Solstice. These same festivities are held in Christian lands today, on the same date -- December the 25th. The date of this Solar Resurrection has never been in doubt.

The Scandinavian Mysteries have their Baldur (the Sun) and their twelve Drotters, representing the twelve signs of the Zodiac; and when the Sun is said to step from his darkened tomb, having formed his Cross, he returns in the full majesty of his Light and Power, which is dramatically given by them in the same ritualistic, mystical tragedy.

Baldur, with many other ancient gods, holds a place similar to that of Hiram. Baldur was so beautiful that he was known as the synonym of Light and Beauty. His vitality and the completion of the temple depended upon the Master Builder, Baldur; just as the completion of the Temple of Solomon depended upon the Master Builder, Hiram. Both were unjustly murdered; and at their deaths, great grief and sorrow prevailed among their followers. Loud were the wails that everywhere ascended to heaven -- a bewailing that belongs practically to all literature of the ancient world. The loss of Baldur, who was slain by treachery and fraud, was lamented as irreparable. Hiram, assassinated by cowardly Craftsmen, had refused to reveal the coveted word and was universally lamented. They belong to the same allegory -- as a typical expression of death by the Sun, or Light. The Acacia was the emblematic of Hiram -- the Mistletoe, of Baldur -- both emblems of spirituality, celestial strength and power.

A search was instituted by Solomon, who sent messengers to the four corners of the world to seek the body of Hiram; and a search was instituted by Odin, who sent his messengers over the world to recover the lost Baldur. Due to the death of Hiram, the principal support of the Universal Temple had fallen; the True Word had been lost; due to the death of Baldur, the Light of the earth was replaced by darkness, and it was required that everyone, dead or alive, should weep for Baldur if he was to be restored to his Celestial Companions. One alone refused. One thing was required for the resurrection of Hiram and one alone, for the resurrection of Baldur.

The Setting Maul used in Lodges today, associated with the funeral furniture, typified the death of the Master Builder, Hiram; and the Hammer became typical of the death of the Master Builder, Baldur. Baldur was placed upon a funeral pyre on board his ship, by the seashore where the Great God, Thor, arose and consecrated the burning pyre with his Hammer. For purification in crematory Rites, a hammer was used in ancient times before the dead were reduced to ashes; and frequently the hammer was buried with the dead. These Rites have been interwoven with many other old sacred customs. Death and its Resurrection into a world of Light belonged to very ancient days, and are found in the Rituals of Fraternities, Guilds and Lodges, as well as in very old heathen temple-worship, and have been made the subject of profound Spiritual Ritualism.

The Judas of Baldur was Loki, who was the personification of evil. Loki instructed the blind Hodur to shoot Baldur with an arrow tipped with the mistletoe -- the only thing that could kill him. Through the gods communing together a way was found to resurrect the spirit of Baldur, so that youth and love might return; for he was ever called "the Beautiful," shedding his Light among all; and like Hiram, he was a true architect, a "Builder of souls." At the death of both, light vanished and darkness prevailed. But darkness has its lesson to teach, for without darkness, light could not be reflected; without evil, good would not be known. The spirit of goodness and beauty may have been slain through craft ignorance; but it is written that "Gods shall again walk with men."

Odinic Mysteries were given in the darkness of crypts, or caves, and represented the wanderings of the soul through the worlds and their spheres, that through the darkness Light might come -- that Light which was to be given each candidate after he had enacted the part of the death, burial and resurrection of a martyred hero. Then -- and then only -- was a candidate reborn without passing the gate of death. This was enacted in all ancient Mysteries.

One of the greatest and most sublime dramas ever given to the world is that of the Sun journeying through the dark to his resurrection; and those taking part in this wonderful Ritual today are the members and officers of Fraternities, or Lodges, who in turn impersonate or become symbolical, not alone of the Sun, but of the Moon, and the Planets.

In the Odinic Mysteries, the candidate, after his hours of wanderings, found himself in a room before a beautiful statue of Baldur; and in the same chamber was a plant bearing seven blossoms, representing the seven planets -- symbolical of the seven officers; and there, on the naked blade of a sword, he took the oath of secrecy, drank of the sanctified mead from a human skull, and was finally permitted to lift the veil -- revealing to him a personification of the Great Wisdom.

The nine chambers of the Odinic Mysteries represented the nine spheres of the universe, (1) all of which were invisible to the senses of man except the sphere of Midgard, the home of human creatures. To both Hiram and Baldur, the entombed body was symbolical of the indestructible forces of nature; and its resurrection represented inherent Immortality; for Divine vitality in man survives. The doctrines of the Immortality of the Soul dates from the time when humanity was a spiritual race. No pre-historic peoples ever denied the existence of the Immortality of the Inner Man -- the true self. All ancient peoples recognized the return of the soul into the physical world, the end being its liberation from that "Wheel of birth," or "Wheel of Necessity," which was accomplished by its becoming initiated into those sacred Mysteries.

The theory of "Eternal Damnation" belongs, in origin, exclusively to the Christians. Ancient peoples could not conceive of eternal punishment for passing sins. In Egypt and elsewhere it was believed that there was a place for the purification of the soul, that it might be freed from sin and so rise triumphantly into the abode of the "blessed." Heaven without death belongs

---

(1) - The highest sphere was the heaven-world of the gods; below this, the world of light and beautiful spirits. In the North there was cold and darkness. The East was the home of the Giants. The earth-world, the world of human beings, was called Midgard. The West was the world of the vanes. The South was the world of fire. And there was the world of dark and treacherous elves; and the world of cold and death.

to the higher consciousness; it is not a Place, for "the soul is without birth and is eternal. When the Initiate emancipates himself from his passions, he must flee from everything sensual that the soul may with ease reunite itself with God." (Porphyry)

Hiram Abiff was the Great Master Builder and represented a form of that Divine energy which must obey creative law. All forms, material or spiritual, have been said to be the result of his handicraft; and if a Mason builds a temple, though it be with a grain of sand, or with a solar system, it becomes a master-building and a habitation in honor of his God.

"The most profound secrets of Masonry are not revealed in Lodges at all. They belong only to the few. But these secrets must be sought by the individual himself. .... If he prefers to treat the whole subject with contempt and to deny any such real knowledge exists, it becomes evident that he not only closes the door against the possibility of his possessing such knowledge, but he becomes impervious to any evidence of its existence that might have come to him at any time. He has no one but himself to blame if he is left in darkness."[1]

The legend of Hiram Abiff and the significance of his death are found to be analogous to that of the Christos, which is symbolically given in the eucharistic Rites of the early churches -- Rites performed with the same secrecy and divine mystery belonging to the third degree in Masonry.

THE APRON

The origin of the Apron can only be truly illustrated hieroglyphically. It is "an extant form of the fig-leaf or skin with which the primal parent clothed herself, and of the loin-cloth of the naked nations."[2] It has been used symbolically for many strange Rites and Ceremonies belonging to the Mysteries; but the first Apron worn was the fig-leaf. The fig-leaf is a trinity in unity, or a triangle; hence its sacred significance.

Nothing was so precious or so sacred to the ancient Priest King as the Apron -- symbol of his Initiation. Thus the Masonic Apron is used today, as a symbol of Innocence and Purification.

The ancient Egyptians wore an Apron that was triangular in shape, and about their necks they wore collars of gold that were, in some instances, set with twelve precious stones representing the zodiac.

The White Apron is the first sacred and precious gift made to the Entered Apprentice. It is square, with a triangular flap. The square holds the lesson of the four cardinal virtues, and the flap, as the triangle, holds the ancient symbol of God. Combined, they represent the spiritual and material worlds, bidding the candidate to rise from his lowly material existence into the higher spiritual world, teaching him one of the greatest of Masonic mottoes, a gift of the Spirit: I SERVE, a SERVICE belonging to universal Brotherhood.

The Apron is the most distinguished badge of a Mason, and should be worn worthily before God. It is shown on countless monuments. It is given to the Entered Apprentice today, as it was given many years ago to the Initiate-- as the greatest of gifts, to remind him of SERVICE.

---

(1) - BUCK; - MYSTIC MASONRY, Page 56
(2) - MASSEY, Gerald; - A BOOK OF BEGINNINGS, VOL. I, Page 118.

The Masonic Apron symbolically represents the sacred number Seven, with the flap, representing Three, or the Triangle, which in its descent is enfolded in the material world of Four; but when the flap is raised, it becomes the ascent, or resurrection into the spiritual world -- an entrance into Light. The Masonic Apron originally was of pure white lambskin -- symbol of Innocence and Purity; but modern innovations have changed this. It was a very old custom for members of a Fraternity to wear white during Lodge hours. It is to be regretted that at present very often the White Apron alone is worn. White is the emblematic color of the Aborigines of America; and when Black Hawk, a prophet, came to prepare the treaty (1833) he was dressed entirely in white. With his hands uplifted towards heaven, he addressed the President, saying, "I call upon the Great Spirit of myself and my forefathers to witness the purity of my heart on this occasion."

THE POINT WITHIN THE CIRCLE

Every Lodge has its symbol of the Point Within the Circle -- a symbol capable of very many interpretations. To some, this Point may signify the individual Brother, and the Circle may show the boundary line of his duty to God and man. Beyond the Circle his passions and prejudices must never betray him. This symbol is recognized by Masons of all religions. Its origin harks back to the Pole Star -- the emblem of Stability or standpoint in heaven, The Point Within the Circle.

In primitive thought THE GREAT ARCHITECT OF THE UNIVERSE began to build the house of heaven, to be duplicated on earth, with the Pole Star for the foundation stone. Primordially, it was the All-Seeing Eye of Astral Mythology. The mountain at the Pole (Meru) was called the Mountain of Seven Steps, or, the Seven Great Stars known as THE FRATERNITY OF THE BUILDERS. The All-Seeing Eye, in Masonry, is symbolical of Deity. It was also a symbol of the Sun, and in its geometrical design, when enclosed in a half circle, became the symbol of the Word of Power.

All life begins in a circle, emanates from a circle, and is full of procreation -- the center of activity. "The mystery of creation is the mystery of ovation." The Point Within the Circle holds a vital place in Masonry and will prove, to any student, to be a mine of marvelous symbolism if he will but meditate freely and often upon it, and all it represented to the Sages of the Past. The Point Within the Circle symbolized to them the first going forth of Light as a Creative Force, from which all things were said to emanate.

The Kabala explains that the Universe was created from the First Great Light which evolved nine others, the Mysterious Three-Times-Three. Each Three, as a Triad embodying an attribute of the Divine Nature, had one special Light or attribute of the Divine which permeated the other two -- even as Wisdom, Strength and Beauty were always associated with the group of Three, derived from one Chief Light.

The first Great Triad was symbolized in and enlightened by the Word of God -- the Light of Wisdom; another symbolized Glory -- the Power of Divinity, Strength; while a third Triad, representing Justice and Mercy, symbolized the moral nature of Divinity and was called Beauty. From the ninth of these proceeds the tenth -- symbol of the Kingdom. From the mystic Three-Times-Three Triangle, the lights are grouped to correspond to the Three Great Pillars as the

Divine attributes upon which the Great Temple was first established, and they stand great and strong in all their Wisdom, Strength and Beauty as the lights around the Volume of Sacred Knowledge, absorbed in the Greater Lights on the altar of the Lodge.

In many ways the mystic has given the Divine and His attributes through form, number and symbol. Pythagoras called the number One, the Central Fire of God, the beginning and the end, the first and the last; and this creative energy of God was very reverently symbolized by a Point in the Center of Immensity. Among primitive peoples the Circle meant Eternity -- boundless Light, in the center of which Deity dwelt.

"It is Infinity we seek, and the Point Within the Circle turns inward, returning to the Point; as it carries with it all the experiences gained through the Point becoming the Circle, and the Circle becoming the Point. The earnest student becomes the Point, and his consciousness, the Circle. One's self is not absorbed into the All, any more than the All is absorbed into one's self; but it is in the blending or merging that Infinity is realized. It all means the expansion, as well as the expression, of consciousness so vast that only through experience can this be known." (1)

In Christian symbolism the Dot became God the Father -- the Eternal Life lying concealed within the germinal Dot. All lines and rows are dots; the line being the outpouring of the dot -- something coming into expression. The two perpendicular lines or pillars on either side of the Circle were known in Masonic symbolism as the great luminaries; the Sun, Fire; and the Moon, Wisdom. (2) Astrologically, they are the signs Cancer and Capricorn. The crux of everything is bound up in the Zodiacal Universe, in conformity with the Laws of God. In the inner Rite of Masonry, those parallel columns represent birth and death -- extremes of physical life. In more recent times they have become symbolical of the two Johns of Biblical lore. The birthdays of the two St. Johns were fixed, by the framers of church Ritual, at the time of the Solstices and were observed as festival days by Druidical Masons.

These feast days in Roman and Episcopal churches are astronomical. Easter is kept the first Sunday after the Full Moon, at the Vernal Equinox.

---

(1) - WIGGS, George W.
(2) - The circle enclosing a central point and placed between two parallel lines is a figure that is purely Kabalistic; the rest is modern.

CHAPTER XV

MASONRY

> Gates of Wisdom need special keys
> with which to open them. Beneath the
> sublime allegories of the Builders of
> the Temples is secreted the Wisdom of
> the Ages.
>
> -- E. V. S

ANCIENT WISDOM comes as a gift of the Spirit, endowed with untold spiritual riches -- a gift to be cherished. Wisdom's tree bears fruit only as it is rooted in the mind, and the "leaves, in the symbolic words of the Apocalypse, are for the healing of the nations," that mind and body may be nourished by all the elements of our system, material and mystical, leading to the "open sesame" of the higher life; for then, and then only, will man begin to build on earth the Living Temple not made with hands. Even the ruins of a fallen temple may become the keynote of an onward spiritual march, through which one may glimpse the grandeur of the Infinite. The true and everlasting Wisdom of ancient Masonry, if accepted and understood, may take man beyond the realms of much of the ancient teachings, for IT ALWAYS WAS, IS, AND EVER SHALL BE.

Symbolism is a divine, celestial language, and through its alphabet can be traced the workings and patterns that have descended from the seats of the Might Ones above, who are ever watching in silence. Symbols are centers of tremendous forces, standing for things beyond the comprehension of those who cannot SEE. Ancients have declared that God walked in the garden above, illuminating all that was there. His permanence is symbolized in the universe, -- and His presence, in life.

Speculative Masonry was the outcome of Medieval guilds; but the spirit of Masonry belongs above and is manifested below. The simple institutions, the usages, and the profound knowledge of nature of primeval peoples have been grossly misunderstood. The Ancients applied their laws of truth, which came to them from above, to their Rites and Ceremonies below -- a mode of attainment direct from Nature, which led to perfection; and these Rites and Ceremonies belong to modern Masonry. A realization of what heaven might be, of what God might be, presaged a glory awaiting primeval man, bringing him close to the friendly lovingness of God. Today the object of Masonry is to inspire man with reverence, that he may also partake of the friendly lovingness of God and feel His nearness.

Somewhere in those misty primordial days coeval with first creations, myths and allegories relative to philosophy and spirituality were born, and with their celestial symbolism, they have been perpetuated through the iron calendars of time and are being unfolded today in Masonry.

Knowledge was apparently concealed in those far-off times. For "the most perfect, that is, the most primitive, forms of the myths and symbols ---

are those which, for thousands of years, have been kept by living memory alone ... whose ritual and gnosis depended on the <u>living memory</u> for their truth, purity and sanctity." (1)

The mode of communication even in that far-away past was from "mouth to ear," and this has continued in the Mysteries and in Masonry today. But so deeply and sacredly were the ancient treasures of knowledge engrafted in the mind, they were not alone given from mouth to ear but were "painfully scored in the flesh by the marks and symbols of tattoo, as if one should bury his jewels in his own body for a safe; so permanently was the record inscribed that it still lives and underlies all literature or artificial registers in the world." (2)

It was the origin of human thought, preserved in Universal Masonry, and belongs to the age of symbolic expression. Therefore, back to the symbol we must go for the truth underlying all things. "The symbolic extends beyond the written or the spoken language of any people now extant." (3)

The symbol in its origin is all-powerful and potent in its influence on the mind, but much has been perverted by the ignorant. It belongs to a universal language -- the Masonry of Nature -- which was the mode of the Immortals. Ceremonial Rites came as a means of memorizing facts in sign-language; for there were no written words. "Myths and allegories whose significance was once unfolded to initiates in the mysteries have been adopted in ignorance and re-issued as real truths directly and divinely vouchsafed to mankind for the first and only time. The earlier religions had their myths interpreted; we have ours mis-interpreted." (4)

"It may be that the beginning of verbal language, with a few simple names for things, sensations and actions, is indicated by the mystical value attached in later times to <u>Names;</u> their primitive preciousness being reflected in their religious sacredness. ..... The passage of Osiris through the underworld is effected by his preserving all the mystical <u>Names</u> in memory. Ra has 75 names; Osiris, 153." (5)

Through awakened memory the old Atlantean Mysteries have come down to us as Masonic, wrapped up in the same symbols and allegories that were known on the old continent, and brought over by Priests into Egypt and other countries as Sun or Fire-Worship. This Great Wisdom had been known even beyond the Atlantean Mysteries, or any knowledge gained from Lemuria, for fundamentally the religion or Ritual of every Greater or Lesser Mystery in the world has come from, and can be traced to that Great World Mother and her Children, known as THE FRATERNITY OF THE BUILDERS, symbolically holding the Wisdom of the ages.

This "mythical Great Mother and her children passed into the legendary lore of the whole world." These Seven Great Stars of the great Fraternity became prototypes of the seven planets which are related in Masonic Lodges to the seven officers that make up the number necessary to open a Lodge, each officer

---

(1) - MASSEY, Gerald; THE NATURAL GENESIS, VOL. I; Page 10.
(2) - Ibid, Page 10
(3) - Ibid, Page 10
(4) - Ibid, Page 13
(5) - Ibid, Page 240.

following out symbolically the significance given to each planet. The Seven Stars play a very great part in the Ritual of all Masonic Lodges and show how easily the Masonic Heaven of the Seven Stars has followed down through the ages.

It is of the greatest interest that signs and symbols used in Masonry today, celestially created, have come down to us through the relics of lost continents. It is claimed there are seven cradles of the human race. It seems futile from such records to try to discover man's first appearance, which is usually called a veiled secret -- a secret lost forever. By tracing backward through interminable ages we find that man appeared as a developed human being on earth at the end of the Lemurian and beginning of the Atlantean Era. Those submerged lands are now revealing Masonic signs and symbols. Masonry, from its incipient age, was established in all its mighty import, revealing below what the heavens declared above.

Tracing the order of Freemasonry to its source has been the endeavor of many an earnest student and writer, its secret Rites being the subject of much inquiry. The enigma has baffled many; yet Masonry survives, teaching the old Truths gathered since the manifestation of man. Sweeping on through the centuries, this Ancient Wisdom emanating from the Great Mother entered the different philosophies of the countries, North, East South and West.

Wisdom and Strength guard the portals of Masonic Lodges today, leading into the Temple Part, the Holy Place, which is filled with beauty and spiritual vibrations. Signs and symbols originated aeons before the word "Freemason" was heard of; but Masons, as Sons of Light, belonged to the beginning of man and the Universe. A true Mason ever seeks the Light, and life itself is the substance of Light -- a living substance which reacts from an invisible center lighting the way towards Infinity.

"Masonry is a peculiar system of morality, veiled in allegory and illustrated by symbols." Masonry is thoroughly Hermetic. Its teachings have blazed a trail through Atlantis, Egypt, India and other great countries, and through the original Holy Kabala. The true significance of allegories and symbols was kept sacred by all ancient Initiates in all countries and in all times. Egypt held a key which brought to her country Pythagoras, Plato, Thales and other great philosophers who remained for years to gather Ancient Wisdom through their Initiations. Pythagoras and Plato were there to study science and religion. Later they went to Greece to perfect their work and gain knowledge of the basis of religion. From its incipient age they found that fundamentally it was purely mystical and that it belonged to a "defined scientific tradition communicated orally to the Initiates or mystics who secretly passed it on from generation to generation."

Masonry is a creedless religion. Today it may be but a shadow of the first great mystery school, but it can be traced back millions or even billions of years to the time "when the temple of the Solar Man was in the making, ... and there, in the dawn of time, were given and laid down the true Mysteries of the ancient Lodge, and it was the gods of creation and the spirits of the dawn who first tiled the Master's Lodge." (1)

In Ancient Stellar cult, temples were built in the form of a double square, symbolical of heaven and earth. Three cubes were placed in the center

---
(1) - HALL, Manly P.; -- THE LOST KEYS OF MASONRY, Page 25

of the temple, one above the other, representing a trinity. Some of these cubes were ornamented with axes. A single axe was called "The Great One" or "The Prince of Peace." Three axes represented the "Three Great Ones" of the North, South, and the Equinox or the middle point. Three cubes and three Masters formed a trinity of great power and might. The origin of the trinity was known only to a few of the Initiated who had entered into the sacred Mysteries. It has been stated that the three pillars of a temple had their origin in these three cubes as a first trinity, that they belonged to the Stellar myths and were represented by Horus, Sut and Shu (The Sun, Saturn and Mars), placed North, South and Center. Later, when the Solar cult arrived, they were made to represent the Sun rising in the East, setting in the West, with a station in the South.

Ptah, in primal astro-mythology, was called the Great Architect of Heaven. Two pillars were placed at the gateway leading to the house of Ptah. They were made stable for eternity. These were placed at the entrance of temples named for two of these "Great Ones" -- Horus, North, and Sut, South. On each pillar four lines were engraved to represent heaven and earth as the double square on which the temple was built. These pillars became known as the Tatt Pillars. Tatt symbolized "in Strength," and "Tattu," "to Establish," meaning the "Place to Establish Forever," which was equivalent to the double square. Similar pillars were placed at the porchway or gates to Temples of Initiation.

In Egypt, back of these pillars guarding the sacred doors, in the mysticism and beauty of the older cult, sat in silence "The Eternal One." Two guards were always standing within and without the entrance to the temple -- the Watcher inside and the Herald outside. We have these pillars in Masonic Lodges today, adorned with a celestial and a terrestrial globe. As a rule the cubes are missing from the interior of the Lodges, but may still be found in the Royal Arch Chapter. In early Totemic ceremonies these pillars were erected when "making a boy into a man" as an Establisher or Creator. This belonged to the cult of the Stars, and was followed by the cult of the Sun and the Ritual of final things, so beautifully given in the Masonic Order today.

In French Lodges these pillars were usually placed North and South, near the West entrance. The Apprentices received their wages at the Pillar of Jachin, North; and the Fellow Crafts were paid in the South, at the Pillar of Boaz; and the Master received his wages in the middle chamber. [1]

King Solomon made a complete copy of the pillars that were placed at the entrance to Amenta for the porch of his Temple, on which the ornamentation and lily work were practically the same. They bore resemblance to the two mystical Pillars of Hermes, which gave the astronomical science of their time. It has been claimed that the Pillars on the porch of Solomon's Temple were called the Tablets of the Law, typical of those placed in the Ark of the Covenant. The Pillar on the right, called Jachin, was "The White Pillar of Light;" the one on the left, called Boaz, was "The Shadowy Pillar of Darkness." They were beautifully ornamented with chain work, with two stories of network enclosing pomegranates and lilies. The pomegranate was a mystic fruit, and became a Divine symbol known as "The Forbidden Fruit," showing the connection with the Ark of the Covenant.

The Ark of the Covenant was built for Jehovah. The name Jehovah is Bi-une, that is, male-female. The Bible states that a large bowl was set upon

---
(1) - Authority: REGULATEUR DU MAÇON, Page 17.

each Pillar, one of which was thought to contain Fire, emblematic of the Father, and the other, Water, emblematic of the Mother, or the divine and terrestrial life of humankind. Between the two Pillars was the door leading to the Holy Place, where those going from earthly labors entered to seek their spiritual refreshment. These Pillars are also represented on the Sephirotic Tree of the Kabala, and when Kabalistically interpreted, mean "In Strength shall my House be Established." Modern significance has been given them in connection with the two St. Johns of the New Testament, as Wisdom and Love, in which "My House shall be Established."

Worship has always found a place in the heart of man. It is with him today as a religious instinct, though perilously near extinction. Even the savage has a Ritual, very simple, very humble, very intense. Religion is a revelation, not an invention of man. It came through the necessities of life, and through it Initiates have recognized the immense value of toil and suffering. Every theology, from the earliest to the latest, has come from a common source, or abstract ideas. Through the progress of human evolution, personality has descended until the racial consciousness or memory seems lost; but beauty of the spirit transcends this personality, and spiritual beauty has been called the trysting place of the Nirvanees.

The oldest religions or philosophies of the world are rooted in the one idea -- the Divine Oneness of God, taught by all nations. The powers and forces so deeply revered were those of nature and nature-gods. Through nature God signed all His Great Works, so simply expressed in the stars, in the flowers, in crystals -- everywhere; for nature is God. No religion since earliest times was ever based upon fiction; dogma alone has killed primeval truths. No creed, no human-born doctrine can compare with nature. All keys lie hidden in the bosom of our Mother Nature. It has been left for the neophyte to deduce an explanation from Mother Nature and be guided by her influence, which seems to be surrounded in modern thought by doubt -- but to the doubter only. Suggestions given in symbol, allegory, or tradition, are most efficacious as instruments of instruction when the inner side of nature is being approached, for through them the neophyte's power of perception is awakened.

Throughout the entire East, religion was more or less a mystery, entirely devoted to symbolism. Philosophers had deeply embedded within them the mystic laws of nature; and though many of the ancient laws had become hidden through the ages, symbols had been preserved. Many ancient laws became separated to meet the needs of the people. Few received the esoteric teaching. The profane have been responsible for much that has been used to undo what was sacred and profound in the ceremonial mystery-teachings of the past. Though some of the brilliancy of the past may be lacking, Masonry interprets the great laws of nature and incessantly strives towards spiritual perfection.

Masonic philosophy can be conclusively proved to be the first spiritual, mystical religion and science -- and it will be the last. Primitive Masons have left us imperishable records of their knowledge. Masonry has within it the truest Ritual of the past -- the same signs and symbols used ages and ages ago to express man's thoughts when he was unconscious of articulate sounds. These he afterwards adopted to express secret meanings, just as they are used today. Of celestial origin, they are divinely perfect. True Masonry is esoteric. "A Mason is not appointed, he is evolved; his Ritual is not a ceremony but something to be lived" and its key lies in service. Out of darkness, or that sleep of the ages, and through Masonry man will learn how to build the Temple of his God, eternal in the heavens, without the sound of the hammer or the voice of the workman. Esoteric wisdom is a living, spiritual thing and faith comes in the Hidden Wisdom of Masonic Rituals. The world recognizes the material; the spiritual sees into the Invisible Cause. Within each human body is a living spark which lights those esoteric powers, and to the seeker of spiritual truths the rough ashlar soon becomes the polished stone, ready for the foundation of his super-structure -- the bettering of the building of the Temple of Humanity and of himself.

Masonry is the science of the secrets of nature, physical and psychic, mental and spiritual, and develops the psychic powers latent in man. The Masonic Lodge is the symbol of the Universe -- a true Temple of Humanity where deep inner truths are enshrined. An almost miraculous knowledge has been concentrated in the hearts of Initiates who lovingly overshadow the lives of those in need.

To a candidate entering Masonry, the polishing of the rough ashlar is the refining of his own nature, bringing his soul to perfection through divine truths. Charity to man gives him the opportunity to make of himself an altar in his own temple, made sacred to the Great Architect. Deep in the quarries of his human heart there are endless resources of great power which "symbolize the Cosmic substance from which man must gather the stones for his temple." (1) The square, the level and the plumb rule can transform the rough ashlar into the triangle or the cube; and then the building begins.

Associations in Lodges today stand upon spiritual and charitable principles -- principles which arose through the Secret Mysteries. Masonic ceremonials imply moral and spiritual concepts; Lodges are symbolical of the Universe; and the Universe is the Great Temple wherein Deity is ever present. The doctrines of Masonry are the most beautiful and uplifting conceivable. The simplicity of early ages permeates their Rites, giving them a majestic beauty. Love is the keynote of their mystic science -- love and charity. Love one another, help one another, is the fulfilling of their law. To be a good Mason is to be a good man. One can become a Mason only through the unfoldment and expansion of the divine power within his own heart, and the longing for the Light, which comes to him upon his entry into a Lodge. Masonic Ritual as we have it has been evolved out of the beginning of all things and has been but little changed; or whatever changes have taken place have been due, practically, to the passing of time — endless time. In the abstract, however, Masonry is the same, founded on the Laws of THE GREAT ARCHITECT OF THE UNIVERSE and the Divine Order of the Heavens, of which its Ritual is emblematic.

The exact science of human regeneration has been called one of the lost keys of Masonry. There are emblems in use today that a few Masons belonging to the highest orders have worked out through a key-system. As our Aquarian Age unfolds, certain lost keys to the old Mysteries will be revealed. For a transcendent science is now arising from the ashes of the past which, in the light of our new art, will transform the whole trend of human thought by destroying all false and irrational teaching. In Masonry we shall find the True Gnosis; and the secret religions of the world will once more include the raising to Initiation by the Grip of the Lion's Paw; for, nothing is ever really lost. The soul knows all things; knowledge is only remembrance; and hope is undying.

---
(1) - HALL, Manly P.

The thread of truth remains slender but is not broken. Few, however, have the courage or patience to go far enough back into the dim past to attempt to separate truth from superstition or disfigured allegory into which much harm has crept, accepting, rather, modern tradition with its allurements. The past holds the profundity of simplicity but not of subtlety.

Much of the Ritualism of Masonry is founded upon the Mysteries of Atlantis, perfected in Egypt. An understanding of its symbolical imagery disentangled many difficult knots. Ritualism is not an empty thing. It reveals ancient worship, and man's dependence upon, and knowledge of God, expressed in symbols -- in voice and clothes -- together with geometrical and numerical combinations. All are designed to be a method of measuring His works.

In Egypt, geometry became deified and the letter "G" according to the ancient Masters still denotes this great science. Therefore, as God geometrizes, we have THE GREAT ARCHITECT OF THE UNIVERSE and blessed indeed is he who knows the spiritual value and power of numbers, for they have preserved within them the Ancient Wisdom.

"Divine cosmogony is to be found pure and truthful in some of the grandest ritual features of the Roman Catholic Church ... for it is so. ... On the other hand, Free Masonry holds to the elemental workings by geometrical display -- i.e., by the harder, more exact, and purer outlines of the same system of problems. As between the two systems, in their ultimate, there is no difference at all. Lord God of a common humanity, loosen the shackles from the bodies and enlarge the souls of man! Let freedom be the seed, and let wisdom, love and peace -- but above and before all, charity -- be the harvest! And SO MOTE IT BE!" (1)

"Mote is purely Egyptian, a rare form for 'May it Be.' .... 'So Mote it Be' is the conservative formula of the Mason, as it was of the Priests of Egypt."(2) Whereas "Peace Profound" answered by "God is with us" is a highly mystical mode of salutation; and though belonging to the Rosicrucians, has its place in Masonry, as it has with the Kabalistic Initiates.

If we trace the Roman Catholic faith under the symbolism of Water, and that of the Freemason under Fire, we find that these faiths came down from the lost continent of Atlantis, from which "we have knowledge of the Lords of Reason, and the Lords of Compassion, ever trying to unfold human consciousness."

Harmonious union of Fire and Water produces Air, which, in turn, represents the Soul, or mediator, the Soul being the link between Spirit and body; and as man is Spirit, Soul and body, his Soul is the mediator between the spiritual and the material. Ancient Initiates divided the Sun into three distinct bodies, and the Mystics tell us that there are three Suns in each solar system analogous to the centers of life in man; Spirit, Soul and body. The properties of the Sun are life, light and heat. They vitalize and vivify the three worlds -- spiritual, intellectual and material. The Spiritual Sun, the Intellectual Sun, and the Material Sun are now symbolized in Masonry by the three Candles, the three Lights, the Spiritual Sun manifesting as the Power of God, the Father; the Intellectual Sun, as the Life of God; and the Material Sun, as the vehicle of His manifestation.

---

(1) - SKINNER, J. R.; THE SOURCE OF MEASURES, Page 320.
(2) - MASSEY, Gerald; A BOOK OF BEGINNINGS, Volume I, Page 178.

It is said "From one Light, three Lights," and these not only lead to, but become, in Masonry, the Master Mason. The three divisions of the Tabernacle represented the three degrees belonging to the Blue Lodge; and there were three Orders of Priests serving, representing the Entered Apprentice, the Fellow Craftsman and the Master Mason. Masonic Ritualism should hold all that was held most sacred in the Ancient Religions.

Ritualism has within itself a highly spiritual purpose. It searches for inner tranquility and peace, and evolves a quiet beauty and understanding. Pain is the spiritualizing principle which develops the inner man. In adversity man is more apt to turn his thoughts to God. He has needed the emotion of sorrow to realize the inner urge towards higher truths -- an urge awakened in his heart which has often led him to the door of a Masonic Lodge.

From the moment he applies for admission the desire is to seek relief by entering into the Light -- that Divine power in everyone known as the Hidden Light, which brings into manifestation a spiritual force awakened through supreme effort and devotion. Upon entering the ante-room of a Masonic Lodge his awaited Initiation begins. From the ante-room, the outer guard gives certain knocks upon the door leading to the Holy Place, the Inner Sanctuary, and these are answered by the inner guard. Later, the candidate will come to know and feel the inner meaning of those knocks, when the outer guard is answered by the inner; for then the lower nature is getting its response from the Higher Self.

From within is asked, "Who is there, and what does he seek?" The reply comes from the outer guard: "He is seeking Light." Then the inner guard addresses the Worshipful Master, telling him that a stranger is outside, seeking Light; whereupon the Worshipful Master says: "Let him be admitted." It is then that the true Initiation begins, and a Son of Light steps forth on the Path to Enlightenment, Service and Love.

Throughout the Ritual of the first three degrees of the Blue Lodge, the symbolic meaning of the rough ashlar is taught. The seven great sciences are given for reflection and study, followed in all its sacred significance by the sublime degree of the Master Mason, which raises man from darkness into the sphere of everlasting Light, or Life. Thirty-three degrees are given in Masonry, leading man ever onward and upward in his ascent of the Tree of Life on the way towards Infinity.

The seven officers of a Lodge are representative of the seven planets, known in primordial days as THE FRATERNITY OF THE BUILDERS; and these first three degrees of the Blue Lodge represented by the Entered Apprentice, the Fellow Craft, and the Master Mason, open the inner significance of the seven planets and call down into the one to be initiated the higher forces corresponding to each officer. The Lodge symbolizes creation; and the three principal officers, the Worshipful Master and the two Wardens, symbolize the three aspects of the Logos; the other officers symbolize the aspects of the human man and his higher consciousness.

Two factors in Masonry -- symbolism and ceremonial -- are very full of detail and accuracy, which are always important is the outward act. The thought which is free from all personality, therefore true and sincere, is needed and helpful in the progress of Masonry. An officer of the Lodge is not as other men, for he is the keeper of a great secret; and the chair in which he sits is reminiscent of the Immortals. The Worshipful Master impersonates LIGHT.

Even among most uncivilized races, Rituals have been known -- very often of great spiritual beauty, directing the tribal thought towards God. Although many signs, symbols and various things of a sacred nature, such as the Lion's Paw, the Ladder, et cetra, have come down through the Mysteries, Masonry lived long before any of them became renowned. Its antiquity may not be reached, as many have thought, through the mythology of Greece or Rome. Masonry belonged to primeval man who, in recognizing Deity, looked reverently towards the heavens, where the foundation of all things exists. Ancient faiths claim millions of years of existence, yet Masonry antedates them all, for its principles, coeval with creation itself, are founded on the laws of heaven; not alone on thoughts expressed, but by the commands of God. The past looms up as darkness but does not preclude all knowledge for throughout the entire world Ritualistic Philosophic Religion, wherever practised, has always had a distinct reverence for the worship of God; and as a religion, Masonry precedes all others.

Interpreters of ancient Masonry are few today, but the number will increase as the undercurrent of spirituality increases. Faithful candidates are those who will bring to mind and study those old, illuminated philosophers and hierophants who worked so patiently endeavoring to open the souls of men to the beauty and glory of the Ancient Arcanum. Temple-Builders are needed. Labor, toil, endeavor, industry -- all could become, in rhythmic measures of time and service, a glorious anthem of the Builders. In the sanctum sanctorum of Masonry are hidden jewels of many, many ages gone by -- ages of wisdom that hundreds of religions have brought to it. Emblematic thoughts alone on the Tracing Board are filled with everlasting truths; and this is where the mysteries of that long-lost Arcanum, whose power lies in its symbols, may be comprehended. Its symbolism is its soul. Man should endeavor intelligently to realize how profound are the designs on the Tracing Board of THE GREAT ARCHITECT OF THE UNIVERSE.

A working of the three Masonic degrees is emblematically given in designs on movable Boards, which change when the candidate passes from one degree to another, and he finds a new Board before him, with a design appropriate for each of the degrees. The Checker Board floor and the Tracing Board of the Dionysiac architects made their appearance about 1,000 B.C. These architects polished crude stones, squared them, and trued them into miracles of beauty; and they gouged out rough ashlars and trued them into universal temples, in veneration of THE GREAT ARCHITECT.

The design on an old Tracing Board that has been preserved in a Masonic Hall in London, England, was apparently taken from an ancient traditional plan. "On one side it shows a Lodge of the first and second degrees; and on the other, that of the third degree. The proportion of the Board is very nearly in the ration of 3:1; that is to say, it is composed of three squares laid in a row, and is consequently of the same proportion as the floor of the tabernacle."(1)

The Tracing Board is for the guidance of the workmen, to aid them in carrying out the plans of THE GREAT ARCHITECT. Mystically it refers to the Charter, the standard of faith. No Lodge is Regular without its Charter, which is placed at the pedestal of the Master.

---

(1) - THE CANON, Page 295.

Geometrically, the Tracing Board fully bears out the statement in the Ritual -- that the Lodge is as long as from East to West, and as wide as from North to South, and as high as from the highest heaven to the center of the earth; and what is of deepest interest is that it seems to have ingeniously contrived to include all the canonical numbers of the universe.

"In Modern Masonry the Deity is symbolized as the equilateral triangle, its three sides representing the primary manifestation of the Eternal One, who is Himself represented as a tiny flame by the Hebrew Yod (י) placed in a circle, as a symbol of Deity surrounded by the circle of eternity."

Each letter of the Hebrew alphabet, which is the basis of a great, fire-born doctrine, is composed of tiny flames, ranging from one to four. The letter "Yod" is the Great Flame which draws to itself or to its form the 22 letters of the Hebrew alphabet. The Masons have accepted this Yod as a symbol of THE GREAT ARCHITECT OF THE UNIVERSE, whose sacred name is written in this divine alphabet and not in the language of man. It has ever been known that all things were created by a Word, and the earliest form of the Word and the Mistress of Letters, was the Great Mother.

The alphabet of Wisdom -- Symbolism -- is taken from the Dot, the line, and the circle in combination; for the key to all knowledge is the Dot in motion -- just as words originated in sound. The most sacred and profound Kabalistic figure is a circle, within which are three Yods and a Tau. It belonged to an age when there was no Trinity as we know it today; for at that time no fatherhood was known in heaven -- only the mother and child. The Tau Cross means "Established Forever." When the equilateral triangle was illuminated with a single Yod, the letter denoted the thought, the idea of God, a ray of heavenly light. It was a point at which thought paused. The Yod is the number-letter 10 -- male and female.

For ages, ignorance has dimmed the mind to the richness of old symbolism and traditions -- perhaps more so to the true meaning of that small letter we know as the Yod, the Great Fire Flame, whose symbolism is not fully forgotten, for its sound and a general knowledge of its meaning have been preserved. The modern "G" has replaced the Yod as the initial letter.

The letter Yod should be within the center of the glory in the East, instead of the now universal and less significant letter "G" given this exalted point in "The Place of Light." In France, the Yod was put in the center of the Blazing Star. It was the germ of life, the basic letter of the entire alphabet, and its value was 10.

The three Mother Letters of the Kabalists are the three Sepharim, "Number, Writing and Speech, by which Jah is said to have created the Universe. Number is Fire (the writing of the Stars); Writing flows like Water; and Air is the basis of Speech. But these are all mysteriously connected symbolically with the Perfect Number 10, of which 0 is the Naught of the Unmanifest, and 1 the First Positive Idea. The Mouth from which issues the Fire of the Spirit in the form of Breath, and also the Water, is, when closed, a horizontal line. When open it is a Circle; thus 10." (1)

---
(1) - FRATER ACHAD, THE ANATOMY OF THE BODY OF GOD, Page 30

"The Creator compounded the world out of all the fire, and all the water, and all the air, and all the earth, having no part of any of them, nor any power of them outside -- in the center he placed the soul."(1)

It is stated that Water preceded and was the cause of the Breath of Life, Water being the first form of Matter in all old mythologies or so-called cosmogonies. It is the Mother Substance, and Mother and Matter are one. Water became the first cause in Egypt, and also in India.

Samothraceans venerated the Circle and consecrated it to the universal presence of Deity. The Chinese used a similar symbol which was bounded North and South by two serpents, equivalent to the two perpendicular lines of the Masonic symbol. "A ring supported by two serpents was emblematic of the world, protected by the power and wisdom of the Creator; and that is the origin of the two parallel lines (into which time has changed the two serpents) that support the circle in our Lodges." (2) The Hindus had as their symbol a perfect Sphere, without beginning or end. A most profound symbol in Masonry is the name -- "Sol-om-on" -- three names of the Sun, a solar Deity -- and trebly so.

It is an extraordinary fact that Rites and Ceremonies corresponding to those of Freemasonry can be found in all Ancient Mysteries, presupposing one original source. The finger points towards Masonry, where the teaching was the most profound; and this Ancient Mystery is readily traced back to the Divine Wisdom emanating from the Great Mother and her Fraternity, which has descended to those who were waiting below.

All ancient hierophants, who were practically Masters of the old world, had their esoteric doctrines and sacred ceremonies. No work could be undertaken without their ritualistic jurisdiction; but Hindus, Gymnosophists, the later Essenes, Greeks and Romans, all copied the Rituals, Grips and Passwords of Masonry. Only through initiations could the meaning of sacred writings and their ceremonies be understood. Vital doctrines were kept from the profane.

Rituals belonging to Greece and Rome and their temple service have been comparatively lost, as much was destroyed by their successors. Very little is left of the ceremonial Rite through which their deities were invoked. A few hymns to their gods have survived; no trace in the temple services of the Pagan cult is left. A few references have been saved from the sacred writings of the Eleusinians Initiatory Mysteries. Slight information regarding the Rituals of these older religions was given at certain unusual celebrations with dramatic intent, forming a final spectacle of the Initiations. But very little is known, even among writers such as Plutarch, St. Clement of Alexandria, Lucien, Apulius, Macrobius and others.

It is a pity that the old Rituals cannot be clearly understood and all difficulties abandoned. Our Priests today barely grasp the meaning of the ancient scriptures which they undertake to expound, unaware of their real significance. They do not know "what the Canon of the church is, or why a certain office or literary arrangement is canonical, and what makes it so." (3) Therefore they deny that the Old Testament and the Gospels are allegorical books and that their followers are unaware of the spirit of the Law.

---

(1) - The TIMAEUS of Plato
(2) - PIKE, Albert; MORALS AND DOGMA, Page 429.
(3) - THE CANON, Pages 5-6.

The Vernal Equinox was, to the ancients, an occasion of the impregnation of the world and was annually celebrated as such, centuries before the Christians commemorated the Crucifixion or the Resurrection. "To the old Pagans this stupendous consummation has been the humanizing of the natural powers of omnipotence, infinity, and eternity, which could only be conceived by some concrete figure, and it brought home to them by analogy the love of God for the earth and the hope of life through death. ..... The supposed analogy between the creative functions of God and man supplied the basis of the principal ritualistic ceremonies of antiquity, and constituted the culminating revelation disclosed to the initiate at the celebration of the Mysteries. ... Initiations were so arranged that the ignorant neophytes were gradually instructed in the hidden truths which were concealed under the characters and events of the mythos." (1)

While these Rites were being performed, to maintain secretiveness the doors were closed, lest knowledge should reach the profane. This was the Glory set apart for the true Initiate. There were many instances of the symbols of the masculine and feminine powers of the universe being commingled as Magic Powers, typically celebrating Cosmic powers revivified on earth, that earth might bring forth during the Spring.

All ancient degrees evolved by primeval man were of profound knowledge and were simply given, but some have become like the broken columns in the old temples. Though much may have been lost through additions and absurd interpretations, old foundations still remain representative of the remote past. The degrees of Initiation belonging to Masonry are but the degrees of the evolution of God in man, and the Ritual should be performed with all the joy and beauty of so profound a revelation.

The three steps or degrees of a Blue Lodge are the paths for man's liberation and attainment. They are embryonic, mental and spiritual. The first degree represents man in his prenatal period -- embryonic; the second (2) degree represents him in the flesh; while in the third degree he enacts the death of the Master Builder, allegorically signifying the transmission of the soul to heaven. From this he arises into a new sphere of life.

Thus, figuratively, the Masonic Ritual represents in these three degrees the epitome of his existence, both cosmic and human. The triune spirit of man created in the Ritual of Masonry is symbolical of the three Grand Masters of the Lodge of Jerusalem. "The Master Builder through all the ages erects living temples of flesh and blood as shrines to the Most High." He sets the atoms to work, or in motion, as it were, thereby building up that cosmic power as it enters the soul of the Builder. It should be the aspiration of all true seekers or candidates endeavoring to reach the heights attained by those old Priests and Brothers, to build within the temple a Cosmic Power, or Light, so profound that, when leaving the temple, it could be translated over the entire world.

Symbols in Masonry were divined by ancient astronomers. Of all the sciences Solomon considered none more useful than the knowledge of celestial

---
(1) - THE CANON, Pages 282-284.
(2) - The sign given in the second, or Fellow Craft's degree, is far older than that given in modern tradition. It was used by the Egyptians many ages ago, at the setting of the Sun.

movements, which were to him more precious than all riches. Also, great veneration was given by him to numbers, as they had their beginning among the stars, radiating Divine powers. The threefold condition, or construction of man may be illustrated in many ways in the Blue Lodge of Masonry. The numbers 3,5,7, regarded as mystic by all the old civilized nations of antiquity, in Masonic Lodges have been adopted to express the Universal Temple. There are three large stars in the constellation of Orion which are particularly adapted to the Blue Lodge degrees through the numbers 3,5,7. Two of these stars are just three degrees apart, the other star, one-third of a degree from the other two. They represent the Entered Apprentices. The Hiades, near Orion, are five in number and represent the Fellow Craftsmen. Near by are the Pleiades, seven in number, representing the Master Masons. The grouping together of these famous stars brings their vibrations to the members of the Blue Lodge, who are to become, in name, Masons. This name "Mason" has been weighed and honored in the great scale of a profound and celestial heritage.

The mystic Three-Times-Three Triangle of the Kabalists shows how Wisdom, Strength and Beauty are divine attributes upon which the Universal Temple was built. In many of the Mysteries an emblematical Triad of Deity was represented by three principal officers of a Lodge and the three Pillars which symbolized Wisdom, Strength and Beauty. In the Hindu temples these Pillars, also known as Wisdom, Strength and Beauty, were placed East, West and South, crowned with three human heads. They referred to the Creator who planned His work in His Infinite Wisdom, executed it by His Strength, and adorned it in all Beauty and unselfishness for the benefit of man. These are represented in solemn ceremonies of Initiation by the three presiding officers, or Brahmans.

"The chief Brahman sat in the east, high exalted on a brilliant throne, clad in a flowing robe of azure, thickly sparkled with golden stars, and bearing in his hand a magical rod; thus symbolizing Brahma, the creator of the world." (1)   The other two Brahmans were equally attired in magnificence, occupying corresponding places of distinction. "The representative of Vishnu, the setting sun, was placed on an exalted throne in the west; and he who personates Siva, the meridian sun, occupied a splendid throne in the south."(2)

Masonic Lodges, bounded by the extreme points of the compass and from the highest heavens to the lowest depths of the earth, are supported by these three Pillars as Wisdom, Strength and Beauty. Similarly in Egypt, the form of the Deity was designated by the attributes of Wisdom, Strength and Beauty. (3) The Sacred Triad has come to us from Atlantis. The three steps belong to the Master's degree and at right angles, as do the three mystic steps of Vishnu.

Every mysterious system practised over the world contained a Triad of Deity and the doctrine of the unity of the Godhead or the Triplicity of the Supreme. Nature, likened to the Equilateral Triangle -- the most beautiful of all -- was assigned the number "Three" -- symbol of the Great God. "The Great A U M that dwells in the Infinite is figured as the equilateral triangle." The Chaldeans assigned their Ain Suph Aur to the limitless light of Chaos and to the great Light of the Equilateral Triangle. This Triangle was the diagram of the creation of the world for the Hindus, and they used it as the model for their temples. It was also worshipped by the Egyptians.

---

(1) - FELLOWS, John; MYSTERIES OF FREEMASONRY, Page 236.
(2) - Ibid.
(3) - A very ancient triangle of Asiatic origin, portraying three human legs springing from a center, was called a Trinacaria (Trinitarian).

"The oracle in Damascus asserts throughout the world a Triad shines forth which resolves itself into a monad." The Masonic Pillars of Wisdom, Strength and Beauty form the equilateral triangle representing the threefold Deity. The Triad of Spirit, Mind and Body is the fundamental Trinity of every religious doctrine. There is a prehistoric adage that the "Trinity is the Unknowable Source of the Unknown Universe." Everywhere in this universe the Trinity upon which it is formed is found in nature; and nature is the revelation of God; and the voice of nature sings into the soul the wonders of God.

The importance of the number "Three" and the Triangle is an almost inexhaustible theme. A sublime Triad -- Light, Life and Substance -- one and indivisible, comes from the first three steps of the Ten Sephiroth, as Infinite Light, Infinite Wisdom, and as "The Great Mother Substance energized by the Divine Will of God" it is resurrection of pure spirit and regeneration of matter. Masonically "this upright Triad, or the Tree of Life, would be Kether, Chokmah and Binah, or the Trinity -- that is, the three chief Masonic Officers, which the Masons do not show, as a Lodge is composed of seven officers or planets, and they should have what is known in the Higher Mystic Orders, the Three Chiefs seated back of the Seven Officers. That is, they should be seated in dignity, in the East of the Masonic Lodge, back of the Grand Master, so that the TRINITY in UNITY, or Father-Mother-Son, could function and pass their three upper rays, as the upright triangle, into the inverted or lower seven rays which would be Jupiter, Mars and the SUN, as the Fire-Principle, and then be reflected into the Form-Principle, or Watery, into Venus, Mercury and the Moon; or, Spirit into Form.

"Jupiter has its polar opposite in Mars, synthesized into the Sun. Venus, the form, has its polar opposite in Mercury, synthesized in the Moon. The Earth has no planetary counterpart. Its counterpart is in the Elements, which are four instead of three. The zodiacal Aries is ruled by Mars on the inverted plane; but if the Triangle were reversed, Jupiter would be the ruler. Jupiter is the Father, or the Individuality in manifestation; and Mars, the Personality. Jupiter is Mercy; Mars, Severity; and they are synthesized in the SUN, or Harmony. For this reason Masons look upon that which they represent as the FIRE PRINCIPLE of the planetary chain, or, Jupiter Mars and the Sun; and when the inverted Triangle is lifted, the rays of the Sun are lifted into Mars as the Personality, to be destroyed, being merged into Jupiter. This enables the Consciousness to be lifted into the Upper Triad (which is upright) into Binah, the Mother, or Love, which is aligned with Chokmah, or Wisdom, and unites with the SUN or the Sphere of the Zodiac, as the Son or WORD into Kether, the Highest Consciousness, the Supreme Light."(1)

A U M is venerated by the Hindus as the most sacred Name of God, their Deity, and it has three aspects: Brahma (symbolically Life-Giving), Vishnu (Life-Preserving), and Siva (Life-Destroying). This Triune God was also represented by the mystic "Y" of the Chinese; and the equilateral triangle was always symbolical of the Triune God. A triple Tau in the center of a circle symbolized the Sacred Name -- the Sacred Triad. A trine within the circle was an emblem of the Trinity in Unity; a circle within the trine, the converse, was an emblem of Unity in Trinity; a point, Deity -- self-existent. Rituals throughout the world are founded on the revolutions of the Sun, Moon and Stars. The Egyptians worshipped astronomy and their knowledge was profound.

---

(1) - WIGGS, George W.

In their ceremonies they reversed the order of the apparent movement of the Sun, to that of the earth around the Sun; and this order of circumambulation is in use in Masonic Lodges today.

Take one of their degrees where the number "six" is repeated: In the ante-room, before entering the Lodge, the candidate is prepared with a rope tied six times about his body. On the door to the inner Lodge, he gives six raps which are answered from within. These knocks have deep esoteric significance. The candidate is admitted and walks six times around the Lodge, moving with the Sun; while the Brothers who are more advanced form a procession and march six times around the Lodge, against the course of the Sun. This proves at almost every point the celestial origin of Masonic ceremonials, for, as above stated, the candidate moves around the Lodge following the course of the Sun, and afterwards the direction is reversed, showing that "this appearance is produced by the actual movement of the earth from West to East around the Sun." This should be known and understood by all Masons.

Some of the higher degrees of Masonry were added at the time when the Ancient Mother and her Sons, THE FRATERNITY OF THE BUILDERS, were said to build the heavens on the square, at the commencement of the solar system. In very early ages Operative Masons were only instructed in part of the Rituals and ceremonies. Their oath related to temple building -- an oath which, it is said, has never been violated. These Operative Masons date back at least 300,000 years. Certain of them had worked in temples and were known as "Companions." They were of a lower order than the Priests, and were never initiated beyond the third degree, but were allowed certain privileges during religious Rites. They were distinct from the "Old Religious Brotherhood" of the Stellar Cult, and had been previously initiated so that secrets would be kept. The term "Companion" was primary.

Totemic sociology survived in Egypt when artisans worked together as Companions, or in company. Neolithic man, with or without a Hero Cult, had Totems. They believed in the elementary powers and the Great Mother who brought them forth. This cult was scattered over the world. They divinized the Great Mother Earth and the seven elementary powers into the Great Mother whose Seven Sons were assigned to the stars. The Totem was first given to the female at the time of puberty. It was needed for recognition, to indicate the tribe or clan to which she belonged, as each tribe was distinguished by the Totem which descended from the female, the Mother of the tribe. In this way the Blood-Motherhood which gave the Blood-Brotherhood was recognized. In the Totemic system each Fraternity had its special sign through which Brotherhood became known. (This is also found in Masonry today). This Mother was later exalted as the mystical Virgin Mother.

Totemic ancestry seems almost lost in the past, or forgotten. "Their clans had a type-sign of signs, and a gesture language, before names could be given." This was prior to mythology. Spirit worship antedated ancestor worship, many ages before eschatology had been perfected. Research proves that ancient Mysteries had a common Neolithic root in the tribal ceremonies of Totemism. In the following order came Totemism, Fetishism and Mythology, an improvement on the former. Then came Eschatology.

Totemic sociology, 800,000 years ago, used the same signs and symbols in use today. Their secrets lie among the stars. An ancient papyrus states that "The God of the Universe is in the light above the firmament; and the symbols are upon the earth." "Totemism is the semi-cultural background of all primitive society." The sole original ancestor of sociology, and in mythology, is the Mother. Sociology always began with the Mother; but after the long interval of a Patriarchal age, it will end in the Matriarchal. Motherhood represented the most ancient stage of sociology.

"The tribes of North America are divided into Totemic divisions, and the Crow Tribe has two interesting 'signs,' tokens of friendship and brotherhood, and if given and answered by strangers, you are a 'safe brother' amongst them, which is important to those brothers of the 18°.

1. In crossing their arms on the breast L U
2. In raising the R H to the side of the H, with the I F pointing to the Great Spirit, and then reversing H A and H D."(1)

This was a Stellar Sacred Sign used ages and ages ago, almost in the beginning.

Masonic Lodges are oriented East and West, proving them to belong to the Solar Cult. "Go from East to West in search of that which is lost" is well known to all Masons. Stellar orientation, North and South, is the oldest of all, and goes back to the Mount of the Mother and her Sons of Light, THE FRATERNITY OF THE BUILDERS. Though eschatological ceremonies are solar, signs and symbols go back to creation. Freemasonry today gives the purest form of eschatology; yet, how very few, when performing the Rites and ceremonies in the Lodge, seem to know of the true and beautiful eschatology perfected in Egypt.

The North was looked upon as the birthplace of all beginnings. The circumpolar paradise is known to the oldest races in the world as the initial starting-point of gods and men. In Egyptian tombs a small aperture opened towards the North. It was their idea that the breath of life came from the North, which created rebirth, re-begetting of the god, or the soul, in the matrix of the tomb for the next life, and the Mother was considered the sole progenitor. The Akkadians had the same idea of the breath of life. The South to them was the funeral point.

Research develops the fact that in philosophic and religious thought Masonry was the original vehicle of Divine Revelation. It came out of the celestial North -- the primordial home of the Great World Mother. The first Mason was symbolized as a woman, the Manifestor of the Seven Great and Sacred Stars which came to be known as THE FRATERNITY OF THE BUILDERS or "Companions."

The Abyss of the North, called the Void, was the abode of Darkness. It was "The Cave of Production" surrounded by the celestial waters, when this Great Mother was called "The Ark of Life;" and out of this primordial Darkness -- that unknown, inconceivable, incomprehensible Darkness -- the Mother, as the "Mistress of Darkness," was the bringer forth of Light, giving birth to creative forces and powers known as gods, which were called the Sons of "The Children of Light." In the language of antiquity Masons were known as the Sons of Light.

The North is the most mysterious and sacred corner of the entire world, and in its dark recesses are concealed many of the deepest, most profound, and

---
(1) - CHURCHWARD, Albert -- SIGNS AND SYMBOLS OF PRIMORDIAL MAN, Page 223

priceless secrets of the soul, of man, and of the Universe. Every ancient tradition of creation came from this common source. "Tradition is the result of the Thought of Humanity in the 'past' focused on the Present, the How and Now. So it is in regard to what we term the Future." One must bring the Divine Idea before the mental vision, no matter how, when, or where, "so long as the great essential is attained -- THAT MEN ARE MADE TO REMEMBER, TO UNDERSTAND AND TO LOVE." (1)

The radiant principle in nature, called Vitality, in Masonry is known as Cosmic Fire, or CHiram (Hiram Abiff). CHiram is the Chaldean name for Hiram. When a candidate crosses the line between the lower and the higher worlds he receives the benediction of Fire. It is claimed that this opens the coils of the mystical serpent and turns the Fire upwards through the central spinal canal which is the road to attainment, to adeptship, and to the "Inner Order" which lies beyond the veil, only to be lifted when all previous transmutations have passed into Spirit. Then consciousness may function on the fourth plane of nature, where the Great Mystery lies. Each brother should seek knowledge of that heavenly Fire, not alone for his own glory but that he may radiate or transmit its blessings to those in need, thereby showing the Great Masonic Way of helping to redeem man. True knowledge of the Sacred Fire is not found in books; it is to be sought within, by means of deep meditation. When found, it must be guarded. It is the Fire which shall illuminate the world.

The vital or Cosmic Force which ascends through this central spinal canal was also called "Fire Oil." In Greek, this Fire Oil is known as Christ; in Masonry, it is the Hidden Christ declared to manifest through the marrow of the bone; and this vital force, flowing up through the central canal, finally reaches the third ventricle of the brain, where a luminous light is born. This third ventricle in the old Masonic Rite was called "The Master Mason's Chamber."

The Uraeus, the Egyptian Serpent, emblem of Fire, was worn on the head of the Egyptian. It is a secret symbol of the zodiacal sign, Scorpio, meaning generation and regeneration. It is the transmuted Scorpio energy of the zodiac which, working upward in the regenerated soul, is called the Kundalini. This serpent was the sign of the Initiates. It is the mystical serpent or Kundalini which lies coiled at the end of the spine. This serpent or vital force was anciently accepted as the magic wand of the spinal canal -- the wand that budded and opened into blossom, and later became the Caduceus with the entwined serpents which, in ascending, are the positive and negative currents of the Super-Solar-Force and, guided heavenward, lead into communion with Divine Love.

This great ascending highway was "The Glory of the Lord." It is the true Tree of Life, its trunk, the rod, a symbol revered by all ancient peoples. The Christians alone forgot. But in that great primeval garden there is still the Tree of Life whose Fruits will nourish and help in the building of the Temple within, for the Great Architect builds from within. In the sacred garden of life, the mind has first to envision its Fruits before the time of garnering.

"The opening of the Tree of Life within oneself is a goal to be reached. This Tree, Kabalistically given, is only the Ten Sephira or the two

---
(1) - PIKE, Albert; MORALS AND DOGMA, Page 515.

pillars of Masonry, which are to be united to a third; -- in other words, the masculine and the feminine are to be brought into unison so that they may ascend through this central canal by opening the seven Chakras, which, when united in the head to the five senses, make twelve; and in uniting with the Godhead, make thirteen -- the number of the Mother. The Ten Sephira are to be united to the Godhead which is above, or Ain-Suph-Aun -- Infinite Space, Infinite Light -- and back to the Godhead, Unity Itself." (1) This third, or central pillar of the Tree of Life, is the same wand around which are twined the twin serpents of time and space.

Oratory originated with Hermes. He was the winged messenger of the gods who became the Caduceus wreathed with serpents, and who, in Masonry, represents the Orator, or the planet, Mercury.

When man profanes the Fruit of the Tree of Knowledge for unjust and unnatural uses, he practically clothes himself in the skin of the beast and can no longer enter the circle or garden watered by the four rivers of Life, for a cherub is placed at the gate with a flaming sword turning in all directions. In the Mystic pentacle of Eden there was an enclosure, by a ring or circle of water, and an island within; and the waters flowed towards the four points of heaven, or into the world. They formed a cross; and in the center of this cross was Paradise.

The earnest seeker and aspirant who through right desire has attained is, as it were, mystically reborn, unfolding or bringing to light that invisible spark of immortality called the Spirit. "Then all that has gone before is obliterated, all gives place to the wonder of wonders, the human made divine." Wisdom's path is not a swept and shaded avenue, but the hard and beaten highway of the world; yet the path of the candidate unfolds gradually into that ideal service of Brotherhood which is the foundation of Masonry; and as God geometrizes, behind the Ritual of Masonry lies the geometry of natural law.

The Will of God must be discovered by man himself; the Great Cyclic Law moves within. The Beauty of creation may not always be understood because of its great diversity; yet nature assures us of individual freedom through order. The Mason is told that the Sun is always shining. It does not travel round the earth, as we conclude, for our convenience; it is we who travel round the Sun, revolving as we go.

Symbolism is based on celestial lore, spiritual and fundamental, far above the dogmas and creeds and petty differences of today. From symbolism have sprung the lesser and greater religions of the world; and upon that old Rock of Ages we find the Father-Motherhood of God, the Brotherhood of man, and the Immortality of the Soul. Truth is eternal; and the ageless FRATERNITY OF THE BUILDERS holds the same truths today as it did millions of years ago -- truths that have trued their way through untold ages without change. They have reached and passed many of the world's Cyclic periods, each age bringing a definite philosophic revelation out of the tangled mysteries of time; and with each a modernized faith has been woven out of many threads. Teachers, using adaptations of the old Wisdom in their attempt to have the people of different ages understand, have far too often seemingly lost to that age imperishable truths through mistaken ideas; but God's Wisdom -- the inheritance of that GREAT FRATERNITY -- never changes. Some teachers have tried to tear away

---

(1) - WIGGS, George W.

the veil before the Great Wisdom, that a few might have a glimpse of the age-old faith; but very few have entered the inner sanctuary, and they were the great Initiate-Philosophers of Freemasonry. "Yet their power is not to be measured by the achievements of ordinary men. They are the dwellers upon the threshold of the Innermost."[1]

A world religion does not belong to one mind or one earthly religion. The home of Wisdom is mystically hidden in the clouds, and secreted within them is the Great Arcanum. The genuine student of Masonry may pierce the clouds for this unspeakable mystery and find the foundations of Masonry, which are mystical. The wealth of Freemasonry lies in its mysticism, which the modern world endeavors to expel. Many modern Masons seem loath to believe in the mysticism or transcendentalism which belongs to true Masonry. Andersen, whose greatly prized Constitutions are used by the Freemasons, was a great transcendentalist; Eliphas Levi was a great mystic and transcendentalist; so also was Albert Pike, who is greatly loved and revered, and through whom Masonry has been raised to its highest standard.

The trials of the neophyte cannot compare with the mountainous trials and miseries which true Masonry has undergone from its inception, when it was revealed through the Father-Mother-God. The impetus for work is ready; a new note is to be struck -- a new Word of power sounded, that man may flee from his separateness. Spiritual unfoldment lies in the gospel of Identity -- in the Brotherhood of this age.

---

(1) - HALL, Manly P.

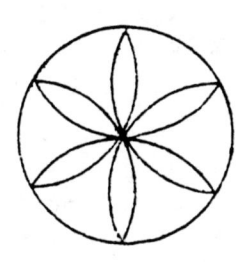

APPENDIX

A
LEGENDARY HISTORY OF MASONRY

B
A PHOENICIAN TRADITION
SANCHONIATHON

C
INTERESTING FRAGMENTS
SUGGESTING THE
ATLANTEAN AND BIBLICAL CONNECTION

A LEGENDARY HISTORY OF MASONRY

WHEN a legend shows more than ordinary exuberance of fancy, it compels our attention. This is well proven in the legend of Masonry, in which we are told that Lemech, the Father of Masonry, "in the order of Patriarchal giants the ninth from Adam, corresponds to the step Yesod of the Kabala; and in this capacity he may be said to be a symbol of the generative powers of the Sun." From a numerical standpoint, Lemech and his two wives form a complete triad. Numbers form a great part of Masonry. Lemech has the value of the side of a rhombus, while Tubal Cain, numerically, has the value of the width of the Vesica. Tubal Cain founded the science of music, and the measure of the Sun's distance computed by the tone. He has been called the first worker in stone or metal.

The first worker in metals, however, does not seem to have been Tubal Cain. Wallis Budge states in "The Gods of the Egyptians" that "it is, of course, impossible to say who were the first blacksmiths that swept over Egypt from South to North, or where they came from," but he is inclined to believe that they came from a country in the East, whose people worked in brick and iron. Nilotic negroes of inner Africa worked in iron and copper. Albert Churchward claims that there were two classes, among them the Gemi tribe (blacksmiths who founded a secret religious society in the time of Totemic sociology).

Operative Masons of the Middle Ages had accepted a sevenfold division of the liberal arts and sciences, an arrangement accepted by Marcianus Capella in the Fifth Century; and in the Eighth Century this same septinary division was adopted by Alcuinus, but with an exception: he placed arithmetic, geometry, music, and astronomy under the term of <u>Mathematics</u>. ("Of these sciences and arts Cassidorus was the author.")

Medieval craftsmen and scientists worked by measure, ponderation and weight, assuming geometry to be the one unchangeable principle, the most worthy, the most honorable. The Cooke manuscript speaks of the great obligation all workers are under to geometry, coming from a time of the highest antiquity; and the legend tells how it came to be invented. There is evidence that this was written by a Masonic writer at the close of the Fifteenth Century, or at the beginning of the Sixteenth. The manuscript has been published frequently. It also shows what a prominent part religion was given in Lodge secrets.

"Good Brethren and Fellowes: Our purpose is to tell you how and in what manner this worthy scyence of Masonrye begunne. .... The words 'Scyence' and 'Masonrye' are equivalent, as they have the same numerical value. .... for for there be seaven liberall scyences of the which seaven it is one of them, and the names of the seaven scyences bene these: First is Grammere; and it teacheth man to speak truly and write truly. The second is Rethorike; and teacheth a man to speake faire in subtill terms. And the third is Dialectyke; and teacheth a man for to discern and know the truth from false. And the fourth is Arithmeticke; and teacheth a man for to reckon and to accompte all manner of numbers. And the fifth is called Geometrie; and that teacheth the Mett and Measure of the earth, and all other things <u>of the which scyence is called Masonrye</u>. And the sixth scyence is called Musicke; and that teacheth a man of songs, and voice of tongue, and orgaine, harpe, and trompe," (which attuned the voices of man to song and joy, teaching him the harmonies not alone of tongue and voice, but of instruments of music then known). "And the seaventh scyence is called Astronomye; and that teacheth a man the course of the sonne, monne, and stars." (This taught of the Fields of Heaven, the Sun, the Moon, and the planets, and the triumphant march of the stars.)

"How that these worthy scyences were first begonne I shall tell you. Before Noyes Floode there was a man called Lameche, as it is written in the Byble, in the fourth chapter of Genesis: And this Lameche had two wives, the one height Ada, and the other height Sella: By his first wife Ada he gott two sons, and that one Jabell and tother Tuball, and by that other wife Sella he gott a son and a daughter." (Tubal and Naamah). "All these children founden the beginning of all the scyences in the world. And this elder son Jabell found the scyence of Geometrie;" (In one of Cooke's manuscripts it is stated: "He was name mast Mason and governor of all Adam's works when he made ye citie of Enoch.") "and he departed flocks of sheepe and lambs of the field, and first wrought house of stone and tree, and is noted in the chapter above said. And his brother Tubal found the science of Musicke, songs of tongue, harpe, and orgaine. And the third son, Tubal Cain, found smithcraft of gold, silver and copper, iron and steel; and the daughter found the crafte of Weavinge. And these children knew well that God would take vengeance for synn, either by fire or by water;" (They knew that the crimes and sins of mankind would be avenged by a universal deluge, either by fire or water, thinking it was the vengeance of God. They were all great astronomers. Masonry is founded upon astrology, the oldest known science.) "wherefore they writte their scyence that they founden in two pillars of stone that they might be found after Noyes Floode;" (That future generations might know what had been discovered, they preserved their science in this manner, and it was found in these pillars after the Great Deluge called Noah's Flood.) "And that one stone was marble, for that would not bren with fire; and the other stone was clepped laterns" (lattress or brick) "and would not drown in noe water." (To withstand the inundation, so that at least one would be preserved).

"Our intent is to tell you trulie and in what manner these stones were found, that these scyences were written in. The great Hermarynes that was Cubys son, the which Cub was Sem's son, that was Noys son. This Hermarynes afterwards was called Hermes, the Father of Wise Men. He found one of the two pillars of stone, and found the science written there, and he taught it to other men."

The Dowland manuscript mentions the discovery of these pillars and states that "Hermarynes or Hermes afterwards found one of the two pillars of stone and found the scyence written there." Hughan also mentions this. It has been written that Hermes concealed his sacred books under a certain pillar said to be hidden in a corner of an Egyptian temple; and there they were found.

"And at the making of the Tower of Babylon, there was Masonry first made much of" (when it was first regularly organized into a corporate body. And, according to Cooke's manuscript, one of Noah's sons built this Tower, as he loved and cherished all Masons. The Tower of Babel was an ancient astronomical temple called the "Temple of the Seven Lights or the Celestial Earth," and was decorated from top to bottom with innumerable stars, proving, as usual, that Masonry had its foundation in the heavens.)

The legend goes on naively to say: "And the Kings of Babylon that height Nimrothe was a Mason himself; .... and this was the first tyme that ever Mason had any charge of this science." (When the city of Nineveh and other cities of the earth, including Oriental cities, were built, Nimrod, at the request of his cousin, King of Nineveh, gave him three score Masons to assist in the building of these structures, also gave him Charges in which they were instructed to remain steadfast and true to one another, to live in harmony, and serve their Master truly for pay, in order that the Master might always have proper worship. This is the first mention of Masons having had Charges given them; and among the Charges was one concerning their secrets. Nimrod's prototype is found among the Seven Great Stars above, THE FRATERNITY OF THE BUILDERS.)

"Moreover, when Abraham and Sara his wife went into Egypt, there he taught the seaven scyences to the Egyptians, and he had a worthy Scoller that height Ewclyde, and he learned right well, and was a Master of all the vii scyences liberall. And in his day it befell, that the lond and the estates of the realms had many sonnes." (And their families increased so rapidly, lawfully and otherwise, it was written, "In his day it came to pass that the sovereign and Lords of the Realm had gotten many sons unlawfully by other men's wives, in so much the land was grievously burdened with them," and they had but small means to maintain themselves withal. Then the tradition goes on to relate how "Egypt has of plenteous generation on account of extreme heat, and in order to remedy these conditions the Pharaohs caused a Parliament to be summoned to suggest some means whereby the children of Egypt might live as gentlemen; but as they were unable to meet this emergency, he therefore caused a proclamation to be made through the realm, that if any man could devise a course how to maintain them, to inform the king, for which he would receive a liberal reward.")

"And they had not competent livehode to find with their children. ... And they did crye through all the realm, if there were any man that could informe them, that he should come to them. After that this crye was made, came this worthy clarke Ewclyde, and said to the Kinge and to all his great lords: 'If yee will take me your children to governe, and to teach them one of the seaven Scyences, wherewith they may live honestly as gentlemen should, under a condition that you will grant me and them a commission, that I may have power to rule them after the manner that the scyence ought to be ruled.' And that the Kinge and all his counsell granted to him anone, and sealed their commission." ... (to which was attached the Seal of Egypt). "And thus was the scyence grounded there;" (He instructed them in the art of hewing stone, and adapted it to the art of building churches, temples, palaces, and other grand structures.) "and that worthy Mr Ewclyde gave it the name of geometrie. And now it is called through all the land Masonrye."(1)

Cooke, in his manuscript, states that this distinguished scientist signalized himself in the construction of ditches or canals to irrigate the land along the River Nile. And there Euclid gave them his admonitions, ordering them to be true to their King, to the Master whom they served, to love one another, to live in harmony together, and to call each other Brother or Fellow; to be diligent in labor, fairly earn their wages, live honestly and with credit, and come and assemble together in the year, to take council in their Craft, as

---
(1) -- From THE CANON, Pages 241-2-3.

to how they might best work, and serve their Lord and Master for his profit and their credit. The wisest among them was to be selected as Master -- not for his lineage, riches, or favor, but for his merit and cunning in his work, that his Lord or employer should be served with fidelity and zeal; and the head of the works was to be called Master.

Euclid compelled them to swear a solemn oath that they would guard their regulations. Each year they were to hold "a convocation to discuss ways of best serving their employers' interests and reflect honor upon themselves. He granted them power to correct any irregularities arising in their craft and to call to account those who trespassed against the science of Masonry."(1)

A long time afterward, the Children of Israel, during a sojourn in Egypt, learned the science of Masonry; and when driven from the land of the Egyptians, they carried their Masonic knowledge to the land of Behest, or Jerusalem. (One part of that land, now called Emens, was then known as Behest.) And there King David began a temple named "Templum Domini," now called the Temple of Jerusalem. King David loved Masons and cherished them, and by every means in his power showed how highly he prized them; and, though he adhered to the Charges of Euclid, as Euclid had given them to the children of Egypt, he enlarged their powers and increased wages.

After the death of King David, Solomon ascended the Israelitish throne and hastened the completion of the temple his father had begun. He sent for Masons from divers nations to the number of four score thousand hewers of stone; and according to the Charges made by Solomon, he selected three thousand of the most expert operative Masons and made them governors or superintendents of the work. There was a king of another country, or region, called Hiram, King of Tyre. He loved King Solomon, and offered him the resources of the Tyrian Kingdom; thus Solomon was able to procure timber necessary for the construction of the temple. Hiram had a son called Aynon (Amon, or Hiram) who was a master of geometry, and Chief Master engaged in the erection of the Jewish temple. He was proficient in carving and engraving, and in all manner of Masonry required for the sacred edifice.

King Solomon confirmed all things concerning Masonry, including the ancient Charges and sanctioned customs of his father's reign. In this way the worthy science of Masonry was introduced into the country of Jerusalem, thence found its way into divers countries and was propagated throughout many kingdoms.

It happened that a curious man, Naymus Graecus, or Naymus the Greek, incited by a zealous impulse to know all and completely master Masonic science, went to the Jewish metropolis and placed himself under the instruction of Hiram -- Chief Master of King Solomon's Temple. Naymus Graecus amassed great knowledge of Masonry and Geometry, and then went to France, greeted there with royal favor by Charles Martell.

---
(1) - HUGHAN, - OLD MASONIC CHARGES.

A PHOENICIAN TRADITION
SANCHONIATHON

A CELEBRATED Phoenician fragment by Sanchoniathon, which has been translated by Philo, is of very great interest. It was preserved by Eusebius as a genealogical account of the first ages. It was read to the Initiates during the celebration of Egyptian and Phoenician Mysteries.

"Of the first two mortals, Protogonous and Aeon, were begotten Genos and Genea. These in the time of great droughts stretched their hands upwards to the Sun whom they regarded as a god, the sole ruler of the heavens. From those, after two or three generations, came Upsouranios and his brother Ousous. One of them invented the art of building cottages of reeds and rushes; the other, the art of making garments of the skins of wild beasts. In their time violent tempests of wind and rain having rubbed the large branches of the forest trees against one another, they took fire and burnt up the woods. Of the bare trunks of trees they first made vessels to pass the waters; they consecrated two pillars to fire and wind; and then offered bloody sacrifices to them as to gods." This worship of the elements and heavenly bodies represented the first species of idolatry.

"After many generations came Chrysor, and he likewise invented many things useful to civil life; for which, after his decease, he was worshipped as a god. Then flourished Ouranus and his sister Ge, who deified and offered sacrifices to their father Upsistos, when he had been torn in pieces by wild beasts. Afterwards Cronos consecrated Muth, his son, and was himself consecrated by his subjects." This was the second species of idolatry -- the worship of dead men.

"Ouranus was the inventor of the Baetylia, a kind of animated stones, framed with great art. And that Taautus formed allegoric figures, characters, and images of the celestial gods and elements. In which is delivered the third species of idolatry -- statue and brute worship. For by the animated stones is meant stones cut into human shape; brute, unformed stones being, before this invention, consecrated and adored. As, by Taatus's invention of allegoric figures, is insinuated the origin of brute worship from the use of hieroglyphics." (1)

---

(1) - FELLOWS, John -- THE MYSTERIES OF FREEMASONRY, Page 119.

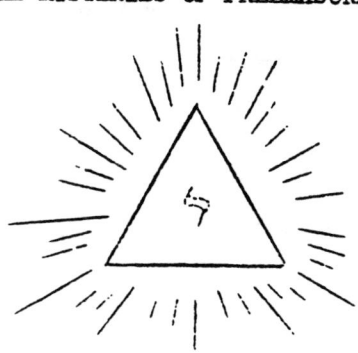

INTERESTING FRAGMENTS SUGGESTING THE ATLANTEAN AND BIBLICAL CONNECTION

ANOTHER very, very old and interesting fragment follows, suggesting the story of Atlantis and the Biblical Genesis:

The Phoenicians preserved traditions, which have come down to us in the writings of Sanchoniathon, of all the great essential inventions or discoveries which underlie civilization.

"The first two human beings, they tell us, were Protogonos and Aion (Adam and 'Havath' -- Adam and Eve), who produced Genos and Genea (Qên and Qêneth -- Cain and Abel), from whom again are descended three brothers, named Phoe, Phur and Phlox (Light, Fire and Flame), because they 'have discovered how to produce fire by the friction of two pieces of wood, and have taught the use of this element.'

"In another fragment, at the origin of the human race, we see in succession the fraternal couples of Autochthon and Technites (Adam and Quen -- Cain?), inventors of the manufacture of bricks; Agros and Agrotes (Sade and Cêd), fathers of the agriculturists and hunters; then Amynos and Magos, 'who taught to dwell in villages and rear flocks.'"

"The connection between these Atlantean traditions and the Bible record is shown in many things. .... In like manner Lamech, both in the signification of his name and also in the savage character attributed to him by the legend attached to his memory, is a true synonyme of Agrotes. And the title given to Agros and Agrotes in the Greek of the Phoenician history, fits in wonderfully with the physiognomy of the race of the Cainites in the Bible narrative, whether we take (the title) simply as a Hellenized transcription of the Semitic Elim, 'the strong, the mighty,' or whether we take it in its Greek acceptation, 'the wanderers;' for such is the destiny of Cain and his race. .... (Genesis iv, 14.)"

Sanchoniathon does not end his tradition as does the Bible, with the three sons of Lamech. Amynos and Magos (Phoenician gods) are succeeded by Misor and Sydyk, who invented the use of salt. "To Misôr is born Taautos (Taût), to whom we owe letters; and to Sydyk, the Cabiri or Corybantes, the institutors of navigation." Misor, Sydyk, and the Kabiri show all these to have originated in the Divine astronomy of the heavens.

---

(1) - DONNELLY, Ignatius; ATLANTIS: THE ANTEDILUVIAN WORLD; Pages 329-30.